American Gadfly

American Gadfly
The Intellectual Odyssey of Paul Fussell

Ronald R. Gray

McFarland & Company, Inc., Publishers
Jefferson, North Carolina

LIBRARY OF CONGRESS CATALOGUING-IN-PUBLICATION DATA

Names: Gray, Ronald R, 1957– author.
Title: American gadfly : the intellectual odyssey of Paul Fussell / Ronald R Gray.
Description: Jefferson : McFarland & Company, Inc., Publishers, 2019 | Includes bibliographical references and index.
Identifiers: LCCN 2019033343 | ISBN 9781476672113 (paperback) ∞ | ISBN 9781476637617 (ebook)
Subjects: LCSH: Fussell, Paul, 1924–2012. | English teachers—United States—Biography. | Critics—United States—Biography.
Classification: LCC PE64.F85 G73 2019 | DDC 801/.95092 [B]—dc23
LC record available at https://lccn.loc.gov/2019033343

BRITISH LIBRARY CATALOGUING DATA ARE AVAILABLE

ISBN (print) 978-1-4766-7211-3
ISBN (ebook) 978-1-4766-3761-7

© 2019 Ronald R. Gray. All rights reserved

No part of this book may be reproduced or transmitted in any form or by any means, electronic or mechanical, including photocopying or recording, or by any information storage and retrieval system, without permission in writing from the publisher.

Front cover photograph © 2019 Shutterstock

Printed in the United States of America

McFarland & Company, Inc., Publishers
  Box 611, Jefferson, North Carolina 28640
  www.mcfarlandpub.com

To Kyong Sook Park
sine qua non

Acknowledgments

I am very grateful to two individuals who bravely hacked their way through reams of my knotty prose: T. K. Allred, the Henry Watson Fowler of the University of Colorado at Denver smart set, and Robert Wyss, expert on all things Italian. They both offered valuable comments and numerous needed corrections to the text. Hats off also to the state of Ohio's wonderful library and information network (OHIOLINK). Finally, *kamsahamnida* to my wife, Kyong Sook, for her support, understanding, and constantly telling me to "go work on your book."

Table of Contents

Acknowledgments — vi

Preface — 1

1. "The Extirpation of Boy Fussell" — 5
2. "In the Eighteenth Century I Found It" — 17
3. Oh! What a Lovely Book! — 32
4. "It Is Simply Part of One's Life" — 68
5. An Essayist at Heart — 81
6. Sheer, Vulgar Experience and the Dropping of the Atomic Bomb — 93
7. "A Touchy Subject": Class in America — 107
8. "The Real War Will Never Get in the Books" — 121
9. The BADness of American Culture — 135
10. The War Continues: An Anthology, Introduction and Lectures — 145
11. Defending "Not a Very Nice Fellow" — 158
12. The Autobiography of a Natural Warrior — 165

Table of Contents

13. A Book about Appearances and Belonging	179
14. A Final Look at the "Good War"	186
15. The Power of Facing Unpleasant Truths	200
Chapter Notes	205
Bibliography	223
Index	229

Preface

The purpose of this book is simple: to argue for the importance and relevancy of the American cultural historian and literary and social critic Paul Fussell (1924–2012). Besides serving as a professor of English at Rutgers and later the University of Pennsylvania, Fussell wrote and edited 21 books on a wide variety of topics, ranging from 18th century British literature to works on the Second World War, poetic meter, British 1920s and '30s travel literature, the English novelist Kingsley Amis and a study of the social significance of uniforms to a sardonic take on American culture entitled *BAD: Or, the Dumbing of America*. But he is best known for his highly influential 1975 book, *The Great War and Modern Memory*, which won the 1976 National Book Award, and is listed by the Modern Library as one of the best books of the 20th century.

Fussell is also noted for *Class*, his acerbic 1983 bestselling guide to the American class system, *Wartime*, an account of the terrible psychological and emotional costs of the Second World War, and two scathing collections of essays on British and American culture, *The Boy Scout Handbook and Other Observations* and *Thank God for the Atomic Bomb and Other Essays*. He also edited two large anthologies on travel and modern war and wrote introductions to reissued classic war memoirs. Finally, he was also a frequent presence on American television, and appeared in several documentaries, including Ken Burn's celebrated 2007 series on World War II.

In a 1977 speech entitled "Scholarship and Autobiography," Fussell admitted that his writings had definite autobiographical elements. For him, the defining event of his life was his horrific experiences as a young rifle company infantry officer in Western Europe during the final year of the Second World War, where he was severely wounded. The war provided a lens through which he viewed everything that came after and left him thereafter obsessed with the concepts of innocence, elegy, and irony. It also made him

Preface

on a personal level an angry young (and later old) man. The war would preoccupy him throughout his long life, but he would not start to write about it until the 1970s and would periodically return to the topic in later books. Fittingly, his final work in 2003 would be on the generation that served with him as infantrymen in Europe from 1944 to 45. Because of his terrible war experience, Fussell adamantly resisted all attempts to glorify, romanticize, or sentimentalize war, and would reject efforts to portray the Second World War as a "good" or reasonable undertaking.

When Fussell returned home from the war in 1946, he resumed his undergraduate studies and read widely and deeply, avidly searching for a conceptual framework within which he could deal with what he had undergone and find some order in his life. He discovered it in the British Augustan writers of the 18th century, finding their critical skepticism, hardheaded empiricism, distrust of theory, concern with form in art and expression, nuance, deep humanism, and use of satire, wit, and irony, to be bracing. He rounded this outlook by incorporating the ideas of modern writers like the English novelist and essayist George Orwell, whom Fussell admired for his intellectual honesty and independence, and his stress on, in Orwell's famous words, the "power of facing unpleasant facts." As this study reveals, Fussell's worldview was remarkably coherent and remained consistent throughout his long career.

As a result, Fussell saw literary criticism as an evaluative endeavor that was intimately connected with ethics and needed to be grounded in the empirical experiences of humanity. He admired American literary critics such as Edmund Wilson, Malcolm Cowley, R. P. Blackmur, Lionel Trilling, and Alfred Kazin who were wide-ranging in their interests and humanistic in their readings of texts, and lamented the disappearance of critics of their quality. Fussell was widely accused of being a curmudgeon, a charge that he rejected, saying that the term suggested that criticism, whether cultural, political, or social, was somehow wrong, and that a curmudgeon was actually a reformer and an idealist. In contrast, he maintained that skeptical, informed, and analytical criticism was the responsibility of any humane and educated person and he did not consider himself a reformer or an idealist. This study will maintain that it is more accurate to view Fussell as a gadfly in the traditional meaning of the word, an individual who stimulates, bothers, teases, and provokes people by consistent criticism. But a gadfly with serious messages.

Although this book discusses aspects of Fussell's life, it is not a formal biography *per se* but rather an intellectual biography that tracks the devel-

Preface

opment of his ideas and those considerations which most significantly informed them. His 1996 autobiography, *Doing Battle*, is subtitled *The Making of a Skeptic*. This study will discuss why he called himself a skeptic, and how skepticism informed his writings. One of the charms of reading Fussell is even though he spent his life as an academician, he had a thoroughly non-academic writing style that was refreshingly clear, jargon-free, interdisciplinary in approach, frequently satirical and ironic, and at times painfully honest (as seen most prominently in his autobiography).

While this book is sympathetic to Fussell, it is also critical. I respect him and even have some fondness for him even although I never met him. I also think these feelings might not have been reciprocated. As his friend the noted British military historian John Keegan put it, Fussell was a complex and unusual person. Like his friend the British novelist Kingsley Amis, about whom he wrote a book, Fussell could be difficult, contentious, and highly opinionated in his beliefs. After he became famous, he enjoyed adopting the pose of an elitist bad boy and shocking people with his exceedingly blunt broad cultural observations (in one interview conducted in his eighties, he expressed regrets that he never bayoneted anyone in the war). While some of his more outrageous remarks came from his impish delight in shaking things up, Fussell also said that he primarily considered himself a satirist and ironist, a person who tried to get people to notice a wrong thing or idea and to think about it, and that he did this through the technique of black humor. He acknowledged that he was a cultural elitist, but also stated that he wanted everyone else to be one too.

Fussell was also a paradoxical and, at times, a conflicted individual. Like most of us, he was a bundle of contradictions, with competing passions and ideas. He hated his time in the military and its emphasis on what he famously called "chickenshit," and distrusted it as an organization, blaming it for the lifelong personal anger he felt. At the same time, he credited his military service for helping to make him the successful writer and academician he later became, was a stout supporter of the atomic bombings of Japan in 1945, and was fascinated with the army's rituals, history, and customs. He spent much of the best years of his life writing voluminously about the subject he most detested: war. His longstanding project was to educate people about the horror of war, but he also vehemently maintained that it was ultimately impossible to do so unless one had experienced it oneself. Moreover, he long tried to reconcile the pull he felt towards the past and tradition with the realities of the present by taking his traditional sensibility and aesthetics and

Preface

adapting and applying them to contemporary topics and concerns. While he was in the main able to bridge much of this chasm, he was not able to accomplish it without some contradiction. As his friend the poet W. D. Ehrhart observed, "Fussell was a curious combination of political and social progressiveness coupled with arch cultural conservatism. He was scathingly critical of cant, hypocrisy, greed, stupidity, and the Powers That Be (be they in academia or business or politics).... But he demanded all things artistic pay visible homage to tradition."[1]

Ultimately, despite all his bluster, grumblings, mockery, and contradictions, Fussell was a deadly serious person and animated by a deep anger over man's chronic inability to accept his limitations and ally himself with his humanity. As with his great hero, the 18th century writer Samuel Johnson, Fussell was, in the broad sense of the term, a moralist. Consequently, he was always on the offensive in his writings, raising important moral concerns, sniffing out and pushing back at what Orwell called "smelly little orthodoxies," and revealing unpleasant truths. Truths that continue to be relevant in today's digitally obsessed, epistemologically-challenged, military-worshipping, and politically correct and identity politics driven times. And this is why Paul Fussell matters.

1

"The Extirpation of Boy Fussell"

On a bitterly cold November morning in 1944, a 20-year-old newly minted infantry second lieutenant from California woke up from a sound sleep at dawn in a densely wooded forest overlooking the French city of St. Die in the Alsace region and cautiously peered towards enemy lines. His command, the second platoon of Company F, which consisted of 40 soldiers and was part of the 410th infantry, 103rd Division in the Seventh Army, had been trucked in the night before in a complicated relief maneuver and this was their first exposure to combat. While this maneuver was occurring, they and the unit they were replacing came under heavy shelling by the Germans. The shelling continued until midnight, and the unit was then ordered to get some needed sleep among the trees.

The images the lieutenant saw that morning shocked him and would fundamentally change and haunt him throughout his long life. He would finally write about it decades later. What he saw were the open-eyed, dead bodies of dozens of very young German soldiers clad in greenish brown uniforms who had been recently killed by the unit his company had relieved. He noted in a 1992 article in *Harper's* that "Michelangelo could have made something out of these forms, in the Dying Gaul tradition and I was startled to find that at first, in a way I couldn't understand, they struck me as beautiful. But after a moment, no feeling but shock and horror. My adolescent illusions, largely intact to that moment, fell away all at once, and suddenly knew I was not and never would be in a world that was reasonable or just. The scene was less apocalyptic than shabbily ironic: it sorted so ill with modern popular assumptions about the idea of progress and attendant improvements in public health, social welfare, and social justice."[1] He also wrote that the alteration of these innocent boys into marmoreal corpses after they had undergone "unbearable fear and humiliation and pain and contempt seemed to do them an interesting injustice. I decided to ponder these things."[2] But the worst was yet to come for this young officer.

The second lieutenant's name was Paul Fussell and he was from a wealthy family that lived in Pasadena, California. His father was a noted Los Angeles corporate lawyer. Fussell had a pampered and sheltered upbringing that included living in an expensive compact British manor house complete with servants and idyllic summers at the family's beach house in Balboa participating in sailing boat races in the family's boat. He would later call his childhood extremely happy, and although he was a mediocre student (but excelled in English), he avidly pursued his interests in photography, journalism, printing, and magic. Boisterous, outgoing, and overweight, he was an odd mixture of earnest preppy and a touch of the class clown for he loved practical jokes. After graduating from high school, he entered Pomona College which then consisted of 800 students, where he contributed to the school's humor magazine. He also was strongly influenced by the writings of the Baltimore satirist and cultural critic H. L. Mencken, and began to affect a world weary, cynical take on life as a result. Fussell also indulged in the usual American male undergraduate activities of drinking, smoking, and chasing girls, and he joined the college's ROTC program, in large part because he thought (incorrectly) that it would get him out of gym (which he dreaded because he was overweight). After graduation, he wanted to be a journalist for *Time, Life,* or *Newsweek.*

When the Japanese attacked Pearl Harbor and the U.S. declared war on Japan, Fussell felt, like most of his classmates, intense anger and wanted to join the fray and fight. He waited to be called for service, which finally occurred on May 6, 1943, during his junior year at Pomona. He then underwent a very long and rigorous (and towards the end annoyingly repetitious) training program that started with a 12-week combat training course at Camp Roberts north of Los Angeles, then 17 weeks at the infantry school at Fort Benning, Georgia, where only one third of the class passed to be officers. He was next shipped to Camp Howze, Texas, where he was attached to a 40-man platoon of the 410 Infantry Division

1. "The Extirpation of Boy Fussell"

(known as the Cactus Division), one of 12 divisions of the Seventh Army, for six months of training. Eventually, in September 1944, his unit was moved to Fort Shanks in New York, where he was issued new equipment and waited to be shipped to France. After a total of 19 months of training, his unit finally took a 15-day blacked out and crowded sea voyage to Marseilles.

In order to discuss how Fussell was forever changed by his war experiences, it is necessary to first discuss in some detail the conditions under which he fought during the conflict. The war in the European theater was entering a key phase when Fussell's illusion-shattering experience in France occurred. The Russians were bloodily but successfully advancing on the Eastern front in Poland, the Ukraine and East Prussia, and the Normandy invasion on June 6 had been a great triumph with the Allies soon capturing large swathes of northern and southeastern France, along with most of Belgium and Luxemburg. But the conflict was far from over. Paris had been liberated nearly three months before, but the Allies had yet to cross the all-important Rhine river, and the fighting in France had devolved into a horrible and bloody slog and a campaign of brute attrition. Casualties, desertions, and disciplinary problems were on the rise. In January 1945, the U.S. Army estimated there were more than 18,000 American deserters in the European theater. The month Fussell arrived in France, the Supreme Allied Commander Dwight Eisenhower acknowledged in his diary that army discipline was becoming bad.

The main reason for this setback was a major conflict that developed between the Allies' basic military strategy and the logistics required to accomplish it. After the Normandy invasion was over, strong disagreements arose between Eisenhower and the imperious British Field Marshal Bernard Montgomery (and, at times, other Allied generals) over the direction of the war. Montgomery was adamant that priority be devoted to what he called "a single, full-blooded thrust" into Germany along a narrow front, with all resources supporting it. Eisenhower contented that only a broad front strategy would work in which pressure was exerted along the 450-mile front through attacks by six Allied armies. He also argued that a broad advance would give the Allies the needed flexibility to attack anywhere and force the Germans to be thinly dispersed everywhere. This strategy was also very much in keeping with Eisenhower's long held belief that the war in the European theater had to be fought and won by a multinational (albeit fractious) coalition advancing on a broad front.

In the end, Eisenhower won the debate and his strategy was adopted. But there was a problem with this approach involving logistics. Simply put, the Allied armies were at a stage of the war where they were ironically a prisoner of their own success; because of the great advances they had made they were outrunning their supply lines. Besides, significantly more transport was required in a broad front rather than a narrow front drive. Complicating matters was the fact that the transportation system in Western France had been practically destroyed by Allied aerial attacks prior to the D-Day invasion in an attempt to softened up German defenses and isolate the beaches at Normandy. As a result, it became extremely difficult for gasoline and diesel fuel, ammunition, and supplies to be moved to the front which stretched from the English Channel to the Swiss frontier. Moreover, for goods to be moved it was necessary for military forces to pause, regroup, advance logistical bases, and start again, a process which greatly impacted upon their momentum and gave the Germans time to recover.

What's more, two serious mistakes made earlier by the War Department plagued the American infantry. The first concerned ammunition supplies which were being consumed much more quickly than what had originally been planned for. The rate exceeded "two tons every minute of every hour of every day, despite incessant rationing in the second half of 1944. By late September, fewer than four rounds per day were available for the largest guns, such as the 8-inch howitzer. By early October, ammunition shortfalls were 'truly critical' across the front."[3]

The second War Department oversight concerned the replacement of front-line troops that had been wounded or killed. Low priority had be assigned to this area because it was believed that air superiority, the size of the Russian army and the advances they had made, and the good quality of American combat troops would carry the day.[4] One historian has noted that "the campaign could have been won more quickly, and Allied forces might have been advanced much further east, if Eisenhower had been given soldiers, and especially more infantrymen."[5]

There was a shortage of officers like Fussell, who later stated that "in six weeks of fighting in Normandy, the 90th Infantry Division had to

1. "The Extirpation of Boy Fussell"

replace 150 per cent of its officers and over 100 per cent of men. If a division was engaged more than three months, the probability was that every one of its second lieutenants, all 132 of them, would be killed or wounded."[6]

On top of all these problems were the appalling weather conditions soldiers were operating under. The winter of 1944 was Europe's coldest in 25 years and the cold would extend well into the next year. While soldiers hated the mud and rain, they feared the cold. The harsh winter affected American soldiers in three ways. First, it impacted upon their personal equipment. "Men had to urinate in barrels and on triggers to get rifles and machine guns operating again. They slept with canteens on their bodies to prevent the drinking water from freezing, while medics carried plasma under their armpits. Rations cans froze solid and could not be eaten when fires were forbidden."[7] The Army's official history would later admit that the clothing issued to front-line troops, which included woolen caps, woolen gloves, field jackets, and long woolen overcoats, were inadequate and failed to protect soldiers from the intense cold.[8] Infantrymen coped by wrapping pieces of blankets under their uniform, scavenging from the clothing of dead German soldiers, stuffing newspapers in their uniforms, and having relatives in the U.S. send them heavy sweaters, thick gloves, and scarves.

Compounding this was the fact that infantrymen had to minimize the amount of items they carried so it would not impede their mobility. In an interview in 2007 for Ken Burns' series on the Second World War, Fussell recalled that infantrymen "had no possessions at all. You would cut everything down to the simplest because you had to carry everything. So when we were marching from one horror to another, I had shoepacks on because the ground was always wet or frozen. I had two pairs of woolen socks. In my pockets, I carried a couple of boxes of K rations. I never had a toothbrush at all. I didn't take a shower for six months."[9]

The cold conditions also greatly impacted upon soldier's health. Army statistics revealed that "hospitals in the MTO [Mediterranean Theater of Operations] treated almost 3,000 GI's for excessive cold, those in the ETO [European Theater of Operations] no less than 27,000. Pneumonia struck some 2,500 GIs in the MTO and more than twice that number in the ETO."[10] Frostbite and extremely painful and debilitating foot disorders like "trench foot" were also major problems.

American Gadfly

The combination of these factors produced a horrific environment for soldiers to fight in. As one noted historian has put it, "If ever there was evidence of the of the terrible price extracted by war, it was the autumn and early winter of 1944–45. Death and destruction were the only constants in a mounting war of attrition that proved nothing more than that men can kill one another by a wide variety of savage means. Soldiers of both sides endured a miserable existence in mud, rain, record floods, freezing snow, thick ground fogs, and the gnawing bone-deep, damp cold that is the signature characteristic of European weather in late autumn and winter. 'Instead of hedgerows, the Allies encountered pillboxes, dense forests, canals, urban snares, and defended villages.' Eisenhower described it as 'the dirtiest kind of infantry slugging.'"[11] Fussell would be plunged into this world for the next four months.

Fussell was not impressed by the soldiers in his company when he first met them in Texas, noting that it was composed almost completely of "hillbillies and Okies, dropouts and used car salesmen and petty criminals,"[12] who had been in the army considerably longer than him. This was the first time in his life he would be working closely with individuals of a fundamentally different social class than he had been exposed to and he initially found the experience bewildering. But he would grow to admire and even to form over time friendships with some of his men, so much so that he would dedicate his most famous book to one who was killed next to him in combat in 1945. But Fussell would also feel some resentment over having to serve in the infantry and would regret joining the ROTC and not taking the path of many of his college classmates and choosing a branch of the military that had higher status. He frequently pointed out in his writings that there was a hierarchy in the military during that period. The air corps took the most promising recruits, then the navy, the coast guard, and the marines had their picks, what was left was taken by the army. At the bottom was the combat infantry, which the army, according to the historian Russell Weigley, filled "with its least promising recruits, the uneducated, the unskilled, the unenthusiastic,"[13] who shouldered the main impact of combat.

Fussell would have a low opinion of the wartime performance of the American military in the European theater, believing that they were not equal to German troops and that they did not realize how bad they were

1. "The Extirpation of Boy Fussell"

and how poorly led. When he was told by an interviewer in the early 1990s that some second battalion veterans did not like the way he portrayed them, he replied, "Well, everyone should realize that a writer is not a nice guy. I was actually very kind. I didn't say how utterly incompetent we were, how badly trained."[14] He would also go so far as to ask in his autobiography whether the ground war conducted by the U.S. in the Second World War was in reality an inadvertent type "of eugenics, clearing the population of the dumbest, the least skilled, the least promising of all young American males?"[15]

Throughout his life, Fussell included his military performance in this indictment and remained modest about his combat leadership skills. How did he stack up? Anecdotal evidence about his wartime performance is difficult to find, but Spilman Gibbs, who was F company's commander said in an interview, "He tried his best. I'll be perfectly frank about it. He should have had a little more drive. I thought he was a pretty good officer, but there were times when he was lacking, let's put it that way.... Fussell wanted to be a good soldier, but I think he was a little bit afraid."[16]

By the beginning of February 1945, the military situation in Europe had turned around. The logistical problem had been largely resolved because the Port of Antwerp was finally operational. American and British forces had defeated Hitler's final major campaign offense on the Western front, the Ardennes Counteroffensive which had been launched in December, and the allies were again advancing. Fussell by this time had settled into his position and had learned some things about his responsibilities. He discovered that the job of a rifle platoon leader was not as powerful as he first believed, and that in reality he mainly just passed on company commander orders, censored letters, and sometimes resolved disputes among troops, and that a leader should never show self-pity. He also learned that each individual has a limited amount of courage and it could not be regained if exhausted, and that men fought not for abstract ideological reasons like freedom or democracy, but for each other, self-respect, and to not let others down.

Fussell also acquired two important but bitter truths about dealing with the effects of combat. First, in order to survive psychologically, a distancing and walling off from normal human sympathy was necessary so that one could directly view the horror of things. Second, it was very difficult to accomplish this, especially if you were a compassionate person, for you had to on a major level dehumanize yourself, and this process was a life altering experience. He also realized that to cope with the constant presence of death required using the principle that "the dead don't *know* what they look like. The soldier is *not* smiling, the man whose mouth drips blood doesn't know what he is doing."[17]

But Fussell also found things in the war that were beyond his comprehension and hard to handle. The first was the terrifying pervasiveness of mortal blunders and accidents, the sheer contingency of events and death during fighting, the limitations of planning, and the stupidity of any type of optimism. Most shocking to him was the unalterable fact that you as an individual were expendable. In addition, it was clear that Germany was defeated and knew it, and it was only now a question of when they would surrender. For Fussell and other infantrymen it was maddening and disheartening that the Germans found it necessary to "pedantically [and] literally *enact* their defeat,"[18] and that people were needlessly dying as a result.

When his company was in action, it was mainly involved in attacking small French towns and clearing them of Germans, sometimes with tragic results. In one incident, mortar fire was ordered on a town that the Germans had vacated, and several French civilians were accidentally killed. When troops entered the town, they were accosted by the civilian's distraught families. Officially, the 103rd Division was "in combat" for 166 days, but most of the fighting was packed into 11 days in Eastern Alsace. Fussell's company suffered a total of 13 soldiers killed in action, 93 wounded during the war.[19]

The war would catch up with Fussell on a clear and sunny early spring day, March 12, 1945, in the Eastern French province of Alsace. The Seventh Army had just commenced Operation Undertone, the object of which was to breach the West Wall of the Siegfried Line and to establish a bridgehead over the river Rhine in the Worms area of Germany. The job of Fussell's unit was to take the town of Gundershoffen and secure a bridgehead over a small river that ran through the town so that an armored column could pass through and reach the Rhine. Fussell had returned to his platoon at the beginning of the month after being away since contracting pneumonia in late January because of the terrible weather. Ever since his return he

1. "The Extirpation of Boy Fussell"

felt strangely on edge and terrified and would later say in an interview that "I don't know what happened. I think it was that I'd had time to think about it in a hospital. I had developed the sense that I had become vulnerable.... By March 15, I was pretty tense and nervous."[20]

That morning, he was rebuked by a lieutenant colonel for hesitating while overseeing his men crossing a road while under machine gun fire. Late that afternoon, he vividly recalled this reprimand and was afraid about taking cover when he, his sergeant Edward Hudson (whom Fussell greatly admired and later dedicated *The Great War and Modern Memory* to), and another officer came under artillery fire from a German self-propelled 88 while they were lying flat on their stomachs on the roof of an abandoned German bunker located under a tree. Suddenly, a shell hit the tree and hot metal tore into their bodies, killing the sergeant and the second lieutenant and severely wounding Fussell in the back and leg. He was transported to the rear on a litter carried by German prisoners, given morphine at an aid station, and then transferred on a hospital train to a packed evacuation hospital, where he had an emotional breakdown and could not stop crying.

When Fussell heard that Hudson and the other officer had been killed in the shelling, he "felt a fury flow over me. It has never entirely dissipated."[21] At the hospital, he underwent a painful operation to remove the shrapnel that had riddled his back and to repair the wound in his leg. Later, when it was determined that this surgery missed some shrapnel, he underwent another operation, the surgeries left him with a long gash in his leg. For his actions, he was awarded the Bronze Star and two Purple Hearts, which he believed he did not deserve.

He spent several months in the hospital keenly reading works by Mark Twain, Joseph Conrad, and Thomas Mann but mainly delighting in the humorous writings of Robert Benchley, Dorothy Parker, and James Thurber. He also fell in love with a nurse to no effect. When he finally returned to F Company in July, none of the soldiers were welcoming or friendly which puzzled him. He would frequently wonder why for nearly 50 years until he found out that it was because the officers in his unit had filed a false official report about the actions of Sergeant Hudson on the day he was killed which resulted in him posthumously being awarded the Silver Star, a fraud which they knew Fussell would have objected to and refused to take part in if he had been there. He also learned that nearly half of his unit, 55 soldiers, were killed or wounded on the day he was hit.[22] His company was disbanded shortly after his arrival and he was then transferred to the 45th Division.

Fussell next spent almost an entire year being shuttled around a variety of positions in camps in France and the U.S. Because he did not have enough points to be discharged (the point system was based on factors such as whether you were married, how long you were in the army, and how many months you were in combat), he could not be discharged, even after the war was over. Consequently, he served as a rifle squad leader, lectured officers at a massive camp near Rheims on the use of flame-thrower in preparation for the planned upcoming invasion of Japan in which his unit was scheduled to participate, and in which he was convinced he would be killed. When Fussell heard that Japan had surrendered in August 1945, he said in a 1999 television interview that he "was so happy that I had to retire to my little tent, closed the curtain and sat there and cried for several hours. It was a very powerful emotional feeling to be redeemed from certain death and get life again."[23]

Fussell also worked during this period as a mess officer at a camp in Texas, taught business English, American and English literature, and public speaking at a military school, helped administer the Army General Classification Test, and was even a lifeguard at an enlisted men's swimming pool. He found all these duties boring and a waste of time and grew progressively angrier and surlier in his behavior. His only solace was in reading, which included much poetry, the works of Henry James and Shakespeare, and publications such as the *Saturday Review of Literature, The New Republic, Harper's,* and *The Atlantic Monthly.* Finally, after three years of army service, on June 17, 1946, he was discharged and subsequently met by his parents at Glendale train station in California.

The Second World War would prove the defining event in Fussell's life and hugely informed what he thought and did after. He would spend much of it wrestling with, writing and lecturing about, and being haunted by, the war's meaning and implications and how his experiences fit in. He would later state that he thought about the war daily and felt that he was still in some way in it, and that a perceptive reader would detect in his writings the pain he felt over this war.

1. "The Extirpation of Boy Fussell"

One immediate result of the war was that he was discharged with 40 percent disability and received a monthly check of $300 until he died in 2012. He would also take advantage of the GI bill to fund his graduate study at Harvard. While he left the army hating it and wanting no part of it ever again, stating that it brought about the "extirpation of Boy Fussell,"[24] he was also grateful for what it had taught him about himself and life, remarking, "my time in combat was the crucial moment in my life. I found out about myself, my strengths and weakness.... Having barely escaped with my life taught me a lot about the conditions of life and death, irony and tragedy, crucial subjects which I had not thought about at all before."[25] He would also claim that whatever ability he had as a literary and scholarly critic and historian was paradoxically due to the army, since its extreme and constant stress on conformity, simplicity, and cant drove him in reaction to realize the importance of independence, nuance, and honesty.

The war also stripped Fussell of many illusions and made him acutely aware of human and personal limitations. It made him a skeptic, strongly critical of institutions and conventional and religious beliefs and an avid believer in intellectual and verbal freedom, the importance of clear thinking and truthful language, and the ability to face difficult facts. Warfare is the most ironic of all human activities and for Fussell, irony as a concept and technique (along with satire) became a basic part of his perspective. Additionally, his war experiences instilled in him the belief that because man is fundamentally flawed, human life destined to failure, and irony a key component of the human condition, only a vision of the world that is deeply rooted in tragic irony is correct.

Most of these beliefs were of course inchoate, not worked out, more visceral than capable of being articulated when he arrived home in 1946. But, as we shall see, further education, wide and deep reading, and reflection would enable him to take these convictions and his war experiences, build upon them, and weld them into a sophisticated intellectual and critical framework which he would use with great skill and effect through his career.

Finally, after the publication of 1975's *The Great War and Modern Memory* and the wide acclaim it received, we shall see that Fussell felt emboldened to write more on the topic of war. This would turn into a long-term mission to educate people about the realities of the Second

American Gadfly

World War and to explain why the real war would never be told. He would firmly and vehemently disagreed with the widely held belief propagated by such writers as Tom Brokaw, Stephen Ambrose, and Victor Davis Hanson that it was a "good war" fought by "the greatest generation," and oppose any attempt to normalize or sentimentalize the conflict. He would also take on in a widely discussed article critics of the atomic bombings of Japan. He would agree that sometimes war is necessary and that the U.S. entrance into World War II was politically justifiable. But Fussell would also maintain that psychologically, experientially, and on a humanistic level it was not, because it was an appalling, brutal, irrational, and dehumanizing endeavor that destroyed not just minds and bodies, but also corrupted and degraded language, culture, and society. Most of Fussell's writings on war were intended for an American audience, for he contended that unless Americans grew up about and began to fully understand what war really entails, the U.S. would continue to have unnecessary ones.

2

"In the Eighteenth Century I Found It"

Paul Fussell was 22 years old when he finally returned to his home in California on June 17, 1946, after three years of army service. Anyone who has fought in a war feels that it in some way changed them, but for him the effect was dramatic and permanent. He later stated that at this period of his life, "the extirpation of Boy Fussell was almost complete,"[1] and that the optimism and innocence which had previously characterized him was gone. As a result of war experiences, his personality had also undergone a big change when he returned for his final year at Pomona College. According to Fussell's 1996 autobiography, where previously he had been gregarious, fun loving, fond of jokes, and displayed an H.L. Mencken-inspired cynical stance towards life, he now made no attempt to be popular and avoided joining any group (rejecting anyone who pressured him to do so) nor did he participate in any sports related activities. He had no interest in gossip and became an angry and rather self-absorbed loner. Moreover, Fussell also developed a special hatred for Southern California's easygoing and aggressively sunny and optimistic ways, concluding that "anxiety and doubt are indispensable to the makeup of the complete person,"[2] and that optimism was a belief no respectable individual should take, given man's flawed nature and the widespread existence of evil.

But there is also a slightly different picture of Fussell during this period. Betty Fussell, his first wife whom he had met at Pomona, has written in her lacerating 1999 memoir *My Kitchen Wars* that he was in reality the golden boy of the campus literary set which met at professors' houses. She notes that "Paul was the star of this group. He was the best writer, the most intense, the most persuasive, the most talented, the most committed.... The war slimmed him and trimmed him and sharpened his wit. He was the genial fat boy no more, and while he ridiculed others, he never laughed at himself."[3]

Fussell now wondered how he could justify his existence, given what he had gone through and his newly acquired awareness of life's brevity. He decided to take a more serious approach to his studies and changed his major from journalism to English. During his senior year, he concentrated on his classes and read widely and greatly and embarked on a search for answers to the moral questions that the war had posed. Intellectually, he became interested in ideas in and of themselves, and not simply for satirical effects as he was before, and he became strongly attracted to writers who were critical, anti-romantic, satirical, and skeptical, like Mark Twain, Ambrose Bierce, Flaubert, and Jonathan Swift. He shifted the focus in his readings "from comedy to irony, and from irony to tragedy and indeed 'art' in any form."[4] He also developed a great appreciation of poetry (he would later state that his understanding of the rhythmic nature of poetry was attributable to his years of taking cello lessons when he was young). He became particularly enthralled with the works of the World War I poets Wilfred Owen, Siegfried Sassoon, and Isaac Rosenberg whom he encountered in Louis Untermeyer's collection *Modern British Poetry*. (In fact, his love of these poets would later result in his most famous book.) He also admired the social and political satire of the American writers E. E. Cummings, John Manifold, and Vachel Lindsay that he read in Oscar William's *A Little Treasury of Modern Poetry*. This newfound love of poetry would never leave him.

Fussell also found comfort from his questionings and anxieties in the works of Virginia Woolf, James Joyce, Aldous Huxley, Ernest Hemingway and Henry James. Because of these readings and his new serious attitude, he decided that his duty now lay in "criticism, meaning not carping, but the perpetual obligation of evaluation."[5] Betty Fussell would write that his devotion then "to literature as an art, a sacred text, was religious. It had saved him in the war, he said.... Art was no ivory tower but a mode of moral action, an activist's salvation from the chaos of war."[6]

As a result, Fussell decided to attend graduate school after his graduation in 1947 and become a teacher (much to the dismay of his father who thought there was no money in it). At that time, a considerable num-

2. "In the Eighteenth Century I Found It"

ber of educated returning veterans were studying English in hopes of becoming college teachers. This was due in large part to the conviction that a careful reading and exposition of great literature could, if properly done, help to bring some rationality, nuance, and decency into a world that had been greatly coarsened by years of war. Thanks to the G.I. Bill, he decided to apply to Harvard, and was accepted.

Fussell arrived in Cambridge in the fall of 1947 with high expectations because of the school's reputation and the positive things his brother Art, who was already a student there, had said about the place. But he did not have an easy time at the school. He quickly discovered that many of the faculty were snobby towards graduate students on the G.I. Bill. He also found the graduate school's three language exam requirement (German, French, and Latin) onerous, the class workload extremely demanding, the quality of most of the teaching poor, and the university's rules concerning punishment for academic misconduct draconian. But he did like Harvard's tradition of leaving students alone, and enjoyed Walter Jackson Bate's course on Romanticism, Harry Levin's on English drama, and Douglas Bush's class on John Milton.

During this period, Fussell published several articles related to his academic interests. They included several notes for the famous journal *Modern Language Notes*, one on the poem "The Windhover" by the 19th century English poet Gerard Manley Hopkins, and the other on T. S. Eliot's celebrated poem "The Hollow Men," as well as a short article on the origins of the term *Iron Curtain* for *American Speech*. He also published a short article for the same journal concerning one of his pet peeves: the fraudulent and misleading use of language. The paper discussed pseudo-medical educational jargon, that is, words like *intern, inservice,* and *clinic* that were used "by educationists, presumably in the hope that some of the slick asepsis of the medical profession will become associated with the traditionally tweedy and embarrassingly unhygienic methods and emphases of humane studies."[7]

Fussell did not concentrate only on academic matters, but also wrote a little poetry, some of which was published (he includes one poem in his autobiography), but he gave up composing poems because he thought himself untalented. But he did find out that he had a gift for poetry criticism and for understanding rhythm, which he partly ascribed to his years of studying the cello. (He once stated that he didn't write fiction because he lacked the necessary interest in other people). Despite all this activity, he would later write that his real "self-defined identity was that of a representative angry young man,"[8] for he continued to emotionally suffer from the effects of his war experiences. As a result, he was very difficult to deal with, aggressive towards others, kept to himself, had few friends, and largely lived a monastic existence. He also scrupulously avoided anything to do with popular American culture, including going to movies. He also did not follow sports, and even refused to listen to the radio because of his dislike of American society and disdain for anything that was popular.

But on June 17, 1949, things changed for the better when Fussell married Betty Harper. They were wed at Cambridge's All Souls Episcopal, a wooden church which dated back to the American Revolution. She had moved to New York after graduating from Pomona College in 1948 to work in the publishing business where he had regularly met her. After marrying Fussell, she left her job and enrolled at Radcliffe College to study English. They moved into an apartment off Copley Square and he prepared for his demanding PhD oral exam, which covered a large swath of English literature.

Surprisingly, given his ability, Fussell barely passed the exam and was warned by the committee that he needed to bone up on his Chaucer, Old and Middle English, as well as 19th century literature. After some consideration, he decided to write his PhD thesis on the theory of prosody in 18th century English literature, because he knew this period well and Harvard's Widener Library held a large collection of commentaries on this topic from this period. It took a year to finish his dissertation (which was fast), which he completed in June 1951. But he did not receive any job offers largely because of the insolent and sarcastic tone he took in job interviews. At the last moment, he was finally able to secure a position only through the personal intervention of one of his professors.

His first job was at Connecticut College for Women, a small liberal arts school in New London which was founded in 1911, where he unhappily but diligently taught mostly freshman English composition from 1951 to 1955. His position was that of Instructor and he was paid $2,700 a year. But he was able to get a revised version of his Harvard dissertation pub-

2. "In the Eighteenth Century I Found It"

lished as a 170 paged Connecticut College monograph titled *Theory of Prosody in Eighteenth-Century England* in 1954. In 1955 he was offered a position at Rutgers University due to this book, which he accepted. Despite this professional advancement, his dissatisfaction and anger remained. He would later acknowledge this, writing that "from the 1950s on, my presiding emotion was annoyance, often intensifying to virtually disabling anger. Anger at my accepting invitations to make changes of identity too fast."[9] He continued to experience great difficulty making the transition from soldier to civilian life. Fussell became angry at himself for not being able to understand this change, angry about his experiences during the war, and angry over what he perceived to be the vacuous optimism and growing materialism of the U.S. This anger would at times come out in his interactions with others, and in some of his writings.

For example, in 1957–58, Fussell was the recipient of a Fulbright Lectureship to teach modern American fiction for the University of Heidelberg. During his stay, he attended a production of Thornton Wilder's *Our Town* and became so enraged by the Germans choosing this American writer to perform that he wrote an article entitled "Thornton Wilder and the German Psyche" for the noted magazine *The Nation*. In it, he contended that "the German canonization of Wilder verges on the irrational—a phenomenon of even greater interest to the political psychologist than to the student of the droll vagaries of public literary tastes."[10] He goes on to essentially accuse Germans of disingenuously using Wilder to paper over the evil they had done since Wilder's view of man in this play was, "spiritual, complacent, coy, charming, and entirely unreal."[11]

During these years, his deep interest in 18th century British literature kept him intellectually grounded. Most of his publications during this time concerned this period, and he ended up publishing five books on the subject, ranging from studies of Augustan poetry and literature, a well-received and still used 1965 guide to English poetic stanzaic and meter forms, to a 1971 analysis of Samuel Johnson's views on writings. He also contributed in 1969 to a jointly written comprehensive textbook on 18th century English literature. Fussell would later state in a lecture before the Friends of the Rutgers University Libraries in 1977 that all these books "were expressions of my uneasiness verging on dismay at being set down in a modern world without theological, metaphysical, or even empirical principles of stability and thus without apparent sources for ethical imperatives."[12] He also called them "disguised autobiographical effusions."[13]

While Fussell was extremely well read and influenced by a host of modern and traditional writers, there is little doubt that he found his intellectual home in these 18th century British writers. They had a decisive influence upon him and helped to form a major component of his aesthetic, moral, and intellectual viewpoint, a belief system that enabled him to impose some needed order on his war experiences and life and provided him with a coherent methodology when he was writing criticism. This is not to say that Fussell got all his beliefs and ideas from these writers, for he was interested in many of the themes and literary techniques that they were concerned with before he read their works, but they furnished the foundation he built upon. As we have seen, because he was attracted to literature that displayed irony and satire and was heavily critical in tone, "I looked for an age and a tradition in which these motifs were dominant. In the English eighteenth century I found it."[14] What these writers did was to help him articulate, clarify, and make consistent certain intellectual and literary tendencies he had previously felt.

In spite of his mixed experiences at Harvard, it appears that the university thoroughly exposed him to this literary tradition in two ways. First, through classes like George Sherburn's on Jonathan Swift and Alexander Pope. Although Fussell considered Sherburn a mediocre lecturer, he did apply himself in the course because of his deep interest in the satire of this period. The famous scholar and biographer Walter Jackson Bate also had a large impact on Fussell since he was a Samuel Johnson scholar, and Johnson was one of Fussell's heroes. In addition to attending courses on the period, the detailed research on prosody he did for his doctoral dissertation also gave him a strong education in the subject.

The best way to describe what elements chiefly constituted Fussell's worldview and the intellectual tradition he largely drew from, is to examine the first chapter of his third book, *The Rhetorical World of Augustan Humanism: Ethics and Imagery from Swift to Burke*, which was published in 1965. In the first chapter, Fussell answers the question "What is humanism?" by listing 12 key postulates. For our purposes, what is interesting about these assumptions is what they reveal about the intellectual underpinnings of Fussell's own belief system as most of them are beliefs he held

2. "In the Eighteenth Century I Found It"

himself and some were frequently used or assumed in his writings. The seven most important of these postulates are as follows.

First, the conviction that both the mind and the imagination are core human attributes and that man is most human "when he uses his mind in a uniquely human way."[15] Intertwined with this belief is a reverence for the practice of literature, for it is through literature that "the mind is exercised by a constant oscillation between things and symbols, between actualities and metaphors of actualities."[16]

Second, the belief that one should be keenly "concerned with the act of evaluation—impelled to order everything in rank.... This *libido aestimandi* is naturally accompanied by hierarchical rather than egalitarian expectations about society and politics; about literary genres and techniques; some of which are conceived to be in the nature of things 'better' than others."[17]

Third, a deep veneration for the past, an understanding of "the historical uniformity of human nature"[18] along with severe doubts concerning humans' qualitative or moral progress.

Fourth, the conviction that assertions and morality are intimately connected, and that "good writing is an index of moral virtue."[19]

Fifth, an intense concern with moral questions and the assumption that man should not be viewed primarily "as a maker or even a knower, but rather a moral actor."[20] As a result, the main concern of the humanist is not simply to describe things, but to offer remedies. Sixth, Augustan humanists contended that in terms of human nature, man should be viewed as intrinsically corrupt and flawed. Hence, "man's dignity arises in part from his very perception of the human flaw. Self-distrust thus becomes a central experience, and satire a central literary action."[21]

Finally, they held that one should be inherently skeptical of any theory of government or human nature which ignores "the experienced facts of man's mysterious complexity ... man's most dangerous temptation is his lust to conceive of his nature as simpler than it is"[22] (or as completely rational).

In conjunction with these assumptions, there are several other beliefs that should be mentioned which were also fundamental to the outlook of these writers and to Fussell's worldview. These include an emphasis on wit, nuance, a robust sense of skepticism, and a hard-headed empiricism and reliance upon common sense that was Lockean in epistemology and asserted that experience and observation were the path to knowledge. They also had a contempt for socially accepted cant and boorishness, a suspicion of abstract metaphysics, theoretical science, and the "specialist," and a focus on what Samuel Johnson called "the business of living."

Fussell noted in his autobiography that he thought his ardent concern with structure and form in literature and expression was a product of his fear and hatred of ambiguity and lack of meaning. This concern was also characteristic of the Augustan humanists, who strongly believed in the importance of form and clarity in art and were suspicious of ornament.

The creed of these individuals can be encapsulated in the philosopher John Locke's famous remark that "our business here is not to know all things, but those which concern our conduct." The Augustans believed that literature had to be intimately connected with social life, a position that Fussell also strongly held. But he of course did not agree with all the tenets of these writers as that would have made him a crank and completely out of intellectual step with the modern world. One major difference between them concerned religion. Fussell remained strongly antireligious throughout his life and rejected the Augustan notion of a divinely instituted order.

Another area of similarity between the Augustans and Fussell concerns the use of satire. For the humanists, satire was an important tool to be employed against individuals that deviated from man's humanity, reason, and conscience. As the introduction to the textbook Fussell co-wrote on 18th century literature puts it, "It is the massive Johnsonian subject of the continuity and dignity of the uniquely human—man's will, conscience, yearning for order and peace—menaced as always by brutality, vanity, and sloth, and stupidity, that provided the materials which the later major writers of the later eighteenth century—like the predecessors in the age of Pope—shaped into works of permanent usefulness and beauty."[23] The Augustans used satire to draw attention to this constant menace and to highlight the importance of core human values. Fussell also frequently and effectively employed satire in his popular writings for similar purposes.

Fussell also shared with these authors a fascination with irony. This complex and at times ambiguous concept will play a very important role in Fussell's writings, and he would refer to it often. Consequently, it is key

2. "In the Eighteenth Century I Found It"

that we understand what he meant by the term. He first became acutely aware of the concept during his war experience when he constantly faced a massive gap between appearance and reality, confronted with what he had previously believed war was like and the horrible actuality he encountered in combat. In an interview conducted in 1996, he said, "I learned by my long immersion in 18th century literature, where the urge is constantly outward from oneself; that is, not to try to undertake deep voyages into the self, but, rather to escape the self, see what's going on and comment on it. Irony is a great help there, to protect oneself from self."[24]

In another interview conducted on C-SPAN in 2000, he expanded on his definition, stating, "Irony is an emotion occasioned by some great gulf, half comic, half tragic, between what one expects and what one finds."[25] He would also write in his autobiography that he was obsessed (ever since the war) with a series of polarities, youth/age, innocence/experience, levity/seriousness, and the chasm that exists between them. Therefore, he frequently employed irony in his writings to emphasize the vast distance between the ideal and the actual.

In the final chapter of his 1971 book, *Samuel Johnson and the Life of Writing*, Fussell discusses Johnson's great love of irony and elegy. The book ends with an observation that was ostensibly about the poets in Johnson's celebrated work on English poets, *Lives of the Poets*, but really, Fussell later claimed, about himself. "For all the variety of satiric or compassionate details with which Johnson discriminates his characters as they play out their literary careers, they are all given enough in common to merge in something like a species. Johnson's species to the *Lives* is the writer as representative man, obliged by his fragility to imitate and to adhere to genres and conventions which he has not devised; tormented by the hunger of imagination only to be always defeated of his hopes; and finally carried away by the very stream of time which it had been his ironic ambition to shape, and by shaping, to arrest."[26]

To further flesh out Fussell's worldview, it is useful to contrast his defense of 18th century values of reason and humanism with that of a well-known and current defender of these values, namely the noted Harvard psychologist Steven Pinker. Pinker, armed to the teeth with 75 "evidence based" graphs, has aggressively and often breathlessly maintained in a recent book, *Enlightenment Now: The Case for Reason, Science,*

Humanism, and Progress, that the enlightenment principles of reason and sympathy have greatly enhanced human welfare, greatly reduced human suffering and been the primary engine of the enormous and widespread progress in the areas of health, prosperity, safety, the environment, equal rights, quality of life, democracy, and peace, and contributed to a rise in moral standards. He further contends that "with our understanding of the world advanced by science and our circle of sympathy expanded through reason and cosmopolitanism, humanity could make intellectual and moral progress. It need not resign itself to the miseries and irrationalities of the present, nor try to turn back to a lost golden age."[27]

Fussell would have found this idea of progress preposterous and exceedingly naive. Though he would have found the notion of experiential, material and technological progress unobjectionable, he would have rejected Pinker's link between progress in this realm with significant moral progress. Moreover, Pinker's blanket assertion that after the Second World War, "romance has finally been drained from war, and peace became the stated goal of every Western and international institution. Human life has become more precious, while glory, honor, preeminence, manliness, heroism, and other symptoms of excess testosterone have been down graduated,"[28] would have drawn a long and scornful laugh from Fussell. His position on the topic of modern war was clearly stated in 1991 when he wrote that "the propensity of the twentieth century to generate wars more extensive, destructive, and cruel than any in history must shake the confidence of those like economists and other social scientists, city planners, public health authorities, jurists, legislators, and actuaries, whose work obliges them to assume people are rational, by their nature free of the urge to self-destruction, and that the general tendency of society is progressive—towards ever greater enlightenment and decency. One need not be a cynic to understand that modern history delivers very different news, and that the modern union of neurotic nationalism and complex technology has defined war in a way unknown before."[29] (And this was penned before this century's American incursions into Iraq and Afghanistan, and the bloody civil wars in Libya and Syria.)

Fussell would have also been appalled by Pinker's assertion that science has much to offer for the field of literary scholarship and its insights should be incorporated into the humanities curriculum. For instance,

2. "In the Eighteenth Century I Found It"

Pinker thinks "cognitive psychology can shed light on how readers reconcile their own consciousness with those of the author and characters. Behavioral genetics can update folk theories of parental influence with discoveries about the effects of genes, peers, and chance, which have profound implications for the interpretation of biography and memoir—an endeavor that also has much to learn from the cognitive psychology of memory and the social psychology of self-presentation. Evolutionary psychologists can distinguish the obsessions that are universal from those that are exaggerated by a particular culture and can lay out the inherent conflicts and confluences of interest within families, couples, friendships, and rivalries which are the drivers of plot."[30] Fussell would speak out throughout his career against what he considered to be the increasing encroachment of science-based and data-driven methodologies upon the field of literary studies which he maintained employed an entirely different approach towards texts. According to Fussell, literary works cannot be quantified because interpreting them involves making evaluative and moral judgements and examining how they reflect and relate to social life. He also spoke out against the diminishing place of the English department in higher education and would argue that Pinker's proposal would ultimately result in literary studies being minimized and marginalized.

Finally, he would take strong issue with Pinker's optimistic characterization of human nature. While Pinker admits that people today can be prone to flaws such as the demonization of others when things go bad, authoritarianism, magical thinking, and intense tribalism,[31] he nonetheless argues that all human problems are resolvable if we have the right knowledge. Fussell operated from a more conservative strain of the Enlightenment and believed that man is inherently blemished, morally tainted, complicated, and cognitively limited (but capable of being self-aware of this condition) and that this nature is at heart uniform and permanent, and as a consequence, the human condition is darkly rooted in the tragic. Moreover, Fussell was deeply skeptical of the capacity of individuals to transcend the limitations of their nature and felt that many human problems are not solvable, and that understanding this fact is the first step to acquiring wisdom. In the end, he would have viewed Pinker's optimism as misplaced and ultimately a clever repackaged and marketed version of scientism and the belief in the perfectibility of man.

American Gadfly

This is not to claim that Fussell was simply an 18th century man trapped in the 20th century, a cultural conservative who was permanently at war with the modern era (which some later critics accused him of having been). He was more complicated and nuanced than this, for he was strongly eclectic in his interests and motivated by a vigorous and sweeping curiosity. Throughout his career, Fussell remained a fiercely independent individual and was informed by a thoroughly secular sense with an epistemology that hearkened back to the British empirical tradition which privileged experience. He once wrote that he owed a sense of debt to the writer Herbert Read who said, "I stand by the English empirical school. I feel their spirit in my very bones and anything new will for me be a development of that great tradition."[32]

As a result, Fussell was deeply skeptical of theories, especially those from the fields of cultural studies and critical literary theory. (He did go through a phase where he touted the New Criticism practiced by Northrop Frye but later regretted it.) Moreover, he distrusted knowledge claims that were not strongly anchored in experience, careful observation, and social life, but he did feel that artistic works in some way should acknowledge tradition. He was also highly eclectic and motivated by a vigorous and expansive curiosity.

Fussell had contempt for and constantly warned people about the dangers of self-importance, pretentiousness, sloppy and utopian thinking, philistinism, delusion, and blind optimism. He was not a conservative but quite liberal and progressive in his politics. (He would state that he remained deeply distrustful of Republicans since he grew up among them in Pasadena and "knew their game," and backed Democrats. Late in life, he would be a strong supporter of Bill Clinton and John Edwards.)

Fussell once wrote that the book he most wished he had written was *Culture and Anarchy* by the English poet and critic Matthew Arnold which was published in 1869. In it, Arnold offers a spirited defense of culture from the criticisms that have been launched against it, such as that it was not practical, a useless type of escapism, and merely a salve for the turmoil of life. Arnold maintained that great art had numerous important functions to play in society and that it was actually an excellent remedy for life's constant anxieties and an effective counter to society's obsession with wealth, power, and misguided faith in "machinery." For Arnold, cul-

2. "In the Eighteenth Century I Found It"

ture "is, or ought to be, the study and pursuit of perfection; and that of perfection as pursued by culture, beauty, and intelligence, or, in other words, sweetness and light, are the main characters."[33] Moreover, intrinsic to any great artistic work is often a critique of the status quo, the intention to set right the viewer's perspective, help them to better comprehend beauty, and recharge their moral inclinations. In short, he contended that culture is a criticism of life, that it helps to keep us honest, our sensibilities and moral inclinations refreshed, and enables us to better understand ourselves. Arnold concludes the work by observing that "everywhere we see the beginnings of confusion ... we can only get back by going back upon the actual instincts and forces which rule our life, seeing them as they really are, connecting them with other instincts and forces, and enlarging our whole view and rule of life."[34]

Arnold had great scorn for what he perceived to be the insularity, boorishness, parochialism, and materialism of Victorian society. He famously divided English society into three groups based upon taste and gentility: Barbarians (the aristocracy, serene, good manners but hostile to ideas), Philistines (the commercial middle class, energetic, moral, but lacking in intelligence and appreciation of beauty), and the Populace (blind and unrefined). Arnold thought the Philistines were the most significant group and held the greatest potential, and that what needed to be done was to both educate and refine them.

Fussell was impressed with Arnold's idea that culture was intimately connected with criticism, also with his criticisms of Victorian society (which in some ways are similar to Fussell's criticisms of aspects of American society), his explication of the many advantages great art brings to the viewer, and especially Arnold's classification of English society according to manners and aesthetic discernment (an approach that Fussell would take in his own book on the American class system).

But most of Fussell's writings involved modern subjects and his later works concerned aspects of American society. He was an acknowledged Anglophile and while he found his intellectual home in the Augustans, it was a home that was also stocked with modern American and British writers, poets, and critics such as T. S. Eliot, Northrup Frye, H. L. Mencken, Ezra Pound, Evelyn Waugh, Lionel Trilling, Kurt Vonnegut, Thomas Hardy, Lincoln Kirstein, W. C. Williams, Malcolm Cowley, Leslie Fiedler, Robert

American Gadfly

Byron, Lytton Strachey, Osbert Sitwell, Frederick Manning, José Ortega y Gasset, James Horne Burns, Peter Quennell, Cyril Connolly, Thomas Pynchon, Joseph Heller, Rudyard Kipling, James Joyce, the historian John Lukacs, the British World War I poets, Kingsley Amis, Edmund Wilson, the journalist and novelist Tom Wolfe, and others.

At the top of the list of modern writers that strongly influenced Fussell was the British essayist, journalist, and novelist George Orwell. He explained in a 1985 essay on Orwell for *The Sewanee Review* why he found him so appealing. When the essay was reprinted in his 1988 collection, *Thank God for the Atom Bomb and Other Essays*, he added the subtitle, "The Critic as Honest Man," to the article's original title which was originally just "George Orwell." Fussell added it to underline the article's main point: that Orwell's nonfiction writings should serve as a model for how criticism should be done. For Fussell, a critic is "an essayist concerned with values,"[35] and Orwell was a master essayist. He specifically admired Orwell's strong-willed intellectual honesty and ability to squarely face "unpleasant facts," and his attacks on literary pretension, platitudes, and mental deceitfulness.

In the article, Fussell comes up with and carefully lays out five of what he calls "critical obligations identifiable as Orwellian"[36] that serious critics should follow. The first is that a critic should constantly read and in a lot of different areas, not just works of literature but also things like signs, labels, catalogs, and even business reports, etc., for "his business is language and its behavior in relation to human beings and their desires. The critic should beware generic snobbery—literature has its social classes just like life."[37] Next, a critic should not be afraid of any orthodoxy, "political, religious, nationalistic, or literary."[38] Third, a critic must find pleasure and delight in reading and writing and be doubtful of conventions and mainstream ways of thinking. Fourth, a critic should be attentive to everything, both large and small topics, and have a wide-ranging curiosity. And lastly, a serious critic must try very hard to be completely honest, no matter the consequences. These obligations, which are not just intellectual, but also moral, were obligations that Fussell himself tried to follow in his own writings.

Moreover, at the risk of complicating matters, there was also in Fussell's perspective a touch of what British sociologist Peter Wilkin has

2. "In the Eighteenth Century I Found It"

called "Tory Anarchism." This term originated with Orwell and was used by him to describe himself and Jonathan Swift. Wilkin has expanded upon this term and argued that modern writers like Evelyn Waugh and entertainers like Peter Cook and Spike Milligan can also be included in this category and contended that they all shared a common set of beliefs. Among these were the use of satire to show their moral and cultural objections to aspects of modern life, a strong sense of nonconformism, a love of irony which was employed, the drawbacks of the society they inhabited, a deep skepticism about social and political progress, and a stress on the independence of the individual. They viewed themselves as provocateurs and contrarians and not revolutionaries, were culturally conservative, hated political correctness, the ubiquity of mass consumer society, were critical of business, and worried about the influence of monetary values on society. They also felt an intense sense of pessimism about the direction the modern world was taking.[39] Wilkin also states that similar figures can be found in other countries. Fussell also shared some of these individuals' beliefs. In addition, as well shall later see, he also wrote a book praising the works of the British writer Kingsley Amis, who can also, in many ways, be characterized as a Tory anarchist.

By the early 1970s, Fussell felt that he had said everything he wanted to say about 18th century British literature, and now wanted to use his honed skills as a critic on topics which had long interested him and were of a popular or unusual and non-academic nature but were engaging to educated readers. The first subject he chose to write about would be different from anything he had previously written about and be based in part on his war experiences. It would also be his greatest work and make him famous.

3

Oh! What a Lovely Book!

During the summer of 1972, 47-year-old Paul Fussell would diligently walk every morning (except Sunday) by the famous massive 15-inch guns which had been removed from a scrapped British warship and now stood guard to the entrance to the Imperial War Museum in London. He would then patiently wait at the front door for a museum guard to escort him to a room furnished with only a chair and a large rectangular table on the museum's top floor to conduct research on his next book. After his arrival, worn cartons containing "little notebooks still stiff with the mud of the Somme or Ypres. Field orders, platoon rosters, copies of letters from young lieutenants to the parents of the dead, mangled identity disks, the string still dark with the sweat of some hopeful boy violently killed over fifty years ago"[1] would be delivered to him and he would spend the day slowly going through them. These boxes contained relics of British infantry activities in France and Belgium during the First World War. Fussell selected this museum to conduct his research in because it contained a world-famous collection of items related to British military actions during this war.

He would later write of these three exciting, research filled months, "I lived in the trenches with the British infantry, accompanying them on their raids, drinking their rum, searching for lice in my trouser seams, and affecting British phlegm as they prepared to jump the bags and charge into machine gun fire. How did they do it? What did they think about it? How did they control their fear? These were questions an ex-infantry officer from another war, but a notably similar one, seemed uniquely prepared to ask."[2] His research, which was supported by grants from the National Endowment for the Humanities and Rutgers University's Research Coun-

3. Oh! What a Lovely Book!

cil, would provide the basis for his greatest book, *The Great War and Modern Memory*, a work that would win him wide acclaim and establish his reputation.

Because this book is considered Fussell's best work (he also thought so and said it was his favorite book), has been so influential and controversial, and is the work most associated with him, it is important to go into some detail about it.

It is pertinent to state again that up until this time, Fussell had never written anything about this war (although he had read war memoirs from the period as a hobby), and his career had taken the path of a conventional but well-published scholar of 18th century British literature and poetry. As mentioned in the previous chapter, he felt at this stage in his career that he had said everything he wanted to about his area of expertise and wanted to move on to another subject. People write books for a variety of reasons, and Fussell, who was an extremely complex person, wrote *The Great War and Modern Memory* for diverse and revealing reasons which served several emotional and intellectual needs he had at the time. In a special afterword to the 25th anniversary edition of the book, Fussell observes, "All books of non-fiction are autobiographical, and this one more than most."[3]

First of all, it helped him to deal with some long-standing questions he had had about his own war experiences. He had been reading Great War memoirs as a hobby and wondering whether his experiences as a young infantry officer were unique and worthy of attention and whether there were any similarities between his experiences and those of the young, literary-minded infantry officers who wrote about war, and if so what he could learn from them concerning the topics of memory, order, and meaning.[4]

In a 1989 interview with the military historian Roger Spiller, Fussell said that the book was "essentially the result of my own war experience and my attempt to make sense of it. Interestingly, I think the idea of that book came to me unconsciously in 1945, when I found myself in Alsace conducting my own platoon war against the Germans in concrete emplacements left over from the First World War. We used those bunkers just as they had been used a generation earlier. I got very interested in the First World War as a sort of prolegomenon to the Second. I wasn't ready to write about my own war, so I thought, I'll put some of my awareness of what combat is like in a quasi-scholarly account of the relation of the First World War to general culture."[5]

Secondly, he penned the work in a spirit of disgust over events that were happening in the U.S. at that time, specifically the Vietnam War and certain fashionable intellectual trends. "During the Vietnam War I had grown sick of hearing phrases like 'body count' from otherwise fairly civilized people. I had listened with silent revulsion to most of the talk about the war, with silent revulsion to most of the talk of the war, with speaker's utter failure to imagine what, regardless of which "side" or ideology it was attached to, the suffering of infantry was like. One of my objects in writing this book was to reawaken the reader's imagination and power of sympathy in a world too far gone in the complacencies of mechanism, scientism, and abstraction."[6] He would also later claim that the book was about the Vietnam War as much as it was the Great War. (It is interesting to note that the book was published in 1975, the year the U.S. left Saigon and ended the war.)

Fussell was also motivated to write this study because it allowed him to explore in depth several literary techniques and polarities that had long fascinated him and that he had dealt with in his studies of 18th century British literature: irony, elegy, and innocence/experience, youth/age, and seriousness/levity. Finally, he would later claim that the book was also intended to be a "satire on humanity in general. It might be called *Gulliver's Travels* because it is a satire on how preposterous people become when they become self-righteous, when their self-righteousness obliged them to kill a whole generation of young people."[7]

Fussell often stressed that readers should view *The Great War and Modern Memory* as the work of an essayist and eulogist and not that of a scholar. While the book's main theme is decidedly large and multifaceted, each chapter can be read on its own. In the preface, he states that it is a book "about the British experience on the Western Front from 1914 to 1918 and some of the literary means by which it has been remembered, conventionalized and mythologized. It is also about the literary dimensions of the trench experience.... I have focused on places and situations where literary tradition and real life notably transect and in doing so I have tried to understand something of the simultaneous and reciprocal

3. Oh! What a Lovely Book!

process by which life feeds materials to literature while literature returns the favor by conferring forms upon life."[8]

Fussell does this by primarily focusing on the experiences and writings of a group of well-educated and mostly upper-class British combatants of the war. They are Edmund Blunden, Robert Graves, and Siegfried Sassoon, each of whom wrote famous memoirs about their experiences, and the poets Wilfred Owen and David Jones. Besides drawing attention to these writers, he also offers new interpretations of their works. But he does not only discuss these poets, he also looks at letters, diaries, popular songs, English and soldier's newspapers, illustrated weeklies, posters, doggerel, postcards, and even jokes from the war. In addition, the book provides a detailed account of everyday life in the trenches on the Western front as well as a very general overview of military operations.

Detailed studies of the literature of the Great War had previously appeared but they had concentrated on establishing which texts were important and constituted the canon, the literary qualities that make them unique, and providing biographical information about the authors. Fussell took a much different organizational approach, and instead of offering a chapter-by-chapter introduction to each writer or group of writers as was done in the past, he organized his chapters on the key themes each writer wrote about. Therefore, the literature being discussed "becomes less an end in itself than a means through which to interpret the war as a kind of literary text. The war is to be read as an artifact, full of symbolic resonance and prophetic power."[9] Moreover, as the distinguished literary historian Samuel Hynes has said, "He was the first critic, as I know, to deal with the war writings of the combatants as *literature*, and at the same time, as *history*."[10]

But Fussell's book is much more than a detailed literary analysis of key writers from the War and the themes that preoccupied them. It also asserts that the war was a cultural turning point in modern history and is an attempt to describe the intellectual legacy of the conflict. Fussell maintains that the First World War was *sui generis* in its conditions and effects—it was the first conflict between industrialized powers, the first global war, touching not just on Europe, but also Africa, Russia, Asia, the Pacific, and the Middle East. Naval engagements occurred as far away as the South China Sea and in the Pacific off Chile. It involved over 100 modern nations and every continent but the Antarctic. In fact, the war was so encompassing that it required historians to come up with a new category of war—world war.

The First World War was also the first modern and mechanized war, and was unique in the terrible scale of its global casualties—nearly 10 million soldiers killed, 21 million wounded, and 6.5 million civilians dead. One respected historian has pointed out, "The destructiveness of the First World War, in terms of the number of soldiers killed, exceeded that of all other wars known to history."[11] In just the first five months of the war, the French Army suffered 1,000,000 causalities and the Germans 800,000. Moreover, the scope of casualties in some of the battles was horrendous. Total British causalities in the Passchendaele campaign between July 31 and November 12, 1917, was 244,897 men. The infamous Battle of the Somme in 1916 resulted in 419,654 British casualties and slightly fewer German losses. (In fact, British armed forces fatalities during the war exceeded those in the Second World War by a factor of three or four to one.) It was also the first war where the majority of casualties were caused by weapons (70 percent of deaths were caused by artillery) and not illness.

Furthermore, it was the first war in which chemical weapons, zeppelins (which killed 1,413 people in raids over England), flamethrowers, the machine gun, barbed wire, steel helmets, gas masks, fighter planes, and tanks were employed, and brought war for the first time to civilian populations through aerial bombardment and unrestricted submarine warfare. It was a war where genocide and ethnic cleansing occurred, a war in which there was a prolonged stalemate on the Western front which resulted in the deaths of millions of British, French, German, and American combatants, and a war in which political boundaries were redrawn and centuries old empires disappeared. It was also a conflict which led to the greatest fall of monarchs in history.[12] Remnants of the War continue to haunt the battlefields of France and sometimes kill. A century later, bomb disposal experts are still defusing the massive amounts of munitions that were used during the conflict. It is estimated that 250–300 tonnes of ordnance remained buried in the hills of Eastern France, most of which could still explode (and do on occasion, killing or maiming farmers). It is estimated that it will take at least another century to get rid of them all.

It is also important to emphasize the special nature of trench warfare

3. Oh! What a Lovely Book!

on the Western front (the focus of Fussell's book). As Christopher Moore-Bick points out, "The deployment of immensely powerful defensive weapons like artillery and machine guns, whose efficiency in killing outstretched that of riflemen, created a deadly environment in which soldiers were deprived of the traditional warrior role of the active combatant.... Death frequently came suddenly and unexpectedly from a high-velocity shell fired by some unseen hands some distance away. Enemy combatants might not be seen for months at a time. In the absence of a personalized foe, aggressive instincts were frequently thwarted. It was especially difficult to witness comrades being killed and to suffer the strains of being under fire oneself without having any opportunity for revenge on the enemy or even escape from the killing zone.... Rather than focusing on killing the enemy, soldiers became primarily concerned with one thing—survival in the face of literally a killing machine."[13]

There is also, which is rarely mentioned, the massive economic cost of the war, which was unprecedented up to that time in terms of the wealth expended by so many countries. By 1916, the central powers were spending a whopping 50 percent of their collective GDP, or $3 billion a month, on the conflict (to translate this number into 2008 terms, multiply it by 20). Great Britain's government alone spent $43 billion on the war. Most of these monies were funded by huge borrowings, and when financial sources were exhausted, governments simply printed more money.[14] Finally, there was the cost to civilization itself. One distinguished historian has noted that the Great War "damaged civilization, the rational and liberal civilization of the European enlightenment, permanently for the worse, and through the damage done, world civilization also ... when the guns fell silent a legacy of political rancor and racial hatred so intense that no explanation of the of the causes of the Second World War can stand without references to those roots."[15]

Because of the terrible and prolonged nature of this conflict, which Fussell believes was historically unique in its horrific conditions, needless killings, and pointlessness, he posits World War I fundamentally changed the outlook of the Western world and greatly molded what it means to be modern. This might at first appear to be an overgeneralization because its outbreak in 1914 seems so long ago (even though the last Great War veteran died in 2014) and battlefield locations today are treated as archaeological sites.[16] *The Great War and Modern Memory* is a work which attempts in a fundamental way to culturally excavate our modern minds.

In 2014, a book was published entitled *The First World War in 100 Objects*. In it, the author writes, "The basis for this book is an examination of surviving objects and the interpretation of their individual narratives.... [Objects] represent a time capsule, a direct link with the time in which they were made. But they are also mute witnesses to events, recording devices that might allow a clearer understanding of a time or event—if only we can read them. Each object has a story, a unique narrative that is there to be interpreted, to be read."[17] Similarly, Fussell in this book is attempting to discern narratives and language rooted in the Great War that have formed the contours of our minds, our, as he put it, "own buried lives,"[18] and helped shape a new, modern consciousness. In addition, Fussell is one of the first authors to examine the topic of remembrance, and how wars are recalled.

In fact, on one level, the title of this book could be accurately titled *The Great War and the Modern Mind* for Fussell wants to show there is a fundamental link between the war and modernity and this link can be found in irony and the language of this war. "I am saying that there seems to be one dominating form of modern understanding; that it is essentially ironic; and that it originates largely in the application of mind and memory to the events of the Great War.... Even if now attenuated and largely metaphorical, the diction of war resides everywhere just below the surface of modern experience."[19]

The Great War and Modern Memory is divided into ten chapters. The initial chapters lay out his thesis and give background information on trench life. Each of the following chapters discusses a feature of the war that has contributed to modern public memory, examines a particular writer that employed this feature, and ends with a discussion of modern examples of this feature.

In the first chapter, "Satire of Circumstance," Fussell jumps right into his main thesis: "Every war is ironic because every war is worse than expected. Every war constitutes an irony of situation because its means are so melodramatically disproportionate to is presumed ends.... But the Great War was more ironic than any before or since. It was a hideous embarrassment to the prevailing Meliorist myth which had dominated

3. Oh! What a Lovely Book!

the public consciousness for a century. It reversed the idea of Progress."[20] He also examines the connection between irony and memory and argues that one key reason why this war was more ironic than others was that it began with such innocence.

Chapter 2, "The Troglodyte World," provides a concise overview of what trench life was like for soldiers on the Western front. He also writes about the importance of sunrise and sunset to their visually restricted lives, and the irony of the front lines being only a short trip away from England.

In the next chapter, "Adversary Proceedings," Fussell examines the phenomenon of the modern habit of gross dichotomizing—"us" and "them," "friend" and "foe," "we" and "they"—and claims it can be traced back to the war. He argues that the static, drawn out, claustrophobic, and paranoia-inducing nature of trench warfare where the landscape is divided into known and unknown, safe and unsafe territory with no-man's land between, fostered a polarizing and binary way of thinking which has resulted in the modern addiction to oppositional terminology, to simple distinctions, and to a loss of nuance, ambiguity, and complexity. While it might be objected that gross dichotomizing can be widely found throughout human history, Fussell counters that it is a proclivity that was brought to people's attention because of the extreme conditions of the First World War, and that this war trained or educated people to be aware of and expect it.

To illustrate this topic, he describes in detail how the writer Siegfried Sassoon skillfully employed this form of thinking to structure his account of his war experiences in his famous trilogy, *The Complete Memoirs of George Sherston*. Fussell writes that what makes Sassoon exceptional "is the brilliance with which he exploits the dichotomies forced to his attention by his wartime experience and refines them until they become the very fiber of his superb memoir of the war."[21] The trilogy, which consists of *Memoirs of a Fox-Hunting Man* (1928), *Memoirs of an Infantry Officer* (1930), and *Sherston's Progress* (1936) is a mixture of a memoir and a work of fiction. In it, Sassoon portrays the coming of age of a pampered, Edwardian, fox-hunting lover, George Sherston, his experiences in the Great War, and his attempts to deal with its aftereffects. Fussell argues that a complex ironic structure is present in the books and polarities are frequently used by Sassoon to highlight this irony. These polarities are not just general ones concerning contrasts between life before the war, during, and after, but also the daily and gritty dichotomies between things like the enemy and "us," line troops and the much hated red-tabbed army staff, the "real" life of the trenches and the "false" life in England, day and night activities, rest areas and trench life, and sunrise and sunset. Sassoon's style and tone throughout the work, which he uses to devastating effect, is understated and restrained, but also visually arresting and closely attuned to geography, light, color, and mood.

Fussell finishes the chapter by cautioning that the modern tendency after the War to find division present everywhere is not simply due to the war, but that it influenced in unique ways how modern people choose to see or communicate certain things. He cites T. S. Eliot's famous concept of a "dissociation of sensibility," E. M. Forster's "only connect" command, the combative writings of Ezra Pound and Wyndham Lewis, the highly politicized and adversary rhetoric of literary criticism, especially in the 1960s and 1970s, and the rebellious and subversive British "Bright Young Things" in the 1920s, as examples of how the Great War's oppositional and battlefield imagery permeated modern thinking and language.

The next chapter, "Myth, Ritual and Romance," offers a comprehensive analysis of the intriguing paradox of how "a plethora of very unmodern superstitions, talismans, wonders, miracles, relics, legends, and rumors ... could take shape in the midst of a war representing a triumph of modern industrialism, materialism, and mechanism."[22] He then examines numerous superstitions, myths, and legends from the war, including the powerful mystical and symbolic importance of the number three; the curious tale of the "Angels of Mons" where British soldiers were said to have been saved from a rout by the Germans in 1914 by the sudden appearance of angelic bowmen by St. George who shot arrows at the enemy; the widely believed stories of crucified allied soldiers and of large bands of army deserters who lived in underground and abandoned trenches; and the famous myth of the Golden Virgin which concerned the forward leaning statue of the Virgin and Child on top of the Basilica at Albert. He also explains the significance of the concept of the romance quest in the war and in the works of William Morris's 1896 novel *The Well at the World's End* and how John Bunyan's 16th century work *The Pilgrim's Progress* provided solace for imaginative and troubled soldiers.

3. Oh! What a Lovely Book!

Fussell turns to the half-English and half-Welsh poet, painter, and essayist, David Jones, to explain this new world of myth and romance created by the war. Jones's most famous work is his 1963, seven-part autobiographical poem *In Parenthesis,* which chronicles the travails of Private John Ball, leading to his wounding in the Battle of the Somme in 1916. Of the five World War I writers discussed in detail in *The Great War and Modern Memory,* Jones's writings are the most difficult, and this is especially true of *In Parenthesis.* Fussell contends that Jones is attempting in this work to solve the problem of how to use traditional meanings to describe the unparalleled realities of the Great War. He claims the poem is strongly conservative and that Jones endeavors to find meaning by directly associating the experiences of front-line participants with tradition through multifarious and dense allusions to a wide body of writers, artists, myths and folklore, including Thomas Malory, Alfred Lord Tennyson, T. S. Eliot, William Shakespeare, Old Testament history, the Arthurian legend, English folklore, Welsh folklore, Roman Catholic liturgy, Norse myth, Samuel Taylor Coleridge, Geoffrey Chaucer, Sir James G. Frazer, the Florentine painter Paolo Uccello, and Lewis Carroll.[23] By linking the war with being "in the tradition," Jones is implying that it is comprehensible.

Fussell thinks this is wrong-headed, writing, "The tradition in which the poem points holds suffering to be close to sacrifice and individual effort to end in heroism; it contains, unfortunately, no precedent for an understanding of war as a shambles, and its participants as victims."[24] He insists that the Great War cannot be understood in traditional terms because it was historically unprecedented and therefore impossible to be neatly fitted to any previous form of explanation, and that Jones ultimately fails in his endeavor to romanticize and elevate it to famous historical events in the past. Fussell does, however, admit that Jones's poem is in spite of this limitation a masterpiece and memorable for its passages where man's humanity is revealed and for its realistic and suggestive physical descriptions. Fussell's interpretation of Jones has received some criticism, but he is innovative in the way he has meshed Jones's poem with the Great War's mythopoeic world.[25]

Chapter 5, "Oh What a Literary War" (the title is a playful riff on the famous 1960s play and movie about the conflict, *Oh! What a Lovely*

War), offers an extremely well researched and fascinating discussion of "the unparalleled literariness of all ranks who fought the Great War."[26] Fussell shows this was because there was a widespread respect for humanistic education and literature in England at the time. Members of the middle and upper classes usually received a good grounding in classical literature—both Greek and Latin—and the great English poets in public schools and universities. There was also widespread interest in popular education and self-education among the lower-middle and lower classes, with schools like the National Home Reading Union and the Workmen's Institutes, created to help people rise in the class system. George Walter has noted, "Thanks to a series of Victorian and Edwardian educational reforms, even those who left school before the statutory leaving age of fourteen were equipped with a level of basic literacy previously unseen in Britain. This literacy was primarily engendered through an engagement with literature of a capital 'L.'"[27]

This chapter also demonstrates how literature in several ways significantly informed the war, from start to finish. Because of the efficient British postal service, the long periods of boredom experienced by soldiers on the line owing to the stagnant military situation, and the many participants dedicated to improving themselves culturally, reading formed a big part of many soldiers' lives. Fussell explains why anthologies like *The Oxford Book of English Verse*, novels by Joseph Conrad, Thomas Hardy, H. G. Wells, and Anthony Trollope, and the poetry of A. E. Housman, were popular, and how these and other canonical works enabled individuals to cope with the war and communicate their experiences to others. As he brilliantly observes, these works of literature helped demonstrate what the war was really like by "literal[izing] what before had been figurative."[28] He also contends that the readers of these works strongly felt that literature was deeply connected with social life, real experience, and not just the prerogative of critics and intellectuals (a belief that Fussell, as we saw in the last chapter, also firmly held).

Fussell also presents an intriguing investigation into the various ways the war changed the use of language, usage, and form-rhetoric. He discusses how the conflict and the military language it produced, the compensatory British style of phlegm and a stiff upper lip, and the charged literary and linguistic atmosphere of the period resulted in a war diction

3. Oh! What a Lovely Book!

that, while mainly metaphorical, continues to live "just below the surface of modern experience."[29] One way this diction can be seen is in the use of words and phrases like *lousy, crummy, breakthrough, over the top, firing line, behind the lines, rank and file, trench coat, sector,* and *no man's land*.[30]

To underscore the unique nature of the literariness of the war, it is useful to contrast it with the American Civil War. Fussell points out that this war was the first in which a very large number of soldiers who fought were literate (the U.S. at that time had the highest literacy rate in the world), but it was not, unlike the Great War, a conflict which was strongly literary and produced a large number of exceptional writers. He lightly touches on the question of why this was the case, arguing that, unlike the British, the U.S. has long lacked an awareness of a national literary canon and a long tradition of first-rate writers, noting that the *Oxford Book of American Verse* was not even published until 1950.[31] Fussell holds that these shortcomings explain why no great war literature was produced by Americans during the First World War, and why the literature that was written by individuals like E .E. Cummings and Alan Seeger was self-conscious, lacking in literary allusions, one-dimensional, and sparse.

The next chapter, "Theater of War," begins with a general discussion of the close connection between warfare and the theater, observing that, especially during anxious moments, soldiers keenly feel the unbelievable irrational and cruel nature of war, which makes it impossible for them to believe that they are actually part of it, and not some actor on a stage. Fussell writes that viewing war in this manner gave psychological comfort to the participant, for "with a sufficient sense of theater, he can perform his duties without implicating his 'real' self and without impairing his innermost conviction that the world is a rational place."[32] He goes on to assert that the British have a particular talent for the theatrical because of their class system and the importance it assigns to role-playing, and their cultural awareness and the influence of Shakespeare.[33] Consequently, Fussell maintains that there is a British tendency to associate memories of the Great War with the imagery and techniques of the theater.

To support this thesis, he turns to the British writer Robert Graves's famous 1929 memoir of the war, *Good-Bye to All That*, arguing that it brilliantly exemplifies this tendency by describing the truth of war in theatrical terms. Fussell maintains that this work has been frequently mischaracterized as being a historically flawed but important war memoir, and that it is really a broad satire strongly influenced by the techniques of stage comedy. These techniques include the use of astonishing coincidences, multiple endings, strange characters, humorous interactions between individuals from different social classes, and irony.[34] He contends that Graves's originality lies in his ability to brilliantly place these comedic and absurd forms into descriptions of the ghastliness of his war experiences. Fussell also states that Graves is a gifted comedian, and the book brims with "delightful impetuosity, the mastery, the throw-away fun of it all."[35]

Fussell's interpretation is novel because, although *Good-Bye to All That* was very popular and received much attention when it was published (so much so that it made it financially possible for Graves to move to Majorca), critical attention has mainly been paid to Graves's poetry and popular novels instead of to this work. When critics have discussed the book, they have often given it only brief attention and concentrated on its biographical aspects and ignore the ironic, illusionist, theatrical, and joking elements in the book. Fussell may have overstated his case that the book is a dark satiric comedy for *Good-Bye to All That* is really several books, including a *Bildungsroman*, a cool and dispassionate but realistic war memoir steeped in folly and knavery, a rollicking autobiography chock-full of fiction and exaggeration, a pointed critique of the values of bourgeois English society that once enthused Graves, and a heartfelt farewell to England, the painful past, and politics, literature, and religion as practiced.[36] But the memoir does also abound in satirical, darkly humorous, and theatrical elements.[37] Fussell's interpretation adds an important dimension to the work and shows how subversive yet revealing the work is about war.

Finally, although Fussell does not note it, it seems quite credible that parts of the famous opening first sentence of the 1929 edition of *Good-Bye to All That* (which was cut in the revised edition) which contains the words "good-bye to you and to you and to me and to all that,"[38] is a satirical allusion to the poet Rupert Brooke's 1910 poem "Dining Room Tea," which begins and ends with the line, "When you were there, and you, and you."[39] This subtle but distinct echo provides further possible evidence for Fussell's thesis for Brooke, who died in 1915 before the real horrors of the

3. Oh! What a Lovely Book!

war began, was infamous for his patriotic and idealistic war poetry, and thus eminently subvertible war poetry.

Although he does not directly state it, it appears relatively clear that, of all the Great War writers discussed in this book, Graves is one of Fussell's favorites, if not his favorite. When he writes that Graves's enemies were "solemnity, certainty, complacency, pomposity, cruelty,"[40] and his distrust of official documents and attempts at constructing a rational historiography of a war, he could have also been talking about himself. Graves's underlying anger, interest in irony and satire, and horror over the sheer contingency of war, mirrors Fussell's own attitude as did Grave's subversion of common beliefs. In a 1998 introduction to the book, Fussell wrote that Graves had a "tough mindedness, a virile sense of the funny, a tendency to disbelieve public truths and to ridicule them, as well as an unerring eye for phonies and a powerful impulse to laugh at them."[41] Here, he also could have been talking about himself, and as we shall see in a later chapter, *Goodbye to All That* served as one of his models when Fussell sat down to write his own account of his war experiences, *Doing Battle*.

Chapter 7, "Arcadian Recourses," delves into the deeply rooted pastoral tradition in English literature and the various ways this rich tradition was used by participants to psychologically deal with the war. Fussell interestingly observes that 50 percent of the poems in the version of *The Oxford Book of English Verse* that many educated soldiers carried in the trenches, concerned flowers, and 35 percent involved roses, and that the anthology contained works from Edmund Spenser to Matthew Arnold. He goes on to show how that the pastoral (the favorite style for elegy), was used in the Great War to indicate the war's horrors as well as to provide comfort and shelter to individuals from it. He demonstrates this by showing the pervasiveness of images of literary pastoralism, shepherds, sheep, birds (larks and nightingale), birdsong, roses (which symbolized loyalty to England), and poppies, in writings about and remembrances of the conflict.

The poet whom Fussell employs to illustrate this theme in depth is Edmund Blunden, whom he calls "a harmless young shepard." He examines Blunden's 1928 pastoral elegy in prose and memoir of the war, *Undertones of War*. Like Sassoon's memoir, the book does not reject the past, for both Blunden and Sassoon loved tradition (while fearing it might be lost).

American Gadfly

Unlike Graves, Blunden is not in revolt against conventional beliefs. Fussell points out that Blunden's book differs from Sassoon's and Graves's accounts because the attention is not on Blunden himself but on the experiences of the battalion he served with. Fussell posits that Blunden's originality lies in his archaism, the way he skillfully uses language, imagery and scenery of the traditional literary pastoral and its focus on pre-industrial England as a model to gauge the unspeakable savagery of the First World War. He insightfully notes that "every word of *Undertones of War*, every rhythm, allusion, and droll personification, can be recognized as an assault on the war and on the world which chose to conduct and continue it. Blunden's style is his critique. It suggests what a modern world would look like to a sensibility that was genuinely civilized."[42]

The next chapter, "Soldier Boys," was precedent establishing because it brought the topic of sexuality for the first time explicitly into the discussion of the British experience of the Great War. Since ancient times, numerous literary and literal associations have been drawn between war and love and sexuality. Fussell contends that because of this connection, the isolating and alienating nature of the war, the lack of women, and the basic human need for attachment, it is not surprising that the experiences of British soldiers in the conflict were often homoerotic. Fussell is careful to state that he uses homoerotic to mean "a sublimated (i.e. "chaste") form of temporary homosexuality,"[43] and that there was little active homosexuality in the trenches. He does note that the British did have a tendency for such feelings, especially in the 19th and early 20th century, and that it was especially pronounced among individuals who were from the upper and upper middle classes and had received a public school education. He also ascribes this homoerotic motif in the war to the influence of the Aesthetic Movement, the Uranians group with their ideal of "Greek Love," and to writers such as Gerard Manley Hopkins, Alfred Lord Tennyson, and the very popular poet A. E. Housman (who was avidly read at the front).

Fussell concentrates in this chapter on the renowned poet Wilfred Owen, who was tragically killed in the last days of the war in 1918. He believes that Owen's poetry conspicuously displays these Victorian and early 20th century homoerotic leitmotifs. For Fussell, the way Owen reacted poetically to the war was unique and vastly different from that of Blunden, Graves, and Sassoon, who all had a "university bent toward struc-

3. Oh! What a Lovely Book!

tured general ideas. Owen, as Bergonzi has noted, "rarely attempts a contrast, nostalgic, or ironic, between the trenches, and remembered English scenes. Rather, he harnesses his innate fondness for dwelling on the visible sensuous particulars of boys in order to promote an intimate identification with them."[44] By focusing the outrage and pity he felt over the war on poor, defenseless, handsome boys, and using his sympathetic imagination, Owen was able to graphically communicate in his verse the reality of the conflict.

Fussell ends the chapter by discussing another homoerotic image that is commonly mentioned when recalling the war—the watching of men bathing—of soldiers momentarily released from the war, stripped of their uniforms, swimming, talking, and relaxing. Fussell finds this common image extremely poignant because the men are terribly defenseless, and because of the visible contrast between their vulnerable flesh and the hard metal of warfare. He also describes how this image has resonated literarily since the war in modern works like *Catch 22* and the poetry of Lincoln Kirstein.

Since the appearance of *The Great War and Modern Memory*, studies on sexuality and the First World War have become more common, and its importance recognized, thanks in part to Fussell bringing attention to the topic.[45] One historian has gone so far as to state in a recent study that sex "is an integral part of the story of the Great War, and particularly of the Western Front."[46]

The final chapter, "Persistence and Memory," depicts the impact of the war on British daily life, including cuisine, subsequent military policy, attitudes towards the press, the devaluation of language, and on British and American writers such as Evelyn Waugh, Norman Mailer, Keith Douglas, Derek Robinson, Ted Hughes, and Louis Simpson. He also gives an intriguing (and graphic) analysis of how the Great War resonates in Thomas Pynchon's celebrated 1973 novel, *Gravity's Rainbow*. Fussell concludes the book by stating that "in this study of a small bit of that culture of the past, I have tried to present just a few recognition scenes. My belief is that what we recognize in them is a part, and perhaps not the least compelling part, of our buried lives."[47]

Sprinkled throughout the book and given prominence in the last chapter are references to the famous 20th century Canadian literary critic and

American Gadfly

theorist Northrop Frye and his book *Anatomy of Criticism*. At the time Fussell was writing *The Great War and Modern Memory*, Frye was considered by many to be one of the top critics in the field. Fussell was intrigued with how Frye's ideas helped explain the complex connection between the Great War and literature and traditional ideas. Specifically, he was much taken with Frye's "theory of modes," and his idea that literature operated in a historical cycle in a sequence of three phases, starting with myth and romance, with high and low mimetic in the middle phase, and ironic in the last, and Frye's notion of the demonic world—the world of pain, confusion, oppression, and the nightmare—and its connection to the world of war. In the final chapter of the book, Fussell relates these phases to aspects of the war. He would later write in 2000 that he found Frye's theory dated and would not have used it if he were to write the book again.[48] But because Fussell's overall analysis is not dependent upon Frye's ideas, the book does not suffer from this change in his thinking.

The Great War and Modern Memory is a brilliant and elegantly written work of scholarship, highly original, full of important insights and sensitive readings of great works of literature, it is refreshingly interdisciplinary and has a bold thesis. It raises important questions about the connection between literature and war, as well as language and reality. Moreover, it also engages readers on an emotional level (a rarity for an academic study) for it is a deeply haunting and haunted book, about figurative if not literal ghosts, the messages they bring from the past, and how their voices have become part of our collective, submerged lives and myths.[49]

When it was published in 1975 by Oxford University Press, *The Great War and Modern Memory* instantly garnered a great deal of attention and praise and was widely reviewed in many academic and nonacademic publications. Noted writers and critics such as Frank Kermode, Geoffrey Wolff, Peter Stansky, and William H. Pritchard wrote glowing reviews. Lionel Trilling, one of the leading American literary critics of the 20th century, called it "an original and brilliant piece of cultural history and one of the most deeply moving books I have read in a long time." The book also won several important honors, including the National Book Award, the National Book Critics Circle Award, and the Ralph Waldo Emerson Award. Even strong critics of the work, like the military historian

3. Oh! What a Lovely Book!

Gary Sheffield, have conceded that it is "the single most influential recent book on the First World War."[50]

More recently, Modern Library named it the 75th-best non-fiction book of the 20th century. In 2000, a special 25th anniversary edition of the book was published, and in 2009, a special illustrated edition was printed by Sterling Publishing. The book has always remained in print and continues to sell well. By 2013, 130,000 copies had been sold, which is a remarkable number for a university press publication. More recently, the famed historian Peter Stansky listed it as one of the five best works on violence and visionaries in a 2017 article published in *The Wall Street Journal*.

James Campbell has neatly described the vast influence this work has exerted. "Quite simply, it is difficult to underestimate *The Great War and Modern Memory's* influence. The book's ambition and popularity move interpretation of the war from a relatively minor literary and historical specialization to a much more widespread cultural concern. His claims for the meaning of the war are profound and far-reaching; indeed, some have found them hyperbolic. Yet, whether in spite of or because of the enormity of his assertions, Fussell has set the agenda for most of the criticism that has followed him.... *The Great War and Modern Memory* marks a fork in the road for Great War criticism. After 1975, criticism largely becomes divided between questions of gender and sexuality and questions of the war's relationship to modernist culture. Both of these directions are present in Fussell in a way they have not been in previous discussions."[51] Moreover, his methodology has been applied to other noted writers who fought in war but did not directly write about it, like the popular fantasy author J. R. R. Tolkien.[52]

Another way of looking at this book's enormous impact is offered by the British writer Geoff Dyer in his meditative study of the 1916 Battle of the Somme. In it, Dyer mentions that when he was preparing for his trip to the battlefield site in Flanders, he reread *The Great War and Modern Memory* and discovered that "it is now difficult to read about the War except through the filter of Fussell's ground-breaking investigation of its dominant themes.... Fussell has himself become part of the process whereby the memory of the war becomes lodged in the present. His commentary has become a part of the testimony it comments on."[53]

American Gadfly

Even today, if you pick up a book on British culture, literature, or military affairs in the Great War, chances are good there will be an allusion to *The Great War and Modern Memory* in it.[54] Furthermore, Fussell's influence can be seen in the titles of many of these studies: *The Great War in Russian Memory*; *The Great War and Medieval Memory: War, Remembrance, and Medievalism in Britain and Germany, 1914–1940*; *The Great War, Memory, and Ritual: Commemoration in the City and East London, 1916–1939*; *The Great War in German Memory: Society, Politics, and Psychological Trauma, 1914–1945*; *The Great War: Myth and Memory*; *The Great War and Memory in Central and South-Eastern Europe, War and Memory in the 20th Century*; *Remembering War: The Great War Between Memory and History in the 20th Century*; *Death So Noble: Memory, Meaning, and the Great War*; and *Britain's Two Wars Against Germany: Myth, Memory, and the Distortions of Hindsight.*

Fussell later said that *The Great War and Modern Memory* was the easiest of his 15 books to write (calling the process a magical experience) and that it was his favorite book. He was also very surprised by its popularity and speculated that it might have been due to readers attempting to recover a lost feeling of religion or elegy, but he remained throughout his life not entirely clear why it so strongly connected with readers, especially those who were not British.

But the book has also over time received criticism, some quite strong, primarily by two groups of historians: military and literary/cultural. Military historians (mainly British) have been the most vocal in their critiques,[55] and Fussell has become in some ways their favorite whipping boy. One problem they have always had is how to treat him. While they are aware that he was trained as a literary historian and critic and not as a military historian, they are forced to treat him using their methodology. (It is interesting that when Oxford University Press published the book they classified it on the back cover as a work of "History/Literature".) In essence, their objections are threefold: they contend that the historical material Fussell presents is far too limited in scope and factually inaccurate, that he employs a dubious and not rigorous methodology when presenting this material, and that he heavily relies upon unreliable material to make his points.[56]

In a widely cited 1994 article, prominent military historians Robin

3. Oh! What a Lovely Book!

Prior and Trevor Wilson launched a blistering attack on the book. At the start, they strongly contended that *The Great War and Modern Memory* is in fact not a work of literary criticism and they question the value of using literary texts to reveal the real story of a war. They write, "Although a Professor of English, Fussell writes as a historian. He puts it bluntly that his literary training and literary raw material equip him to lay bare the realities of war. Conventional historians, in his opinion, only dress up the distorted, fanciful version of official apologists. This raises an issue. If diplomatic documents and battle narratives will not explicate all facets of modern war, will literary sources reveal the entire story? Or is modern war too complex and perhaps too self-contradictory to be wholly revealed even by imaginative writings and personal accounts?"[57]

There is little that Prior and Wilson like about the book. They contend that Fussell neglects to show that the war was actually fought for worthwhile purposes, that he excludes other military theaters besides that of the Western front (like the war at sea and in the air), and the vast mobilization of the British economy and industrial resources for war purposes—endeavors which they claim were not futile or awash with irony. They also point out that Fussell completely ignores the Allied victory in 1918 (and the reasons for it) and is careless in some of the numbers he cites (for example, his assertion that the British army had a casualty rate of 7,000 soldiers a day throughout the war—which they say would have been impossible), and that while he is very hard on British commanders in the war, he completely ignores the incompetency of German officers. Prior and Wilson are also offended that Fussell "feels entitled to pass judgements on the causes of the war, the chronology and changing nature of the war. He even feels able to generalize about the worthlessness of wars beyond this particular conflict."[58]

But their main objection is over the way Fussell characterizes the British army, saying that he erroneously depicts it as consisting of "only two elements: irresponsible commanders who keep well clear of danger while sending their foot-soldiers to purposeless graves, and their victims—who if they survive—grow increasingly disillusioned with the war and with those on their own side who direct or applaud it."[59] The topic of the performance of British commanders has received increasing attention since the publication of Fussell's work. Today, most military historians believe that British strategy and tactics on the Western front during the war, while appalling during the initial years, did eventually during the final years of the war show a "learning curve" in which the army was able to successfully adjust to the new form of warfare being waged, and that this adjustment hugely contributed to the Allied victory in November 1918.[60] Specifically, they argue that success was largely achieved on the Western front using the techniques of a "bite and hold" strategy, which helped solve the long standing trench warfare problem of how to make a military breakthrough. This strategy entailed employing a large but short creeping barrage shortly before infantry attacks on a wide front and the infantry advancing not more than 1,500 yards. Then the infantry consolidated itself behind a standing artillery bombardment which would hold off any attempted German counterattack. Progress was slow, but the strategy was highly effective given the nature of trench warfare. Close coordination among units was key since it involved the deployment of three types of existing technology: aircraft, radio (wireless), and artillery, along with massive logistical preparation.[61]

These historians have also made a concerted effort to change the widespread perception (like Fussell's) that the British High Command was mainly composed of officers (like Commander-in-Chief of the British Expeditionary Force in Flanders and France, Field Marshal Sir Douglas Haig) who were criminally incompetent, out of touch, too tradition bound, and unwilling to adapt to conditions. They insist that the High Command was in fact more competent than previously believed, but greatly hampered in their choices by the extremely limited and static tactical battlefield conditions, the lack of viable options to attack the Central Powers other than the Western front, ineffective voice communications, and the limitations imposed by coalitional warfare. Consequently, they insist that the attrition with maneuver approach they adopted, as costly as it was in human life, was the best and most effective strategy that could have been chosen under the circumstances. More broadly, they also claim that the Great War was necessary, the Allied cause was just (the prevention of Germany dominating continental Europe and controlling the Channel Ports), and the Allied victory was essential in obtaining this goal.[62]

Another common criticism of Fussell's analysis is that he took the war experiences of a very small number of soldiers—well-educated, mainly

3. Oh! What a Lovely Book!

upper class, highly articulate, and dissident—to accurately represent the experiences of the British army as a whole, and that the great majority of front-line soldiers were in fact from urban and rural working and lower middle-class backgrounds. They also point out that 8.9 million British citizens were mobilized for the war, and these soldiers displayed a wide variety of reactions to the war, and that many did not display the attitudes of the writers Fussell cites.[63]

Military historians have also taken issue with Fussell's portrayal of ordinary soldiers as passive victims, doomed to a terrible fate, and lacking agency. Tony Ashworth, in his book *Trench Warfare 1914–1918: The Live and Let Live System*, has held that many of them did in fact have choices, albeit limited, to influence the war and increase their odds of living through the war. Ashworth's analysis rests upon the concept of what he has called a live and let live system which was developed by some soldiers in which a truce was established "where enemies stopped fighting by agreement for a period of time: the British let the Germans live provided the Germans let them live in return…. Truces were usually tacit, but always unofficial and illicit [and illegal].… The unofficial policy of live and let live was the antithesis of the official kill or be killed."[64] Ashworth lists three ways this system worked: first, by open exchanges of peace, second, by a refusal to engage in aggressive action (he points out that there were sectors on the front which were generally quiet where this approach was tacitly observed), and third, by what he calls ritualization, where participants attempted to act in a non-lethal matter and hoped it would be reciprocated.

Historians have also criticized Fussell for his contention that the Great War was *sui generis*, an unhistorical event. They maintain that it was not fundamentally different from other prior conflicts. One historian has written that the scale of the war set it apart, but that it was ultimately "a war of a very traditional type." Another has stated, "It was not history's longest or bloodiest conflict. It was shorter than the Second World War and cost only one-fifth as many lives. Indeed, the military stalemate on the Western Front ensured that the armies lacked the opportunity to rampage over enemy territory, burning cities and destroying crops and livestock."[65]

Moreover, some critics have questioned the validity of Fussell's heavy reliance on the memories of the veterans he cites. British historian Dan Todman has observed that we cannot automatically presume their memories to be accurate or useful as Fussell does. He argues, "This can be a difficult subject for the non-combatant historian to tackle. There is a temptation, meeting veterans in person, on screen or on the page, to grant them an aura of instant credibility. They have seen and done things most of us have not.... Co-opting veteran's experience may be an obligation, but it is also a validation."[66] Todman raises the problem that memories might be too selective, can be influenced by outside sources or fabricated, and are capable of changing over time.

Finally, Fussell has also been attacked for what critics perceive to be his overtly rosy, romantic, and nostalgic depiction of prewar England as a golden age of stability, confident values, peace, prosperity, optimism, and steeped in "never such innocence again." They point out that the period was really one of radical change, division, doubt, intense nationalistic rivalries, massive income inequality, and protest. The popular historian Barbara Tuchman once formulated a rule, based upon careful research about the topic, which stated that "all statements of how lovely it was in that era made by persons contemporary with it will be found to be made after 1914."[67]

Several of these objections are valid. Fussell does make some mistakes about historical facts and his grasp of and comments about the strategic and tactical nature of the Great War and some the decisions made by the British High Command have been shown to be incorrect. (He would later acknowledge this.) But it should be said in his defense that he cannot be completely faulted since *The Great War and Modern Memory* was published in 1975, several years before revisionary accounts of the war began to appear in large numbers and became accepted by the historical establishment.[68] It appears that he heavily relied upon British historian A. J. Taylor's *Illustrated History of the First World War* and the famous military historian B. H. Liddell Hart's *The Real War: 1914–1918* for his discussion of military matters. Both books were strongly critical of the British High Command's conduct of the conflict. Fussell's use of these works is understandable for as Dan Todman has stated, "since both of these works are accessible, [they] have often been used as authoritative sources of opinions on the war."[69] (It should be noted, though, that Fussell's discussion of what life in the trenches were like in chapter two, "The Troglodyte World"— remains generally accurate).[70]

3. Oh! What a Lovely Book!

Moreover, in Fussell's defense, there has been some criticism of aspects of the revisionist view. The respected military historian John Keegan has maintained that while the British army displayed much variation in tactics during the conflict, one central and brutal fact remained true about the fighting on the Western front: "The simple truth of 1914–1918 trench warfare is that a large number of soldiers unprotected by anything but cloth uniforms, however they were trained, however equipped, against large masses of other soldiers, was bound to result in very heavy casualties among the attackers. That was proved to be the case, whatever the variation in tactics and equipment.... The basic and stark fact was that conditions of warfare between 1914–1918 predisposed towards slaughter and that only a different technology, one not available until a generation later, would have altered such an outcome."[71] Furthermore, some proponents of the revisionist school fail to factor in the significance of the Allied blockade of Germany, the failure of the German submarine campaign, and the arrival of American troops in France, upon the outcome of the war.

Fussell addressed the question of why he only focused on the Western front for his analysis and ignored air and naval warfare and what was occurring in areas and continents in the preface of *The Great War and Modern Memory*, stating that when we think of the Great War, our ideas primarily are based on images of trench warfare in France and Belgium. Furthermore, this is the region the most famous writers and poets of the war wrote about.[72]

But there is clearly a "two cultures" problem that has hindered many military historians from fully understanding the position Fussell is putting forth. He views the Great War through a lens that is intellectually steeped in the humanistic, iconoclastic, highly skeptical and ironic 18th century Augustan literary tradition which he greatly admired, and emotionally steeped in his horrific experiences as an infantryman during the Second World War. As a result, underlying Fussell's analysis in this book is his intense hatred of war in any form, and any attempt to sanitize or sentimentalize the horror, brutality, and pointlessness associated with it. In short, he believed that he was exposing truths about war through the writers he selected that military historians failed to capture because of their (in his eyes) limited methodology and cold-blooded focus on military necessity. Although he never directly addressed the conclusions of the revisionist view of the war, he would have undoubtedly felt that these historians were far too accepting of the tremendous losses suffered by the British and the costly blunders and weakness of the British High Command and too willing to justify them on the grounds of the tactical and weaponry improvements slowly made by the military.

Fussell always steadfastly kept his eye on the butcher's bill, the cost and human consequences of war and how it profoundly damages not just bodies, but also minds, and by implication, societies. (This would also be a theme that he would emphasize and further explore in his later books *Wartime*, *Doing Battle*, and *The Boys' Crusade*.)[73]

Fussell's deep emotional attachment to this belief can be seen in a passage from his 1996 autobiography where he says that in *The Great War and Modern Memory* he wanted "to make the reader's flesh creep. I wanted my readers to weep as they sensed the despair of people like themselves, torn, and obliterated for a cause beyond their understanding. I had cried so often while writing the book that to steady myself I often had to take a long walk and breathe deeply after writing some heartrending passage."[74] This concern can also be seen in the fact that he dedicated the book to Technical Sergeant Edward Keith Hudson, who, as described in chapter one, was killed standing next to him on March 15, 1945, the day when he himself was severely wounded, and in the picture he chose for the cover of the book which he accidentally found in the Imperial War Museum. It shows a worried young British soldier appearing "aware of being doomed to a meaningless death."[75]

Historians use a different epistemology: they aim to objectively impose order and institutional structure upon events, and heavily rely upon verifiable historical evidence that is gathered by using professional standards. In contrast, Fussell, who stated he was not a historian, analyzes myths and literature, uses elements of popular culture, equates experience that is closest to the action with authority and privileges this experience, is deeply skeptical of official documents, is not afraid to use emotion in his analysis, and writes as an essayist and eulogist.

It is difficult not to believe some of the intense negative reactions Fussell's writings have induced in military historians is largely because they fail to understand this deeply humanistic (and ironic) and elegiac literary sensibility he is operating from. This misunderstanding can be seen

3. Oh! What a Lovely Book!

in the comment of one historian who has alleged that "rather than conduct wider research, Fussell simply expresses his own prejudices in the most violently sarcastic way."[76]

One example of how some historians have failed to comprehend his ironic writing style can be seen in Prior and Wilson's flabbergasted reaction to his statement that eight million people died in the Great War because two people (the Archduke Ferdinand and his wife) were shot. Now clearly, Fussell is not being that simplistic here; he would freely admit that this assassination did not occur in a political vacuum and that there were a host of other reasons why the conflict began, but he would also argue that the fact that such a catastrophic and global war was precipitated by the murder of two relatively minor individuals *is* highly ironic.[77] Furthermore, Prior and Wilson also seem immune to the literary/aesthetic points Fussell raises. For instance, they dismiss his description of how sunrise and sunset have historically an important literary association in British writing and occupied a special moral and aesthetic significance for many soldiers because of the confining nature of trench warfare and its constructed view. Prior and Wilson crudely mock (and unfairly characterize) Fussell's analysis, stating, "Dawn, in Fussell's view, has never recovered from what the Great War did to it."[78]

They also do not like Fussell's remark that every war is worse than expected and ironic because the means employed are glaringly incommensurate with its assumed goal. This is an understandable statement given Fussell's humanistic assumptions and concern with the human price of war. But they misinterpret the statement, writing, "Many historians no doubt, of the sort Fussell dismisses, would hesitate to claim knowledge of 'every war' or even the great majority of wars."[79] They then question whether the wars that Prussia fought in the 19th century to create an unified Germany "at a relatively small outlay in life and treasure,"[80] could be called "worse than expected" and constituted an "irony of situation."[81] Fussell would remark that it does to those who were killed or grievously wounded during the wars.

Finally, Prior and Wilson observe that "one work of literature missing from Fussell's pages and denied his seal of approval is F. E. Manning's *Her Privates We*—arguably the greatest First World War novel about combat experience by a British writer. Its omission is not accidental. Manning's book does not fit his profile."⁸² They are correct that Fussell does not discuss this work (but it is mentioned once in the text, and he quotes a poem by Manning). If Prior and Wilson had done a little homework, they would have realized that Fussell wrote a special introduction to a Penguin reprint of this novel in 1990, four years before their article. In it, he enthusiastically praises the book, arguing that "few writers about war are better than Manning in rendering the fear of battle and registering the way men try to command it by rituals and rationalizing.... What would it be like to be an extraordinarily smart, articulate person caught in a catastrophe requiring deep moral analysis but apparently quite resistant to it? This book answers that question."⁸³

What's more, many of the more traditional historians vehemently dislike his attempt to expand the scope of military history by taking an interdisciplinary literary and cultural approach which incorporates works of literature, elements of popular culture, and gender, and not military documents, the precise movement of armies on the battlefield, the strategic and political decisions made, as primary sources.⁸⁴ This resentment can be seen in an outburst by Peter Hart, the director of the Imperial War Museum and Great War oral historian. In his 2008 book on the Battle of the Somme, Hart complains about what he calls the "crude sentimental approach" to the war, where "the overall context of the Great War had long been forgotten and the teaching of the subject reduced to an adjunct of English literature that can be brutally summarized in just five words: 'the pity of it all.' Politicians are portrayed as Machiavellian, but simultaneously weak, generals are stupid, soldiers are hapless victims and war poets are latter-day saints made flesh."⁸⁵

This is not to say that Fussell thinks discussions of purely military matters cannot be used to complement a humanistic account. He frequently praised the writings of noted military historians such as John Keegan and John Ellis and was especially taken with writings of the renowned historian Martin Gilbert, going so far as to say that the historical tradition he was employing was based on Gilbert's emotionally based books on the two World Wars. "It is as if Gilbert's 'objective' historiography is not merely impossible but inhuman, offensively heartless and insensitive. To him the writing of history is not a science but distinctly one of the humanities, and only those with deep feelings for the human predicament should try

3. Oh! What a Lovely Book!

it. His work and that of others in his emotional tradition has earned these writers the contemptuous designation 'the Boo-Hoo Brigade,' as one London newspaper ventured to stigmatize them.... I would like to think that this book [*The Great War and Modern Memory*] as a whole, has added a few volunteers to the Boo-Hoo Brigade."[86]

Fussell was quite aware of the epistemological pitfalls involved in using literature to capture the complexity of war. In fact, he touches upon this very topic in several sections in the book. In chapter five, entitled "Problems of Factual Testimony," he discusses "one of the cruxes of the war ... the collision between events and the language available—or thought appropriate—to describe them."[87] In the book's final chapter, he freely acknowledges that "the memoir is a kind of fiction.... The further personal written materials move from the form of the daily diary, the closer they approach to the figurative and the fictional. The significances belonging to fiction are attainable only as 'diary' or annals move toward the mode of memoir, for it is the ex post facto view of an action that generates coherence or makes irony possible."[88] But, he also says, "These memoirs are especially worthy of the closest examination because, for all the blunt violence they depict, they seem so delicately transitional, pointing at once in two opposite directions—back to the low mimetic, foreword to the ironic—most interestingly—to the richest kind of irony proposing, or at least recognizing, a renewed body of rituals and myths."[89] Furthermore, Fussell insisted the falsehoods in writings by subversive authors like Robert Graves actually reveal deep truths about the war. As he says of Grave's war memoir, "If it really were a documentary transcription of the actual, it would be worth very little, and would surely not be, as it is, infinitely re-readable. It is valuable just because it is not true in that way."[90]

Fussell realized that an epistemological tension exists between the limitations of human memories and the use of these memories to realistically characterize a war. He was well aware of the contradiction between the assertion that only the men who were witnesses to the war have the authority to comment upon it and the reality that such a claim is ultimately compromised by the very nature of memory and language. But he would also insist that these articulated memories contain a recurrent set of images and themes that offsets this limitation. Moreover, he felt that the closer to the action an individual was, the greater the chance of them knowing the truth of war.

American Gadfly

In terms of the criticism that he relies too much upon a small, unrepresentative group of soldiers to illustrate the experiences of all British combatants in the war, it needs to be pointed out what the expressed purpose of *The Great War and Modern Memory* was in the first place: to discuss the British experience on the Western front and "some of the literary means by which it has been remembered, conventionalized, and mythologized."[91] In order for Fussell to accomplish this goal, he had to rely upon soldiers who expressly wrote about and were articulate about their experiences. Although, as Fussell notes in chapter five, this was a war that was unique in the literariness of all the ranks of soldiers because of the widespread demand for popular education and the fact that it was the first major European conflict in which a large number of well-educated young men (many of them college educated) from the upper and middle classes who had been inculcated with a cultural tradition of English literature and classical learning served, nevertheless the number of individuals who actually wrote about their war experiences (or even wanted to discuss it in any form) was very limited. It was writers like Sassoon, Owen, Blunden, and Graves who have influenced the way the war has been and continues to be viewed (and remembered) by the general population, and who have strongly contributed to its conventionalization and mythologization in the modern mind. In addition, he limits his analysis to the Western front for the simple but defensible reason that this is the military theater where images and ideas of the war that formed modern memory directly come from and not the other campaign regions.

In regard to the criticism that Fussell's contention of the Great War was *sui generis*, he would have agreed that the bloodiness of the conflict was not necessarily unique (in brute numbers), nor the limitations of staff officers or many of the tactics and strategy employed, in world history. But he would have also pointed out the military firsts associated with this engagement (as mentioned in the first part of this chapter). Moreover, as he stressed in this book and other writings, this was the first example of a total war, complete with massive, global fronts, and massive armies from many countries that extensively used modern weapons technology. These elements would be harbingers of future modern 20th century conflicts. Furthermore, he would opine that these military historians neglect the traumatic, deep, and long terms effects of this war upon culture and fail

3. Oh! What a Lovely Book!

to properly factor in how war is not only a military but also a cultural phenomenon.

Finally, regarding the objection that Fussell paints too rosy, nostalgic, and "innocent" a picture of what prewar English life was like, he does go a bit overboard. But, as the well-known historian Ian Kershaw has recently stated, "Still, the image of a 'golden age' was not merely a post-war construction. Despite Europe's internal divisions and nationalistic rivalries, all countries shared in the unimpeded movement of goods and capital as part of the interwoven, global international capitalist economy.... Confidence in continued stability, prosperity and growth was widespread.... An age of new technology was on show.... Commerce, prosperity and peace seemed to offer the unlimited continuation of this dominance. The future looks bright."[92] Kershaw notes that this belief seemed warranted since Europe had not had a general war for nearly 100 years, and it was hard to conceive that much of the progress made would be lost in a short period of time.

Concerning Fussell's stress on the innocence of the prewar world, Samuel Hynes, who, also like Fussell, quotes Philip Larkin's famous poem "MCMXIV" in his book *The Soldier's Tale*, writes of the special metaphysics regarding the war embedded in the poignant line "never such innocence again" in the poem: "'Innocent' means "unacquainted with evil." What he [Larkin] knew was what narratives of those innocent soldiers tell us. For them, it was all new, all strange and irrational, and we feel the newness in their narratives—the scale of it all.... It isn't new for us, and it never will be again, because in their war an army of literate men wrote their stories, to instruct us in the true nature of war, as men who are there see it and feel it, and so prepare us for other wars ahead."[93]

But ultimately, as one of the great contemporary historians of the Great War, Hew Strachan, has stated, strictly speaking, "Fussell's book is not military history, but his critics (John Terraine, and also Robin Prior and Trevor Wilson) attack it as though it is. Fussell was a literary critic, and his insights illuminate the literature of the war. The proper criticism of the book therefore needs to attack its own terms."[94]

Literary and cultural historians and critics have objected to Fussell on different but also sometimes similar grounds as those of military historians. Many have found his approach to be too narrow and exclusive in the material he used. First, they also found fault with the small pool of writers that he picked to study and generalize from, and some have accused him of having an elitist and even sexist bias. Specifically, they point out that the conflict produced an amazingly large amount of poetry (one researcher has discovered that 2,225 English Great War poets published works),[95] that much of this verse was penned by civilian poets, and that women formed a significant portion of this number. Elizabeth Vandiver has maintained that classical literature and its appropriations into English literature did have a big influence on many of these poets and gave them rich material for tropes and images to use (a point Fussell also stressed as we have seen). These poems were written for a variety of purposes, offered varied political views on the war both pro and con, and many did not protest the war. Vandiver also contends that the accepted canon regarding Great War poetry should be expanded and not only include upper-class poets who were critical of the war but also these other poets.[96] Fussell is also criticized for privileging the writings of combatants in the war and of either ignoring or only treating civilian culture as a foil, which some have believed had a greater importance than is appreciated.

Finally, Fussell's ideas regarding the influence of the war on modern memory and the development of wider cultural movements and modernity have also come under critical scrutiny. Jay Winter, in a widely discussed study of British, French, and German soldier and civilian styles of remembrance and commemoration of the war, has contended that the process leading to modernity was of a continuous nature and not a jarring break (which he implies is Fussell's position). Winter shows through an examination of literary, architectural, and artistic sources that these styles did not reject but actually utilized traditional forms of reference and drew from 18th and 19th century religious and romantic imagery, metaphors, and ideas, as well as classical forms. He posits that people resorted to giving these traditional themes new forms and meanings in order to privately and publicly express their mourning and grief over the war and to help them heal.[97]

Fussell's reliance upon the writings of soldier poets over that of civilians is not that unusual. Prior studies of Great War literature also did this because it was widely held that only war tested, uniformed poets could give people the real and disturbing truth about warfare, because poetry

3. Oh! What a Lovely Book!

had "a more direct conduit to raw experience than either fiction or nonfiction."[98] Fussell would later offer a defense of using soldier poets in another book, writing that "of all writers, it can be assumed that poets are especially sensitive to the adequacy of language to register honest experience, and it was the poets of the Great War who protested most effectively against human debasement and verbal fraud. Perceiving that the protest on behalf of sense and humanity was largely the work of poets.... But to be effective as protest, poetry must be read, and by large numbers of people. The soldier poets of the First World War happened to write at a moment remarkably favorable to both the writing and reading of poetry. Both they and the readers who were sophisticated assumed that major public awareness could find a lodging in lyric poetry."[99] (Interestingly, according to Geoff Dyer, one major reason why *The Great War and Modern Memory* was so popular in England was that Fussell approached the War through the experiences of poets, and that for many Britons this is how they are first exposed to the conflict.)[100]

Fussell said that he selected the poets he discussed in the book because they "most effectively memorialized the Great War as a historical experience with conspicuous imaginative and artistic meaning.... I have dealt with poets of very high literary consciousness."[101] This approach of course dovetails with his deeply rooted, and hard-headed belief in the primacy of experience and his conviction that only combatants (who at the time were all male) could truly know what war was really like. Consequently, from his perspective, he would contend that although a large number of poems were published during the war and many of them were by women and not necessarily against or critical of the conflict, very few of them had the characteristics necessary (as mentioned above) to become assimilated and part of the collective modern memory of the 20th century, which was the topic of the book. While Fussell's methodology is in some ways understandable, it is also limiting and prevents a more comprehensive picture of the war's impact from being shown. The ultimate question to be finally resolved is how limiting it is to his thesis. He would later be more amenable to including other voices (including female ones) and sources, including those from civilian culture in his anthology of writings on war, *The Bloody Game*, and his follow up to *The Great War and Modern Memory*, *Wartime*, but the charge of Fussell having an elitist bias would be one commonly made against him. (This criticism will be more fully addressed in Chapter 7.) Nonetheless, it would always be Fussell's bedrock and non-negotiable conviction in his writings on war that only individuals who had actively participated in combat knew the reality of war and that their observations had the greatest possibility of truth. (This belief would also be frequently questioned by critics of Fussell's books and will be examined in greater detail in Chapter 10.)

Winter's position concerning the development of modernity is largely convincing. Other scholars have argued that much of the foundation for modernity was laid in the early 20th century, years before the outbreak of the war. But it also should be mentioned that Fussell's view of modernity is more nuanced than critics have realized. As Robert Darby has rightly observed, "Whatever historians of cultural modernism may have written, it seems to me that Fussell's use of the term modern is entirely innocent: all he means is memory, particularly as expressed in literature, since the First World War. So little is he focused on modern*ism* that he regards the avant-garde experimentation of David Jones's *In Parenthesis* as 'an honorable miscarriage' (p. 144), and clearly prefers the prose of Sassoon and Blunden and the verse of Owen, all of whom wrote in traditional idiom. It is the moral content in each case that matters."[102] In addition, Fussell is not simply claiming, as Winter implies, that the war represents a complete cultural break with the past, for he explicitly states in *The Great War and Modern Memory* that the "dominant movement in the literature of the Great War ... was to a myth dominated world ... towards a revival of the cultic, the mystical, the sacrificial, the prophetic, the sacramental, and the universally significant."[103] In other words, Fussell believes that while the war ushered in irony and new forms of modern understanding, it also retained certain elements of traditional mythology.

The disagreement between Winter and Fussell regarding the influence of modernism and traditionalism generally comes down to what types of primary source is taken to be representative of the war. Fussell uses elite sources, and relies upon highly educated and articulate writers, poets, and artists, while Winter essentially relies more upon mass audiences, and high and middlebrow accounts. But there is no reason in the end why Fussell's position cannot be amended, and the argument made that the Great War ushered in culturally new forms, meanings, and a sense of historical dislocation, accelerated certain modernist elements already present, and also gave new meaning, form, and continuity to certain traditional motifs. Winter himself has acknowledged that his and Fussell's approach are not inherently incompatible.[104] As he points out, "The overlap of languages and approaches between the old and the new, the 'traditional' and the 'modern,' the conservative and the iconoclastic, was apparent both during and after the war. The ongoing dialogue and exchange among artists and their public, between those who self-consciously returned to 19th century forms and themes and those who sought to supersede them, makes the history of modernism much more complicated than a simple, linear divide between 'old' and 'new' might suggest."[105] While Fussell would concede the presence of traditional form and themes, he would also give prominence to the modernistic elements.

All in all, *The Great War and Modern Memory* has successfully weathered the test of time, albeit in somewhat battered form. Although problems with some of Fussell's descriptions have become apparent, such as some of his details regarding military matters, the, at times, highly selective nature of the material he uses, and the too wide scope of his thesis, the book nevertheless continues to remain a very useful starting point for any investigation into the literature of the Great War and its impact upon modern society and culture, and it remains a good sourcebook for material. As the noted Harvard historian Drew Gilpin Faust has put it, "We continue to ask questions and accept the framework of Fussell's analysis even as we push back against its boundaries and note its limitations.... It has created a language of perception and understanding that has shaped all our subsequent writings and thinking about the war."[106] In addition, it is a book that continues to fascinate and haunt readers due to the quality of its writing and tragic subject matter.

This book is being written in 2018, the centennial anniversary of the end of the First World War. An avalanche of books has been published on aspects of the war during the last few years, especially in England, with numerous ceremonies held and documentaries shown in remembrance of the event. (One easy way to gauge how England remains haunted by this war is go to YouTube and type in World War I. A plethora of British produced documentaries, lectures, and commemorative events will quickly appear.)

American Gadfly

Samuel Hynes has written, "The First World War remains our favorite war—the one we most want to know about, the one that most moves us. Why is that? Is it that we all have an appetite for passive suffering and for stories of betrayal? Or for the witness of man's capacities to endure the unendurable? Or is it perhaps that we have come to see that war as the end of something that was worthy to survive in the world and didn't?"[107] While Hynes's observation might not be true of large swathes of the U.S. (whose citizens are notoriously bad at history, the average American would probably find it difficult to even state when the Great War was fought), it is certainly true of Europe and informed individuals. *The Great War and Modern Memory* is a good book to begin with if one is curious about or simply wants to know more of what all the fuss is about.

In his April 21, 1976, National Book Award for Arts and Letters acceptance speech for the book, Fussell said that he wanted to "erect a memorial to the men whose imaginations I have lived for many years, and your award delights me because it means that this little military cemetery I have made will now have lots of visitors."[108] He also described his approach to literary criticism and took some shots at the academy for the way it interpreted literature, noting that his approach "tries not to lose touch with actual humanity and with the facts of social life. The criticism I have written is not mathematical. It is not structuralist. It is not metaphysical, or even philosophical. It knows that literary structures behave interestingly, but it also knows that human beings behave more interestingly."[109] He finishes by lamenting the disappearance of critics of the caliber of Edmund Wilson, R. P. Blackmur, and Lionel Trilling, who had the ability to read the humanity in literary texts, and recovered "the actual pulse of life that beats everywhere in literature and that constantly solicits us to listen for it."[110]

For Paul Fussell, this book, as his first wife Betty Fussell put it, "catapulted him out of the narrow pigeon coop of English literature and onto the postwar landscape of both sides of the Atlantic."[111] (He would later modestly say that the book's great popularity gave him "some emotional if not intellectual success.")[112] It gave him the confidence (and cachet) to branch out to other topics, some of them of a non-academic and popular culture nature, and to write for mainstream publications such as *Harper's, The New Republic, The Atlantic Monthly,* and *The New York Times.* His

3. Oh! What a Lovely Book!

writing style and attitude also changed, and became more pointed, polemical, and satirical as he began to address wider audiences, and he slowly began to assume the role of an iconoclastic public intellectual. But the topic of war and its tragic consequences would remain a major preoccupation for him and a subject that he would return to often in his future writings.

4

"It Is Simply Part of One's Life"

At first glance, Fussell's next book, *Abroad: British Literary Travelling Between the Wars*, might seem an odd choice. As with *The Great War and Modern Memory*, there were autobiographical reasons behind this decision. One night after a long discussion with his wife over what he was going to write about next, they concluded it should be on travel since it was one of his passions. He had learned long ago that in order to successfully write a book it was necessary for an author to have a passion for the subject being discussed. He had always loved traveling and considered it an essential part of a liberal education, and shared Evelyn Waugh's conviction that "one does not travel, any more than one falls in love, to collect material. It is simply part of one's life."[1] Moreover, he also wrote the book to pay homage to what he believed was the last grand age of travel, and to capture "what it felt like to be young and clever and literate during the final age of travel"[2]

After Fussell received a Guggenheim Fellowship in 1977 for this project, he soon travelled to London, Iran, Egypt, and Eastern Turkey. When he was in London, he came across Robert Byron's neglected 1937 travel book on Iran, *The Road to Oxiana*, in a bookstore and was so bowled over by the work that it would form an important chapter in *Abroad*. He had briefly touched upon the topic of travel before. In 1963, Fussell had published an article entitled "Patrick Brydone: The Eighteenth-Century Traveler as Representative Man," which discussed in detail Brydone's two-volume British travel book *A Tour Through Sicily and Malta* which was published in 1773. In the article, he praises the mock-heroic tone of the book and concludes in typical Fussell fashion that "perhaps no image in

4. "It Is Simply Part of One's Life"

the *Tour* made so powerful an appeal as the image of man who underlies these repeated patterns of comic reversal: despite his capacities for brisk locomotion, observation, and reportage, man is limited and frail, as his occasional awareness of some vague loss should remind him. It is this theme of the permanent limitations of man which allies writers so different as Swift, Burke, Johnson, and Hume, and it is Brydone's expression of it which helps account for the popularity of his *Tour* and which gives him for us the appearance of a consummately representative man."[3] This is also a theme that would be directly or indirectly expressed in virtually all of Fussell's writings, including *Abroad*.

Fussell contends in *Abroad* that certain works of British travel writing composed between the wars should be taken seriously and celebrated, and that these travel books should be considered as constituting an important literary genre. To support this thesis, he takes his usual interdisciplinary approach, utilizing insights from the fields of literary criticism, sociology, cultural history, biography and autobiography to make his point. Although *Abroad* is about travel writing in 1918–39, it is also in some ways similar in content to *The Great War and Modern Memory*. Fussell's other self-described major obsession, war, especially the First World War, has a strong presence throughout the book. He demonstrates that the war influenced the way people viewed travel and was a major factor motivating them to travel abroad during this period.

Fussell discusses many writers and books published during this time, but he primarily concentrates on works by Graham Greene, Evelyn Waugh, Norman Douglas, Robert Byron, and D. H. Lawrence. He chose to primarily focus on English writers because he believed they wrote the most sophisticated and cultured travel books of the period. The initial chapters in *Abroad* provide background information about what motivated the British to travel overseas in such large numbers between the wars. He attributes much of this impulse to the desire to escape from the terrible conditions on the Western Front during the Great War, writing, "The fantasies of flight and freedom which animate the imagination of the 20s and 30s and generate its pervasive images of travel can be said to begin in the trenches."[4] Fussell quotes Graham Greene who says that the literary travelers of his generation, like Waugh, Robert Byron, himself, and others, grew up reading adventure stories and because they did not serve in the

Great War, looked for adventure overseas. Another war related factor which impelled the English to travel overseas was the contempt people felt towards aspects of post war British life during this time, for many felt that the war had wrecked the country. Fussell presents a chart based upon adjectives George Orwell used to describe facets of English society during the 1920s and '30s to illustrate the intense dissatisfaction individuals felt. As a result, people were impelled to go abroad, and numerous British writers left the country.

Interspersed among Fussell's discussions of the British writers are interesting short chapters on a variety of travel related topics. These topics range from the virtues of travelling alone; the connection between travel and romance; the English fascination with the Mediterranean and the Southern European region; the famous Blue Train which took passengers from London to the Riviera; the relationship between travel writing and quest and pastoral romances; the importance of the essay in travel writing; the popularity of heliophily (sun worship); to the history of the passport (which only became a requirement for travel in 1915); and how the political phenomenon of frontiers being redrafted and shifted during this time produced "an awareness of reality as disjointed, dissociated, fractured"[5] among writers and artists.

Fussell claims there were several characteristics that made the English at this time such unique and captivating travel authors and travelers when compared to other nationalities. Among these were their special drive to travel, their belief that travel was a necessary part of life, their national snobbery which was a product of their class system and Britain's history of imperialism, and their strong desire to escape from the self and dashing sense of phlegm and pluck.

One of the chapters that had received a great deal of attention by critics and readers was "Sancte Roberte, Ora pro Nobis." It discusses the eccentric writer, historian, and art critic Robert Byron and his 1937 work *The Road to Oxiana*. As previously mentioned, Fussell had discovered the book in London on a research trip and considered it one of the finest examples of modern travel literature. *The Road to Oxiana* is an account of a 10-month journey Byron (who was distantly related to the poet Lord Byron) took in 1933–34 through the Middle East to Oxiana, a country that was part of the border between the Soviet Union and Afghanistan. The trip involved trav-

4. "It Is Simply Part of One's Life"

elling through Venice, Nicosia, Beirut, Baghdad, Jerusalem, and Tehran. Fussell was particularly impressed with Byron because he found in him many of the personal qualities that he himself greatly valued: dogged independence, a vigorous and unending curiosity, a gift for finding things that were interesting and then thoroughly educating himself about them without help, and a well-developed scorn for hypocrisy and phoniness. He also approved of Byron's modernistic and eclectic literary style, and lively sense of humor. He also thought the book provided a highly informative guide to Iranian archaeology. (Fussell put the book to the test when he was visiting the ruins of Persepolis in Iran and found it to be both accurate and informative.)

In this chapter, Fussell goes so far as to proclaim that Byron's work "is the *Ulysses* or *The Waste Land* of modern travel books. One reason this can be said is that its method is theirs: as if obsessed with frontiers and fragmentations, it juxtaposes into a sort of collage the widest variety of rhetorical materials: news clippings, public signs and notices, letters, bureaucratic documents like *fiches*, diary entries, learned dissertations in art history, essays on current politics, and, most winningly, at least 20 comic dialogues."[6] (*Abroad* would spark new interest in *The Road to Oxiana*, so much so that it was reprinted in in 1982 and 2007 by Oxford University Press, which introduced the work to an even wider audience than it was exposed to when it was first published. Both editions contained a special introduction by Fussell.)

Fussell maintains that the writers of these English travel books were the last masters of a literary form which was to be dispatched by mass tourism and politics. In chapter six, "From Exploration to Travel to Tourism," he draws a hard and controversial distinction between travel in the past and the mass tourism of today, asserting, "travel is now impossible and tourism is all we have left."[7] He holds that travelers between the wars viewed the activity as work, involving preparation that is similar to studying, and viewed it as being "the adornment of the mind and the formation of judgement."[8] For them, travel always carries the possibility of mishaps, and "implies a variety of means and independence of arrangements."[9] In contrast, according to Fussell, the tourists of today are motivated to go abroad to increase their social status back home, are primarily focused on shopping and spending, and are in search of erotic possibilities.

American Gadfly

Ocean liners have been replaced by massive and gaudy cruise ships, and people are now forced into increasingly packed airplanes after traversing through anonymous and uniform looking airports. The uncomfortable and misadventurous experiences and the strong sense of travel as intellectual exploration has been replaced by the safety, efficiency, and predictability of tourism. Fussell also believes that today's mass tourist industry is based upon the passivity of the tourist. For many people now travel in tightly controlled tour groups where they are comfortably shuttled and hurried along to often pseudo-places where they are accosted by touts. Moreover, the average tourist does little preparation, does not read travel books (the quality of which has greatly declined), and if they do read, peruse only commonly available low-quality guidebooks.[10]

Abroad makes a good argument for granting literary respectability to travel writing. It is also an excellent example of how interdisciplinary literary criticism can be effectively used and interesting connections made. Fussell's discussions of writers are insightful and biographically well researched. The book also shows his great ability to take a subject that has either not been taken seriously or overlooked and making it relevant and illuminating. The works he analyzes can also serve as benchmarks on how to measure current travel writing. Fussell has clearly done his homework, for although *Abroad* is a relatively short book, it abounds in allusions to a plethora of travel writers and things related to travel. But his literary judgement is not unerring. Even though *The Road to Oxiana* is undoubtedly a uniquely structured, inventive, informative, and at times, dryly and slyly humorous work, is it really that deserving of all the praise that Fussell heaps upon it? In fact, the book today comes off as being rather tedious in its welter of details and meandering, nor is it as funny or witty as many critics would have us to believe, and Byron does come off on occasion as rather too clever for his own good.

Fussell is also harsh about W. H. Auden and Christopher Isherwood's 1939 work, *Journey to a War*, which describes a trip they took through war-torn China in 1938. He maintains that it belongs to the "decadent stage" of travel writing, and complains that "the narrative is disturbingly discontinuous, interrupted by jokiness, nervousness over what literary mode is appropriate, and self-consciousness about the travel book genre itself ... the narrative is eked out by poems that don't really belong, and

4. "It Is Simply Part of One's Life"

nothing is rounded off."[11] In truth, the book is quite entertaining and informative. While Auden and Isherwood's time in China was short (they left London in January and returned in July), both men continually encountered during the visit a large number of intriguing and often eccentric individuals, including Chinese, British, and German military officials, missionary doctors, war correspondents and journalists, Chinese intellectuals, businessmen and hotel owners, ambassadors and consul generals, and singsong girls. Moreover, they met high ranking politicians including governors, the well-known communist party official Zhou Enlai, the powerful head of the Chinese national government, Chiang Kai-Shek, and his infamous wife, Soong Mei-ling, and even the extremely powerful Shanghai triad boss Du Yuesheng, as well as the celebrated war photographer and photojournalist Robert Capa. They also did much hard traveling, often by train under arduous circumstances, and came under aerial attack by the Japanese. They visited Hong Kong, Wuhan, Xian, Shanghai, and Canton, and even made a trip to the front lines.

In addition, *Journey to a War* has an engaging narrative and is full of fascinating encounters. Auden and Isherwood were good at depicting the contrast between the sheltered lives of British expats in Shanghai and Canton and the lives of ordinary Chinese. Auden and Isherwood also provided compelling snapshots of what China was like during this tumultuous time. For example, in a visit to the British consulate southern city of Wuhan, they observe that "in the early evening there is usually a little knot of spectators around the gates of the consulate, peering into the garden, where the neat, athletic figure of the Consul General is to be seen, practicing with his golf clubs. The exquisite accuracy of the Consul's putting seems somehow very reassuring amidst all the chaos and inefficiency of wartime China. Perhaps the Chinese onlookers feel this, too."[12]

It is puzzling Fussell disliked this book given that it is written in an ironic literary style he liked. Isherwood, who wrote most of the text (Auden provided the poetry, which he later conceded was mediocre, and took the accompanying photographs), was noted for his highly ironic and off-center writing style. As one critic has noted, "Most descriptions in Isherwood's work are, in fact, written from an angle that is oblique to ordinary perception. Not only the ordering and arrangement but also the choice of words serves to bring about a slight but constant displacement of the reader's expectations, and it is Isherwood's accomplishment that even the most apparently random word or phrase contrives to fantasticate the entire passage of which it is a part."[13] *Journey to a War* contains examples of this technique at work. Isherwood will set a scene in which the conversation or description falls on conventional or semi-conventional lines, and then at the end he will ironically undercut or even subvert what had just been said or done.

For example, this technique can be seen in Isherwood's description of a conversation which occurred with the prominent British travel author Peter Fleming. "At supper we drank cognac and began an argument on the meaning of the word Civilization. Had China anything to learn from the West? Peter thought not. 'The Chinese,' he kept repeating, 'have got everything taped.' 'Surely,' I protested, 'you can't pretend that the coolie is well off, in his present condition? Isn't he ever to hear Beethoven? Or see your wife act?' [Fleming was married to the actress Celia Johnson]. 'Oh,' said Peter airily, 'he's got them pretty well taped.' Auden was more for providing the coolies with meals from a really good French restaurant. He had decided, finally, against Chinese food."[14] In short, Isherwood also understood a key point that Fussell emphasized in his writings, namely that a strong sense of irony is an essential component in any attempt to capture the reality of war and the effects it produces.

Critics liked *Abroad,* and the book added to Fussell's growing reputation as a literary and cultural historian. Today, it is considered a classic and precedent establishing work on the topic of travel literature. *The Washington Post* said it was "in some ways an outgrowth of Fussell's equally brilliant *The Great War and Modern Memory*."[15] The distinguished historian and biographer Peter Stansky wrote that "it is hard to imagine the case for travel writing, a genre worthy of a place alongside poetry and the novel, being made more impressively.... [*Abroad*] "might serve as a coda to its distinguished predecessor, looks back again and again to the first war to explain the peculiarities and excitements of the postwar reaction, not least among them the phenomena of travel and travel writing."[16] Edward J. Curtin in *America* stated that it "is a vivid and solid argument for travel writing as a serious literary genre.... Fussell tells [his story] in an entertaining and enormously engaging way."[17]

Travel writer, novelist and critic Jonathan Raban felt that Fussell

4. "It Is Simply Part of One's Life"

deserved some praise, but he also had some deep reservations about the book, declaring, "*Abroad* is an exemplary piece of criticism. It is immensely readable. It bristles with ideas. It disinters a real lost masterpiece from the library stacks. It admits a whole area of writing—at last!–to its proper place in literary history."[18] But he strongly disagreed with Fussell's position that travel and travel writing has been destroyed by mass tourism and the rise of the tourist industry. He holds that Fussell, "Having restored the travel book to critical life, goes on to perform a premature burial over its remains ... it's one essential condition isn't a private income, rough terrain, English hauteur, tramp steamers, Baedekers, the cheap franc or any other of the incidentals on which Mr. Fussell dwells with valedictory nostalgia. It is the experience of living among strangers, away from home. When that ceases to be a matter of any interest, Mr. Fussell will be welcomed to have his funeral."[19]

Fussell's tone in the book also gave rise to some angry letters to the editors of newspapers. In one to the *Los Angeles Times*, a reader attacked him for his "superciliously superior snobbish attitude in unfavorably contrasting tours (tourists) with independent travel (travelers).... Many of us do not sit in ivory towers with time to read about history and travel.... I am not embarrassed to have a guide help me to zero in on the background and the importance of historical places.... We attempt to maximize the two or three weeks a year available to us to learn about the world we live in."[20]

Fussell was frequently accused by many of his critics of being a snob and elitist starting with *The Great War and Modern Memory*. While this charge will be addressed later, suffice it to say at this stage that he had long called himself a cultural and not a class elitist, and that he wanted people to demand more of, and to educate, themselves, and become one themselves. He does address one aspect of this charge in *Abroad* saying, "Already I hear the complaint, 'What snobbery. These experiences are all right for the rich and leisured, but how about others?'"[21] He notes that travel between the wars was much cheaper than today, and that being a traveler during this time cost considerably less than being a tourist today. During the 1920s the pound (and dollar) were stronger than other continental currencies and expenses in Europe were very low, (which was a major reason why so many Americans flocked to the continent). As a result, the great British travel writers "made their money take them very far, less because they were equipped with capital than because they were equipped with intelligence, energy, and curiosity."[22]

Fussell does, on occasion, paint with a very broad brush (he always claimed in defense that it was part and parcel of his satirical style) when discussing present travel writing and tourism. His blanket dismissal of today's travel books is clearly too sweeping as is his characterization of the tourist industry. Rabin in his review calls Fussell's critical remarks about tourism tetchy nonsense and banal. And some of them are. But Fussell also raises some issues worth examining. The affordability and easy accessibility of international travel has resulted in the guidebook essentially replacing the travel book. There is no doubt that guidebooks can provide useful and needed information. What is troubling about them is that they often form many traveler's perception of what they experience and how they view the country and can even be a barrier to understanding a place. As Fussell correctly observes, a good travel book is concerned with seeing, inquiry, and learning, and written in a critical and witty tone. But a guidebook, which is usually compiled by a committee of writers, is based on the business model, and is mainly focused on consuming. Most if not all guidebooks are heavily tilted towards bargain (in the middle- and upper middle-class sense) places to stay, eat, and to buy things, and getting tourists to places which replicate what they would find at home. They often provide the minimal amount of easily digestible (which is quickly forgotten by the tourist) cultural and historical information. Likewise, they are commonly designed to mesh comfortably with the itineraries of people on carefully choreographed group tours.

To Fussell, the decline in the use of travel books by tourists and the rise in the use of guidebooks to replace them has resulted in an essential part of travel being lost, namely preparation. For the travel book provides in the words of Norman Douglas, "an interior, a sentimental or temperamental voyage, which takes place side by side with the outer one,"[23] that is, it supplements the descriptions of locations, scenery, and consuming that a good guidebook gives.

Publishers who have attempted to move away from the standard guidebook business model eventually give in and adapt its format. A good case in point is the widely used Lonely Planet series. When the first guide-

4. "It Is Simply Part of One's Life"

book, which dealt with Asia, was published in 1975, it was intended for backpackers and travelers on a limited budget and offered an attitude that was strikingly different from that of the usual guides. As the series took off, it stood out because the publisher often selected well-travelled and idiosyncratic individuals from a wide variety of backgrounds to be writers. The guides were low priced, simply printed, and usually contained a good amount of historical and cultural background information on the countries they described. The places they recommended readers visit in countries would not necessarily be on the usual traveler's route, and the shopping and eating section of the books was decidedly budget minded. But over time, the consumption section of the guides has become much larger. Five-star hotels and eating establishments are now commonly mentioned (they were largely ignored in the past), and it is now common for much space devoted to upscale Western bars and restaurants. The writers for the series today have more professional backgrounds, and are less well travelled, interesting, and rooted in the country they describe. And the price of the guides has sharply increased.[24] The company has expanded to include books, a magazine and television series, and it now has a very strong Internet presence. The Lonely Planet guides of today generally contain more information than they ever have, but in terms of content and layout, they are now slicky produced, visually arresting, and look very much like any other guide on the market. As a result, they have lost the characteristics that made them initially so appealing and unique, and earned the scorn of much of the audience that was initially attracted to them. Accordingly, they are today commonly carried by upper income tourists on group tours.

This is of course not to say that good travel books have not been written since the golden age of travel or are not being written today. Clearly writers such as Bruce Chatwin, Alan Booth, Jan Morris, Gavin Young, Colin Thubron, Wilfred Thesiger, Geoff Dyer, Tim Mackintosh-Smith, Ryszard Kapuscinski, and Norman Lewis are comparable in many ways to the writers Fussell touts. But they are, or were, the top writers. With the rise of mass tourism and the Internet and the resulting phenomenon of what one critic has called "the cult of the amateur,"[25] an avalanche of self-appointed travel writers have aggressively made their opinions heard (and sometimes with a large audience) in blogs, and the boundaries between travel writing and guidebooks have further blurred. Ultimately, Fussell does have a point that real travel requires good preparation (and contrary to what the author of the letter to *Los Angeles Times* says, there is always time for some background reading if you want to make it), curiosity, and the inclination to go off the well beaten and closely chauffeured path.

Fussell returned to the topic of travel and tourism in 1987 when he edited a massive, more than 800-page anthology of travel literature for Norton. The collection contains travel writings starting with Herodotus and includes such noted travelers as Marco Polo and Christopher Columbus, writers from the 18th century age of the Grand Tour, accounts by Charles Darwin, Henry James and Mark Twain and popular authors from the 1920s and 1930s. The book ends with selections by such tourist age writers as Lawrence Durrell, Truman Capote, Jan Morris, V. S. Naipaul, Claude Levi-Strauss, and Paul Theroux.

Fussell also expands on several of the points he raised in *Abroad*. In the book's introduction, he explains why people find travel so exhilarating, saying that it offers the excitement of escape, enables people to learn new things, including the important value of humility, enhances the senses, and induces a bit of shame because of the freedom it gives them over people who do not have the opportunity to travel. In addition, he contends that traveling is an ironic experience for it makes you realize how insignificant you are. It also can induce melancholy, for "all the pathos and irony of leaving one's youth behind is implicit in every joyous moment of travel: one knows that the first joy can never be recovered, and the wise traveler learns not to repeat successes but tries new places all the time."[26]

Fussell also further explicates the special qualities a good travel writer should possess. These include a strong and roving curiosity, stamina, the drive to instruct, a devotion to language, and the ability to construct a vivid autobiographical narrative. He concludes, "Successful travel writing mediates between two poles: the individual physical things it describes, on the one hand, and the larger theme that it is 'about,' on the other. That is, the particular and the universal.... A travel book will make the reader aware of a lot of *things*.... At the same time, a travel book will reach in the opposite direction and deal with these data so as to suggest that they are not wholly inert and discrete but are elements of a much larger meaning, a meaning metaphysical, political, artistic, or religious—but always, somehow, ethical."[27]

4. "It Is Simply Part of One's Life"

That same year, Fussell published an article entitled "Bourgeois Travel: Techniques and Artifacts" for a book on travel by the Smithsonian Institution. In it, he discusses the novel topic of how major societal changes and developments in the transportation field have impacted upon travel luggage styles since the 18th century. He contends that these changes can be seen in the fact that while luggage in the past was elegant, heavy, and complex, and a person traveled with several trunks, today's luggage is plain, simple, lightweight, and uses light fabric, and a tourist now travels with minimal luggage, usually only one bag. He surmises that these changes are sociologically revealing and that from these objects "a future archeologist can infer something like the social history of the past two centuries."[28]

He also examines the changes over time of the popularity of certain tourist locations, concluding that a study of why so many people found them captivating and wanted to visit them would help us "to appreciate how central to the modern experience are exotic fantasies and desires—for escape and the foreign, for the novel, the exotic, the non-industrial, the archaic, and the luscious—which can be satisfied, for the moment, at least, by travel."[29]

The article is accompanied by numerous and intriguing photographs of well-made travel related paraphernalia, including travelling beds, writing, eating, and scholar's kits, dressing cases, travelling beds, elephant hide and bed trunks, bandboxes, sketchbooks, carpet bags, hat boxes, traveler's clocks, porter's badges, colorful luggage labels, and even luggage for a hot-air balloon.

Fussell made a final stab at sharpening his travel/tourist distinction in a 1988 essay, "Travel. Tourism, and International Understanding." In this piece, he admits that travel and tourism have a lot in common—both are forms of escape, it enables an individual to break free from their usual identity and experience the fun of learning new things, and virtually everyone who first goes abroad when they are young, goes as a tourist. But he insists that stark differences between the two remain. For him, tourism is safe, predicable, calming, social, optimistic, utilitarian, externally directed (by guides, schedules, and tour directors), and presupposes the dutifulness of the participant. Consequently, "it soothes, shielding you from the shocks of novelty and menace, confirming your view of the world rather than shaking it up. It obliges you to not just hold conventional things but to behold them in the approved conventional way ... it invites, or rather, requires an obsession with things that are not travel—the mechanics, rather than the objects and sensations, of displacement."[30] These things include matters like currency rates, the conditions of hotels and the food provided, the cost of items, and conflicts with other members of one's tour group.

In contrast, travel is self-directed, unpredictable, demanding, often difficult and not really relaxing. The traveler is driven by strong intellectual curiosity, seeks places that make them question their beliefs, and is intensely aware of the important messages the past presents. Fussell also argues in the essay that tourism is now being surpassed by a new stage which he calls "post-tourism," which is marked "by boredom, annoyance, disgust, disillusion, and finally anger."[31] This new type of traveler believes that a clear understanding and explanation of the world and other cultures is highly problematic. Fussell believes that this new perspective can be seen in the writings of the French anthropologist Claude Levi-Strauss, and the travel writers and novelists Paul Theroux and V. S. Naipaul, who often focus in their works on their bad travel experiences and on exposing dreadful truths about locations (while often implicitly enjoying it at the same time) and the difficulties associated with understanding people from different cultures.

Fussell obviously has little patience with this new development, finding its deep skepticism epistemically limiting. He also makes the important point that you do not have to find a place attractive to understand it, and that true international understanding can be reconcilable with dislike. He ends the essay noting that the personal qualities of disinterested intellectual inquiry and a free mind that is curious for its own sake is necessary for being a genuine traveler.

5

An Essayist at Heart

Although Paul Fussell wrote numerous books, he liked to view himself as primarily an essayist in the grand tradition of the British man of letters, where essays were broad based, literate, involved ethical, social and cultural commentary, and were intended for educated people. There is an element of truth to this claim, for he covered a wide range of the subjects and was mainly concerned with ethical and cultural matters in these writings. Moreover, several of his books like *Class*, *Wartime*, *Doing Battle*, and *Uniforms* originated as essays, and he said that his best work *The Great War and Modern Memory*, "was the work of an essayist."[1] Fussell had long lamented the decline in importance and popularity of the essay. In *Abroad*, he noted "the virtual disappearance of the essay as a salable commodity,"[2] and claimed that if you wanted to cause a big laugh in a publisher's office, bring in a manuscript of essays. On one level, his writings can be viewed as an extended defense of the essay as an art form.

Fussell's popularity was great enough that he was able to get published two collections of essays and reviews during his lifetime. He also wrote numerous essays and book reviews for *Harper's*, *The New Republic*, *The New York Times*, *The Southern Review*, *Saturday Review*, *Boston Globe*, *Chicago Sun-Times*, *Sewanee Review*, *The Atlantic*, and *Gentleman's Quarterly* in the U.S., and such British publications as the *Times Literary Supplement*, *New Stateman*, *Encounter*, *The London Review of Books*, and *Spectator*. His book reviews covered a lot of ground, ranging from travel books, biographies and studies of traditional and modern literary figures, contemporary novels, military history, and social trends, to autobiographies, and collections of famous writer's letters and essays. (He was also a consulting editor for Random House and a contributing editor for *The*

American Gadfly

New Republic and *Harper's*.) Moreover, Fussell provided blurbs for books, including one for Donald Trump's future National Security Advisor, H. R. McMaster, who had written a well-received 1998 book on the Vietnam War, *Dereliction of Duty: Johnson, McNamara, the Joint Chiefs of Staff, and the Lies that Lead to Vietnam*, which he called "a stunning book: eloquent and highly effective. The word noble would not be going too far."

In addition, Fussell penned introductions to reissued classic Great and Second World War memoirs by Robert Graves, Alfred Hale, E. B. Sledge, and works of literature and literary criticism by Siegfried Sassoon, Frederick Manning, Diana Trilling, and John Horne Burns, and an introduction to an anthology of Second World War poetry. He also prepared, wrote an introduction for, and edited a special, abridged edition of Sassoon's Sherston memoirs. Moreover, he wrote reviews of the movies *Patton* and *Saving Private Ryan*.

Fussell's guiding philosophy concerning the writing of essays and reviews can be found in the forewords to his essay collections. In the first, *The Boy Scout Handbook and Other Observations*, which was published in 1982, he argues for a George Orwell inspired, multi-layered approach to writing, stating that cultural, ethical, literary, political and social commentary essentially can be the same thing, and that the audience for one is in many ways the audience for all.[3] He also has a very broad definition of what constitutes a work of literature, holding "that regardless of its social status or intellectual pretensions a thing is literature if it's worth reading more than a couple of times for illumination or pleasure."[4] In his second collection, *Thank God for the Atom Bomb and Other Essays*, which was published in 1988, he acknowledges and warns the reader about the frequent adversarial and challenging nature of his essays: "Looking over these pieces, many of which are about war, I see they propose another sort of battlefield.... This is not a book to provoke tranquility, and readers in quest of peace of mind should look elsewhere."[5]

The Boy Scout Handbook contains 34 essays and reviews and *Thank God for the Atom Bomb* has 14. They cover a wide scope of subjects and books and reveal Fussell's roving curiosity and ability to successfully cross disciplinary lines. Their range can be seen in the table of contents page in the first collection where the essays are grouped into five categories: 'Americana,' 'Hazards of Literature,' 'Going Places,' 'Britons, Largely Eccen-

5. An Essayist at Heart

tric,' and 'Versions of the Second World War.' The pieces in both collections reflect Fussell's major interests: famous and forgotten American and British literary figures, travel related matters, both World Wars, and cultural and social trends in the U.S.

Five essays in *The Boy Scout Handbook* stand out and have garnered attention. The first concerns the 1979 *Official Boy Scout Handbook*. Fussell begins the essay by accusing literary critics of being too focused on only a few educable classics and consistently ignoring popular worthwhile works of humanistic criticism. Specifically, he is interested in the "vigorous literary-moral life that constantly takes places just below [these classics] ... [and is displayed in] the intersection of rhetoric and social motive."[6] In other words, the culture of organizations such as the Elks, Knights of Columbus, and the Boy Scouts. He then argues for the importance of the Scout's famous handbook, praising its common sense, practical advice, moral tone, and emphasis on engagement with the world. Fussell goes so far as to claim that that this work "is among the very few remaining popular repositories of something like classical ethics, deriving from Aristotle and Cicero.... The constant moral tone is the inestimable benefits of looking objectively outward and losing consciousness of the self in the work to be done."[7] (It is easy to see why he was taken with this work, for many of these values were also the values his Augustan era heroes had held.)

Several essays in the collection regarding the Second World War are also intriguing. In "My War," Fussell graphically describes his own war experiences and how they had forever changed him, formed his attitude towards war in general. (Parts of this piece would be later used in his autobiography *Doing Battle*.) In "The War in Black and Blue," he sensitively examines three famous and four unknown combat photographs from the conflict and discusses what they reveal about the War. He also contends that "now is a good time to interpret them, before they begin to look as if Matthew Brady took them and before those who can never forget the look and feel of what they depict are gone."[8]

"The Regrettable Decision of Herman Wouk" offers a new take on the writer's popular novel *War and Remembrance* about the Second World War. While he strongly derides Wouk's ability as a novelist, he does praise him as a military historian, declaring that the sections in the story where he describes military strategy and tactics in naval engagements like Midway and Leyte Gulf are first rate and that Wouk could have had a fine career as a military historian. In "Time-Life Goes to War," Fussell offers a trenchant critique of the popular Time-Life series on the Second World War, asserting that they sanitize, overtly dramatize, and often offer an upbeat view of the conflict. He does not blame the authors for this flaw but the format of the series, with its *Life* magazine-like photographs, padded picture captions, stress on intense human-interest stories, and lively chapter titles, observing, "These books don't falsify the war. They falsify the conditions of real life in all times and places. But that's what they're supposed to do, for as we know mankind cannot bear very much reality, nor is it the business of a flourishing brickyard to deliver any."[9] (He would later elaborate upon these points in his book *Wartime*.)

"Notes on Class" provides a concise examination of the American class system. In it, Fussell cleverly (and humorously) lays out a typology of the system, maintaining that there are "perceptually" at least nine classes, and describes each class's defining aesthetic and behavioral characteristics, language, and physical appearance. This essay would form the basis for his popular and controversial 1983 book *Class* which further explores the subject. Finally, there is "Being Reviewed: The A.B.M. and Its Theory," a caustic and satirical but also serious sendup of aggrieved writers who complain about the bad reviews they receive and write letters to the editor of publications strenuously defending the value of their work. His point is simple: authors should have the grace not to complain and simply bear the criticism for it comes with the territory of having something published. The essay contains numerous funny and actual examples of writers committing this sin, and an analysis of the conventions these frequently highly defensive letters to publications take. Fussell also gives advice in the essay on how to handle both a bad and good review and gets in some jabs at the notorious narcissistic classified ads in the personal sections of publications like *The New York Review of Books*.

Fussell is not the only critic to make this point regarding author's complaints about reviews. In 1935, the great literary critic Edmund Wilson wrote in an essay entitled "The Literary Worker's Polonius: A Brief Guide for Authors and Editors" that an "author has no justification for expecting serious criticism from reviewers, and that, in becoming elated or indignant over anything that is written about his books, he is wasting his nervous

5. An Essayist at Heart

energy ... he should read his reviews, not as the verdict of the Supreme Court of critics, but as a collection of opinions by persons of various degrees of intelligence who have happened to have some contact with the book. Considered from this point of view, there is occasionally something to be learned from them."[10]

"The Purging of Penrod" is about attempts by some publishers to purge the seemingly racist passages in the 1914 novel *Penrod* by the American novelist Booth Tarkington so that readers will not be offended, and the dangers of political correctness and literary censorship. The essay is more relevant today than it was when it first appeared as is its conclusion, "the past is not the present: pretending it is corrupts art and thus both rots the mind and shrivels the imagination and conscience."[11]

As would be expected, Fussell is also engaging when writing about travel, and the collection has five essays on the subject. Among the more interesting are "Terrors and Delights of the Traveler Abroad," which contains a four-page list of fears and joys that travelers experience abroad, including "that one's bribe will be disdained.... Finding that all the clichés about a place are true."[12] In "Latin America Defeats Intelligent Travel Writer," Fussell scolds the well-known travel writer and novelist Paul Theroux for his very negative and superior attitude in his book *The Old Patagonian Express*, contrasting him with the more tolerant attitude of Graham Greene and Evelyn Waugh in their travel works. He notes that Greene and Waugh "could tour through horrors and make something other than occasions for superior disgust. Their sympathy was wider than Theroux's, their involvement in history was deeper, their belief in the redemption of mankind by common sense was less certain, and perhaps their knowledge of themselves more profound. Theroux never says of the messes he observes: 'That's me.'"[13]

Finally, "A Place to Recuperate" is a curious work of Fussell's imagination. In it, he envisions an idyllic imaginary small European city on a big lake where one might stay in order to recuperate from an illness. (The piece was sparked by an incident when he fell ill of pleurisy on a trip in Israel and had to decide where he would go to convalesce.) Fussell describes in detail what this city would be like—its architecture (Baroque or Palladian or Romanesque), central park (oval shaped, with a large fountain and a covered bandstand with twice weekly concerts), restaurants (offering Italian or French food), hotel (renowned, has the appearance of a big 19th century British country house, and contains a great bar, a billiard room, well-furnished and tasteful guest rooms with no Bibles), cafes, shops (which do not sell cameras, electronic goods, dildos, drugs, or funny T-shirts, numerous well-stocked bookstores (one has all the volumes of the Modern Library, World Classics, and Everyman's Library series), lakefront (where you can view fishermen going out on their boats), and weather (bright and clear, warm during the day and cool at night, perfect for sleeping). Fussell would later write that he actually received letters from people inquiring where this town was located because they wanted to visit it, not realizing that it did not exist.

But there are also pieces, especially those dealing with British writers, that today seem dry and mediocre. One essay that conspicuously fails is "Can Graham Greene Write English?" an attack on the British novelist. Fussell asserts that Greene does not deserve the acclaim he has received, and accuses him of numerous sins, including having an overdramatic and Manichean view of life, of being incapable of creating realistic characters, of having corny themes in his stories, and even of not writing English correctly. At the end of the essay, he gives an "expository writing" examination where the reader is asked to correct eight grammatically incorrect passages from Greene's autobiography *Ways of Escape*. Regrettably, the entire piece comes across as being unfunny, petty, and mean-spirited.

The essays in his second anthology, 1988's *Thank God for the Atom Bomb and Other Essays,* generally have more heft and depth than the ones in the first collection. There are fewer of them, but they are frequently longer than the pieces in the first collection. In the foreword, Fussell readily provides a long list of the specific targets of his essays (referring to them as "the enemy"). They include "habitual euphemizers, professional dissimulators, inadequately educated academic administrators, censors, artistically pretentious third-rate novelists, sexual puritans, rigid optimists and Disneyfiers of life ... humorless critical doctrinaires with grievances (Marxist, Feminist, what-have-you), the sly rhetoricians of the NRA, exploiters of tourists, and, of course, the President."[14]

The essay for which the collection is named, *Thank God for the Atom Bomb,* has received the most attention and will be discussed in detail in the next chapter. Other memorable pieces are his essays "George

5. An Essayist at Heart

Orwell: The Critic as Honest Man" and "Travel, Tourism, and International Understanding," both of which have previously been discussed. "Indy" presents an amusing and perceptive description of the Indianapolis 500 car race which occurs in May at the Indianapolis Motor Speedway in Indiana. Fussell views the famous race from the perspective of what it reveals about social class and society in America. He observes that followers of motor racing often have class worries about how it ranks with other sports, that the official sponsor of the event, the United States Auto Club, has anxieties about crowd discipline, that brand names on clothing worn by spectators, pit crews, and drivers, and on signs, and cars is ubiquitous, not only for commercial reasons but because it confers status on the bearer or owner, and that rituals form an essential part of the event. He also discerns there are three social classes among the spectators and is greatly impressed by the large size of the audience (400,000) and the amount of noise and excitement they generate. Based upon what he has seen and heard, he surmises that "the essence of Indy is in its resemblance to other rituals in which wild, menacing, nonhuman things are tamed. I am thinking of the rodeo and bullfighting."[15]

In "A Well-Regulated Militia," Fussell presents a topical and very clever *reductio ad absurdum* argument against absolutist defenders of the Second Amendment and organizations like the National Rifle Association. This amendment states that "a well-regulated Militia, being necessary to the security of a free State, the right of the people to keep and bear Arms, shall not be infringed." He does this by taking the amendment at face value, giving it a "close reading and thus focusing a lot of attention on the grammatical reasoning of its two clauses."[16] Fussell then takes the amendment, based upon this careful reading, to its strict and logical policy conclusion, and deduces that Congress should as a result enact a bill that requires any person who owns a gun and does not belong to the police or military to join the Militia of the U.S., participate in weekly drills and target practice, and a yearly six-week rigorous training program (because the Amendment uses the term *well-regulated Militia*) conducted on military lines and involving bivouacs, hikes, obstacle courses, and instruction. He further maintains that the law should require that members of the Militia perform duties conforming to the Militia's identity as a volunteer force (emergency relief, border protection), and crowd control at sporting events. Failure to fulfill these requirements would result in an individual's right to possess a firearm being curtailed. Anyone electing to not enroll in the Militia can opt out by being paid $1,000 per gun and turning them in to the federal government. The essay is a funny and well-constructed lampoon of some of the specious arguments advanced by absolutist supporters of the right to bear arms.

"Writing in Wartime: The Uses of Innocence" concerns the book *My Sister and I: The Diary of a Dutch Boy Refugee* which was published in 1941 before the U.S. had entered the war. It was purported to be the diary of a Dutch boy named Dirk van der Heide and chronicled his miraculous journey from Nazi occupied Netherlands to England and then the U.S. The diary was a major best seller and sold over 52,000 copies, received great reviews, and inspired the popular song "My Sister and I." Fussell came across the work when he was doing research for his book *Wartime* at the Imperial War Museum, in London. He read and was moved by it but sensed that "something odd was going on.... What was really teasing was the book being written by a twelve-year-old Dutch boy anxious to portray as Good Samaritans, noble in every way, not so much his own people as the British. Why, one couldn't help wondering?"[17] As a result, he did some checking in New York and London and discovered that the publisher's records regarding the book had been removed or sanitized. He then put notices in publications asking for information on the writing and author of *My Sister and I* and received numerous responses. While most of them were not helpful, one respondent, a woman who worked in a New York publishing house, recommended Fussell contact the popular novelist Nancy Wilson Ross for information. He subsequently did and Ross revealed that her husband, the American writer Stanley Preston Young, who was in 1941was a strong pro–British interventionist, was the real author of the book and the Dutch boy did not exist. Fussell concludes in the piece that *My Sister and I* was in reality a sophisticated work of British propaganda intended to drum up support for the U.S. to enter the war in support of Britain.

Interestingly, Fussell's theory about the authorship of this book has recently been supported by new information. Several years ago, the late distinguished Chinese art historian and UC Berkeley Professor James Cahill wrote in his blog that he too was told by Ross that Young (who died

5. An Essayist at Heart

in 1975) wrote the book, but that Young "had not intended his piece to be taken as a genuine document: he meant only to write an imaginary but moving account as a Dutch boy might have told it. But it was wrongly taken as a true reminiscence and quickly got out of hand, to the point where he was unwilling to acknowledge his authorship of it and lose the value it had for a cause he believed in: convincing Americans that they should come to the aid of the British."[18] Cahill also said that Ross's personal archive at the University of Texas at Austin bears out his claims. Cahill's confirmation is helpful, but it is apparent that it was Fussell's persistent digging and the publication of his article that helped solved this mystery.[19]

The title of the essay "A Power of Facing Unpleasant Facts" comes from George Orwell's famous essay "Why I Write" in which Orwell argues that that the ability to squarely confront distressing truths is a requisite for living an honest life. Fussell states that these unpleasant facts include "that life is short and almost always ends messily; that if you live in the actual world you can't have your way; that if you do get what you want, it turns out not to be the thing you wanted; that no one thinks as well of you as yourself,"[20] that you will be entirely forgotten after a generation or two, that to do well in this world you have to do some things that are worrying and difficult to deal with, and that in the final analysis, you are not really that important. To drive home the prevalence of this human tendency to feel anxious about and avoidant over facing unpleasant realities, Fussell describes Orwell's own efforts to challenge individuals like his publisher to face disturbing facts, and writes about an incident that occurred when he was teaching at the University of Pennsylvania where a professor at the Wharton School of Business was caught disposing of copies of the school's student newspaper that contained an article about an instructor at the school being charged with rape because he did not want the story known during the university's alumni day.

Fussell also returns in this essay to a topic that he previously discussed in a piece in his prior collection—writers who complain about the negative reviews they get and their inability to accept critical remarks about their works. He finishes "The Power of Facing Unpleasant Facts" by noting that people who are good at things like politics, administrating, and writing, welcome criticism, are not frightened by and do not spurn it, for they fully understand that it comes with the job. For him, talented people busy themselves with their craft, and have little concern with their reputation and drawing constant attention to themselves. Fussell's point appears well taken, but it can also be effectively argued that it is considerably less common than he would like to believe, given human nature and the fact that gifted and successful individuals are also extremely ambitious, and that this ambition is usually closely connected with concerns over their reputation and status and how to protect and maintain it.

The anthology, not surprisingly, also has essays on war and its effects. There are readable and thoughtful pieces on the British poet Edmund Blunden, a concise history of pastoral writings and the form they took in First World War literature, a crisp overview of the influence of wars on the transition in literature from the chivalric to the anti-chivalric and from traditional romance to modern irony, and an exploration of changing 20th century attitudes towards warfare in verse as reflected in Jon Stallworthy's *The Oxford Book of War Poetry* and Studs Terkel's *The "Good War."* The collection also contains a comic and surprisingly sympathetic account of Fussell's visit to a nude beach in Yugoslavia.

Fussell's collections are, like most essay collections, a mixed bag. *Thank God for the Atom Bomb* is a far better anthology. But a fair number of the pieces in both books hold up well. These display the famous hallmarks of Fussell's approach: his gift for finding subjects that have been overlooked or offering new angles on old controversies and discussing them in an engaging, informative, and at times provocative manner. The essays are clearly written (a rarity for an academician), draw upon information from different disciplines, and he stays refreshingly clear of literary theory and cant. Though his often satirical and exceedingly blunt tone can sometimes come off as sententious and overwrought, his purpose is usually serious and moral: to incite thought and to inform. Some of the essays (particularly in the first collection) now seem dated and are not illuminating, but the best of them continue to be relevant and instruct. One might strongly disagree with some of the conclusions he draws (and on occasion it is easy to do so), but it is hard to doubt his sincerity.

The Boy Scout Handbook and Other Observations received mixed reviews, but even critics of the book acknowledged Fussell's ability to pen a good essay. *The New York Times'* Michiko Kakutani wrote that it was "a

5. *An Essayist at Heart*

spirited work of criticism. Consistently erudite, often outrageous, and almost always readable.... Mr. Fussell is a gifted literary critic, who eschews the fashionable structuralist inspired arguments of academia for broader based social and political commentary."[21] Katkutani also praised Fussell for his intelligence and talent for understanding larger cultural trends. *The Christian Science Monitor* said that Fussell "writes with a clarity and a sense of humor that effortlessly illumine the serious and moral concerns of his books. This latest book continues the fine record he has established as a cultural and literary critic.... He sees and makes the connections that reveal the wider implications of subjects."[22]

But the American essayist Noel Perrin was generally not impressed, saying that the collection is not of the same quality as *The Great War and Modern Memory* and *Abroad*: "Of the 34 essays, two are brilliant, another 15 range from good to very good and the rest are, well, readable."[23] He accuses Fussell of making several misstatements and of sometimes posturing for the sake of unconventionality. But Perrin does praise him for his special literary perspective and willingness to discuss books critics ignore. And *The Nation*'s reviewer liked the essays dealing with war, but was disappointed with many of the other pieces, contending that they often lacked depth, were at times too narrow in focus, sarcastic, and lacking in generosity. He concludes that "although none of Fussell's essays approach Orwell's or Edmund Wilson's at their best, [the book] does contain a number of pieces worth reprinting. One would not have expected less. But one might have expected more."[24]

Thank God for the Atom Bomb and Other Essays received a great deal of attention and favorable reviews. The *Boston Globe* said it displays "wit, anger, simple curiosity, jauntiness, irony and a general grumpiness ... like Orwell, Fussell demands intellectual honesty, like him, too, he operates with the street-smart empiricism of one entirely free of such systematized orthodoxies as Marxism, Structuralism, or Americanism."[25] *The Washington Post* reviewer wrote, "I am not sure why I enjoy Fussell's essays so much—they are clearly not on par with his longer studies on war and travel ... [his] insights might not be epiphanies but they establish Paul as a lively delightful writer."[26] *The New York Times* opined that Fussell "is out to get post-modernism, dishonesty, hypocrisy, and the passive voice ... this frequently irritating man, when he silences his sarcasm, can write a suspenseful detective story or a meaningful piece of investigative journalism on Indy."[27] And the *Chicago Tribune* stated in a review titled "Honestly Amusing Jabs at the Self-Righteous" that Fussell as a popular essayist is "flawed, sometimes preachy, overquotes others instead of making his own points, but nonetheless is well worth reading ... his strongest virtue is that he can't stand cant."[28]

6

Sheer, Vulgar Experience and the Dropping of the Atomic Bomb

Paul Fussell was 56 years old in 1981 when he published in *The New Republic* the most controversial article of his career. Provocatively titled "Thank God for the Atom Bomb," it offered a spirited defense of the atomic bombings of Hiroshima and Nagasaki in Japan in August 1945. It would be the most contentious, debated, discussed, and widely anthologized of his essays. The title appears to have come from a chapter in William Manchester's 1979 autobiography, *Goodbye Darkness: A Memoir of the Pacific War*, where Manchester describes the horrific fighting that occurred between American and Japanese soldiers who were often entrenched in deep caves on islands during the final months of the war. Manchester writes, "You think of the lives which would have been lost in an invasion of Japan's home islands—a staggering number of American lives but millions more of Japanese—and you thank God for the atomic bomb."[1]

Fussell expands on Manchester's point and approaches the controversy regarding the bomb from the perspective of unfettered personal experience. His thesis is simple and involves "the importance of experience, sheer, vulgar experience, in influencing, if not determining, one's view about the use of the atomic bomb."[2] By experience, he means "having to coming to grips, face to face, with an enemy who designs your death,"[3] i.e., the experiences of infantrymen, marines, and sailors who directly fought in the Second World War. In other words, Fussell wants to introduce what he considers to be fundamental but often overlooked considerations into the debate about the morality of the dropping of the bombs, namely the savage reality of the War at the time and honesty about what one would have really thought if immersed in it.

Fussell contends that how one feels about the bombings is intimately connected with how close one was to the events, and that "in general, the principle is, the farther from the scope of horror, the easier the talk."[4] Moreover, he strongly believes that the bombings were necessary, ended the war, and saved many lives.

In the article, Fussell takes on five critics of the use of the bomb. Most of them maintain that the U.S. should have waited before using it because Japan was close to surrendering. The noted economist John Kenneth Galbraith argued that the Japanese would have surrendered by November, and all the U.S. needed to have done was wait two or three weeks. Historian Michael Sherry claimed that more time was necessary between the test explosion in New Mexico and the actual bombings as it might have meant more serious thought given about using it. And historian David Joravsky contended that the use of the bomb was irrational and should have never occurred, and that the U.S. should have demonstrated self-restraint, waited several days, and seriously considered what the decision would mean.

Fussell's responds to these critics by pointing out what waiting would have meant in terms of human lives, noting that at the time, kamikazes were sinking American ships and allied causalities were averaging over 7,000 a week. In addition, allied prisoners of war were being systematically starved to death in countries held by the Japanese, and there existed a standing order for them to be killed if the allies launched an invasion of Japan. Fussell believed that Japan was not ready to surrender, and waiting would have accomplished nothing and only resulted in even more unnecessary deaths.

He also finds it relevant that these three critics were safely situated far from the "scope of the horror." Galbraith worked in Washington in the Office of Price Administration during the war, Sherry was at home in the U.S., and while Joravsky was in the army at the time, he had no combat experience and was on his way to the Pacific when the Japanese surrendered.

Fussell also addresses the remarks of the philosopher J. Glenn Gray, author of the 1959 book *The Warriors: Reflections on Men in Battle*. In it,

6. Sheer, Vulgar Experience and the Dropping of the Atomic Bomb

Gray states many American soldiers felt both shock and mortification when they heard about the bombings because they fully understood what it meant in terms of suffering and unfairness. Fussell finds this comment particularly offensive and patently wrong, saying that the majority of soldiers felt, like him, immense relief and had absolutely no reason to feel ashamed. He also observes that Gray, though he served in the army, was an interrogator in the Counter Intelligence Corps, and therefore worked at headquarters and not on the front lines.[5]

Finally, Fussell accuses these critics of being intellectually dishonest and concerned with conspicuously showing how morally sensitive and discerning they are, and he indicates how they were placed socially so that they did not have to be down in the muck with ground forces where brute self-interest is the norm, nor compromise their moral purity by dirtying themselves with the moral complexities war presents.

Fussell acknowledges the unpleasant and *ad hominem* nature of his remarks but says in defense that it is fundamental that people fully understand "what's at stake in an infantry assault is so entirely unthinkable to those without the experience of one, or several, or many, even if they possess very wide-ranging imaginations and warm sympathies, that experience is crucial in this case."[6]

Fussell's own wartime experience enters the discussion because he would have been a participant in Operation Cornet had it occurred, that is, the invasion of the main island of Honshu which was slated for March 1946. The first invasion, Operation Olympic, was planned for November 1945 and would have involved the landing 766,700 infantrymen, who were already in the Pacific, on Japan's southernmost home island, Kyushu. Cornet would have been considerably larger, using 1,026,000 infantrymen and involved a massive air bombardment campaign before the invasion. Forty divisions would have been employed for the landing and follow up (by way of contrast, 12 divisions were used in the initial landings at Normandy in France in the 1944 Overlord invasion). The entire operation against Japan, code named Downfall, would have been the biggest amphibious campaign in history. Fussell was 21 years old when this was going on in a staging area in Germany preparing for the invasion still suffering from the wounds in his back and his leg he had received several months before (the army still judged him fit for combat). The plan was for his division to be sent back to the U.S. for retraining, and then on to the Philippines to prepare for the final push in March. Operation Cornet would have involved fighting across the largest level area in Japan, the Kanto Plain, the political and economic center of Japan's empire, where 18 million people lived, and then driving north to take Tokyo. Military planners assumed that it would take a full year, to November 1946, for the Japanese to surrender.

At first blush, Fussell's article might appear to be the knee-jerk and unreflective opinion of a member of a local branch of the Veterans of Foreign Wars, but his position is more nuanced. Firstly, he writes that he is acutely aware that the bombings were a "vast historical tragedy and every passing year magnifies the dilemma into which it has lodged the contemporary world."[7] He also mentions how horrible the event was for the victims of the bombs, describing in some detail the book *Unforgettable Fire: Pictures Drawn by Atomic Bomb Survivors*, which contains graphic watercolors and drawings of the Hiroshima bombing by middle-aged and elderly survivors.

Moreover, while Fussell points out the brutality of the Japanese army during the war, he also acknowledges "there was much sadism and cruelty, undeniably racist, on ours."[8] He references the collecting of Japanese skulls by American soldiers, the killing of Japanese prisoners, the extraction of dental gold from dead and sometimes living Japanese soldiers, and the widely held belief among Americans in general that Japanese were subhuman and yellow monsters.[9]

He warns throughout the article about the dangers of making *ad hoc* judgements about the events without taking proper account of the times and the political and military context in which decisions were made. In addition, he contends that "the stupidity, parochialism, and greed in the international mismanagement of the whole nuclear challenge"[10] should not make people misconstrue the reasons why the bombs were dropped. He concludes the essay by stating, "The past, which as always did not know the future, acted in ways that ask to be imagined before they are condemned. Or even simplified."[11]

On a basic level, Fussell's position is understandable given that his viewpoint is grounded in the experiences of the ordinary combat soldier. But it is still possible to raise questions about some of his claims. His cen-

6. Sheer, Vulgar Experience and the Dropping of the Atomic Bomb

tral premise which equates war experience with absolute authority is questionable. As Robert Jay Lifton and Greg Mitchell have pointed out, "What is problematic about Fussell's thinking is not his insistence on the value of personal history but the certainty with which he rejects all other historical considerations—including evidence of what was happening elsewhere at the same time."[12] They contend that what was occurring at the time in Washington and Potsdam is also relevant and that Fussell's argument rests upon the idea that it was historically inevitable that the invasion was going to occur. "With that insistence, he cannot consider any possibility that the bomb may have not been the necessary ingredient for the war to end and his life preserved."[13]

Fussell further opens himself to this type of criticism when he states in the article that inquiring into whether the dropping of the bombs was needed is "surely an unanswerable question (unlike was it effective?), and one precisely indicating the intellectual difficulties involved in imposing a *ex post facto* rational and even a genteel ethics on this event."[14] This seems too strong, for it is still possible, even granting Fussell's emphasis on experience, to raise the question of whether it was necessary for the bombings to have occurred. While the question might not be answerable with complete historical certainty, a careful examination of the decisions made by the government officials involved in Washington as well as what was going on in Tokyo at the time would clearly be revealing. Specifically, issues concerning whether the Allies' demand of unconditional surrender from Japan helped perpetuate the war, how close Japan was to surrendering, how much of a factor the entry of Russia into the Pacific theater was in the decision, and the question of the targets chosen (both of which had large civilian populations), are all worthy of investigation.

The month after Fussell's article appeared, *The New Republic* published an exchange of views between historian Michael Walzer and Fussell. Walzer raised the relevant question of limits during wartime, arguing that for Fussell, "there are no limits at all; anything goes, so long as it brings the boys home."[15] Walzer then maintains that in fact "there is a code. Hiroshima was a violation of that code.... If Harry Truman's first responsibility was to American soldiers, he was not without responsibility elsewhere, no man is."[16] Fussell responded by stating that the argument ultimately concerns sensibilities, between that of "the ironic and ambiguous

American Gadfly

(or even the tragic, if you like), and ... the certain.... I'd call one sensibility the literary-artistic-historical; I'd call the other the social-political-scientific,"[17] and that it is virtually impossible for these vastly different sensibilities to agree. He also contends that the bombs were a very complicated moral circumstance which frequently occurs during wars, one in which lives were saved by killing others. Finally, Fussell observes that Walzer was 10 years old when the bombs were dropped.

In order for Walzer's argument to be consistent, it also needs to be extended to the incendiary area bombing raids over Japan done by the U.S. Walzer maintains that the atomic bombings were terrorist acts because their underlying purpose was not military but political, and they were designed to inflict enough civilian causalities that the government would be forced to surrender.[18] The incendiary raids on Tokyo, which at that time, mainly consisted of wood and paper structures, were also mainly directed at the civilian population and the number of people killed was even greater than that of Hiroshima. During a raid that occurred on March 9–10, 1945, it is estimated that around 100,000 civilians died and a million were left homeless in the intense firestorm. It turned out to be the most destructive bombing raid in world history, and Tokyo's greatest disaster. (The damage to Tokyo was so severe that if you saw pictures of what the city looked like after the bombing and compared them to pictures of Nagasaki and Hiroshima, it is difficult to tell the difference.)

A total of 67 Japanese cities were bombed, and around 410,000 Japanese were killed.[19] These raids were conducted by B-29s which had been stripped of guns and armaments and excessive weight and loaded with firebombs flying at a low attitude (the Allies had air superiority at the time) attacking urban areas. The horror of these bombings was so pronounced that Curtis LeMay, the American general who oversaw them, stated after the War that if the U.S. had lost the war, he would have been tried as a war criminal. As the historian John W. Dower has observed, the War in the Pacific was literally "a war without mercy."[20] (It also should be pointed out that this strategy was not unusual: in Europe, civilian populations had been expressly targeted by the Allies in area bombing saturation missions. Some historians have even estimated that the controversial U.S./British bombing of the German city of Dresden resulted in the deaths of more people than the bombings of Nagasaki or Hiroshima.)

6. Sheer, Vulgar Experience and the Dropping of the Atomic Bomb

Of course, the key difference between these bombings and the atomic bombings is that the atomic resulted in survivors dying months, years, and decades later because of the effects of radiation emitted. While it has been argued that this fallout was not known at that time, it appears clear that even if it was, the bombs still would have been dropped.

For Fussell, these points, while appalling, graphically showed what modern wars were really like, why they needed be avoided, and provided further moral support for the point that using the bombs was necessary to stop the bloodshed. He would have agreed with Henry L. Stimson, who was Secretary of War and intimately involved in the decision to use the atomic weapons. Stimson writes in his memoirs that "in recommending the use of the atomic bomb he [Stimson] was implicitly confessing that there could be no significant limits to the horror of modern war. The decision was not difficult in 1945, for peace with victory was the prize that outweighed the payment demanded."[21]

It is important to discuss at this stage how well his argument stacks up today from a historical standpoint. The answer is very well. Space limitations prevent a detailed discussion of this complex topic but the historiography regarding the bombings has considerably shifted from when his article first appeared. At that time, the revisionist view on the bombings was strong, and there was a widespread belief that it was not necessary and immoral, that Japan was ready to surrender and would have done so if they could have kept their emperor. It was also held by some that the U.S. government knew this but dropped the bombs in order to intimidate the Soviet Union and keep them out of the Pacific theater. Additionally, it was contended that President Truman had inflated the casualty rates the U.S. would have suffered in an invasion of Japan. Revisionism was prominent from the 1980s through the 1990s. Then the discussion began to change, and new studies appeared, "often based on hitherto unavailable documents, that countered many revisionist arguments about the bomb as a diplomatic weapon in 1945, the likelihood that Japan would have surrendered before the planned U.S. invasion had the bomb not been used, and the allegations that projected casualty figures for the projected invasion of Japan were lower than those cited by the supporters of the decision to use the bomb."[22] Furthermore, "these scholars provided powerful support, based upon military considerations, for Truman's decision to use atomic bombs against Japan ... [these] new books and articles in effect refocused the discussion back on the issue of how the bomb was used to end the war as soon as possible, with the least cost in American lives."[23]

There is no doubt that Japan was defeated by the time decisions were made about using the bomb. As Winston Churchill wrote in 1953, "It would be a mistake to suppose that the fate of Japan was settled by the atomic bomb. Her defeat was certain before the first bomb fell and was brought about by overwhelming maritime power. This alone had made it possible to seize ocean bases from which to launch the final attack and force her metropolitan army to capitulate without striking a blow."[24] The power of deciding when Japan would surrender rested with eight individuals—six were members of the Supreme Council for the Direction of War, and the other two were the Emperor and the Lord Keeper of the Privy Seal. According to documents, allied codebreaking intercepts, and interviews with these individuals after the war, there is no strong evidence that Japan was going to surrender soon. Rather, the guiding strategy was for Japan to fight on for as long as possible and avoid total defeat, and wear down the Allies, with the hope of negotiating favorable surrender conditions.

Furthermore, research has shown that if Japan had been invaded, soldiers like Fussell would have very likely encountered extremely strong Japanese resistance which was based upon a sophisticated homeland defense plan named Ketsu-Go. The country still had two and a half million regular troops based on the home island. Every male between the ages of 15 to 60 was conscripted, females between the ages of 17 to 48 were armed, and thousands of aircraft were available to be used as Kamikazes. Decoded Ultra military intercepts have revealed a large buildup of Japanese forces in Kyushu in late July and August.[25]

The question of how many casualties the U.S. would have suffered in an invasion remains a hotly debated topic. Truman in his memoirs estimated that an invasion would have cost 500,000 American lives. (It is very difficult to calculate what the Japanese military and civilian rates would have been, for obvious reasons.) The U.S. Joint Chiefs of Staff had difficulty calculating it because there did not exist a reliable method of foreseeing casualties. The projections that were made were based on the casualty rates suffered by American troops during the bloody battle over

6. Sheer, Vulgar Experience and the Dropping of the Atomic Bomb

Okinawa which was the largest land-sea-air engagement in history, and rates for the campaigns in the Pacific up until that time and in Europe. One widely cited report by the Joint War Plans Committee estimated that the two invasions would have resulted in 40,000 dead, 150,000 wounded, and 3,500 missing in action, for a total of 193,500 anticipated casualties. But as historian Robert James Maddox warns, "the report itself is studded with qualifications that casualties 'are not subject to accurate estimate'" and the projection 'is admittedly only an educated guess'... subsequent Japanese troop buildup on Kyushu rendered the estimates totally irrelevant by the time the first atomic bombs were dropped."[26]

Whatever the actual numbers would have been, officials assumed the fighting would be vicious and bloody. The three month Battle of Okinawa, which had just wrapped up, was the most brutal engagement between the Americans and Japanese in the war and resulted in the deaths of 23,000 Americans, 91,000 Japanese, and 150,000 Okinawan civilians, and demonstrated the horrifying reality that the closer the Americans came to Japan, the higher the U.S. causality rate. Compounding this was the fact that Japanese soldiers almost never surrendered, and that no organized unit of the Japanese Imperial Army surrendered during the entire Pacific War until the Emperor ordered them to do so at the end of it.

There is also no strong evidence that the bombs were primarily dropped to check the Soviet Union. While Russia was an area of concern for Truman and other government officials regarding postwar conditions in Central and East Europe and worries over Soviet gains in East Asia, there exists no corroborating information that the weapon was used to practice "atomic diplomacy" against this country.[27] In terms of other options that could have been used to end the war, a test over an unoccupied area, like the ocean, was rejected because it carried the chance that it might not have worked. As Fussell notes, two days before the Hiroshima bombing, 720,000 leaflets were dropped on the city warning people to get out because an attack was imminent. (But obviously few people took it seriously enough to leave.)

A blockade and bombardment strategy would almost certainly have prolonged the war and resulted in large civilian casualties. Military planners decided that on August 11 the U.S. bombing strategy would change and concentrate on selectively targeting Japan's railroad system instead of using the previous incendiary approach. The problem with this was that Japan in the fall of 1945 was on the cusp of experiencing mass famine as a result of the Allied destruction of their transportation system. Thus, additional bombing over time would result in a famine that would have killed more people by starvation than the number killed by dropping the bomb.[28] In addition, it was believed by Army Chief of Staff George Marshall and others that a blockade and bombardment approach would almost certainly lead to a time-consuming and protracted war, would not be popular on the home front, and would eventually result in a unsatisfactory negotiated peace with Japan.

Fussell was correct in stating that waiting to drop the bombs would have entailed a large number of deaths. Besides the deaths of allied military personnel, it would have also meant the death of civilians. Richard Frank has noted a frequently overlooked harsh reality, "looming over all the debate of these military and political considerations is the reality of what Japan's war of aggression was doing to the Chinese and other Asian peoples. There is no way to assess with assurance the monthly price extracted from them in death and suffering. It might have exceeded one hundred thousand per month in China alone. Arguments that alternative means could have ended the war without atomic weapons in 'only' three months need to be held against this reality."[29]

Several questions about the event remain unresolved. One of them is how much of a contributory factor to Japan's decision to surrender was the late entry of the Russians into the war? The Hiroshima bomb was dropped on August 6, Russia entered the war on August 8, Nagasaki was bombed on August 9, and Japan's surrender was announced on August 15.[30] Another question concerns whether the unconditional surrender demand of the allies was justified. Arguments have been made that if the U.S. had explicitly stated that Japan could have retained the Emperor (which it eventually did), Japan would have surrendered. Michael Kort has maintained that the U.S. was more flexible about this matter than has been assumed, and that Japan should have explored this possibility diplomatically. Kort concludes that "however one judges the policy of unconditional surrender as it affected the war before July 26, the Potsdam Declaration, Japan's last chance to surrender before the bombing of Hiroshima, demanded it more in rhetoric than fact."[31]

6. Sheer, Vulgar Experience and the Dropping of the Atomic Bomb

There is also the question of targeting, and whether the bombs should have been dropped on a purely military target and not major cities with large civilian populations. In May 1945, General Marshall recommended that, in part because of concern over the international stature of the U.S., that the "weapons might first be used against straight military objectives such as a large naval installation and then if no complete result was derived from the effect of that, he thought we ought to designate a number of large manufacturing areas from which people would be warned to leave."[32] This recommendation was rejected by officials because they concluded that a larger densely populated urban area which contained lightly covered buildings was needed in case the bomb became lost due to poor placement and in order to inflict "profound psychological impression on as many of the inhabitants as possible."[33] In other words, as one historian put it, they thought "the bomb would have to be used in an area where there was a large number of civilians to witness its effects. This recommendation ruled out ... the use of the bomb against a strictly military target."[34] This decision was based on the judgment that the dropping of the bomb would give Japan a massive shock and lead them to the chilling belief that the U.S. could destroy the entire country (if necessary).

One element greatly limiting the selection of bombing targets was that there were very few cities that fit the requirement which had not been bombed by this time. Ninety percent of Japanese homeland targets had been attacked during the final three months of the war and only one-fifth of the bombs were dropped on industrial cities that had any military significance. (It should be noted that both Hiroshima and Nagasaki did have some military importance. Hiroshima was an important army headquarters and military depot, and Nagasaki was a key port, an industrial city that produced war materiel, and naval headquarters.)

There are two other factors that have been frequently overlooked by critics of the bombing and that undoubtedly had a strong influence upon Truman's decision to use the bomb: conditions on the home front and the military's ongoing demobilization and deployment policy. By then, with the war in Europe over, there was a strong sense of war weariness and unrest in the U.S. and intense pressure on the government to readjust priorities. The recent book *Implacable Enemies: War in the Pacific, 1944–1945*, notes that "for Americans, the growing conviction of the inevitability of Japan's defeat and horror at its cost in the Pacific seem more repugnant and less meaningful than the war against Germany. As a result, the public focus after V-E Day shifted to reconversion, rather than to Asia, as Americans began a difficult transition to a civilian economy.... Political, labor, opinion, and corporate elites pressed harder and more insistently for the elimination of wartime regulations and the transition to a sustainable civilian economy. In this transformed setting, the Army, the most pervasive arm of the government, had become the nation's principal target of criticism and scapegoat."[35] Consequently, "arrayed again the Army were a bitterly determined enemy, a restive public, and increasingly assertive political leaders. Under these circumstances, it is not surprising that Truman and Marshall understood that the atomic bomb had been indispensable and that it alone had brought the kind of victory they sought."[36] It also appears clear that if the American public in this environment had learned that the government had a weapon that could have ended the war quickly but elected not to use it, there would have been a tremendous backlash and Truman would probably have been impeached.

What's more, during this period, the army was attempting to put in action the complicated and logistically demanding policy of demobilizing 2,000,000 soldiers who had fought in the Pacific and Europe and had accrued enough points on the bitterly contested army point system and of shipping them home while replacing them in depleted units with low point troops, training the remaining soldiers on how to fight the Japanese, and then moving them to Asia as quickly possible. This entire operation was extraordinarily complex, for the redeployment process alone entailed efficiently moving troops across two oceans and three continents, on ships, trains, and planes in a timely manner. There were deep concerns by the military whether this plan could be successfully carried out, for there was a shortage of ships and other forms of transportation, as well as worries about whether the redeployed soldiers would have enough time to be properly trained, the impact of this redeployment on unit morale, and how these troops would be supplied in the invasion, given the vast distance involved.

In the end, the atomic bombings were the "best" of all the options that were available, options that were all bad. It seems to be quite evident that although a myriad of reasons led to the dropping of the bombs, Truman's

6. Sheer, Vulgar Experience and the Dropping of the Atomic Bomb

primary motivation was to end the war as quickly as possible. Moreover, given what is now known, Secretary of War Henry L. Stimson, who was heavily involved in the decision to use it, and who of all of Truman's close advisers displayed the greatest awareness of the terrible and unique nature of the weapon, probably got it right when he concluded, "The decision to use the atomic bomb was a decision that brought death to over a hundred thousand Japanese. No explanation can change that fact and I do not wish to gloss it over. But this deliberate, premeditated destruction was our least abhorrent choice."[37]

Perhaps the biggest mistake that was made regarding the use of the bomb was the failure to take a hard look at the implications for the future if it was employed. For most of the participants in the decision, it was simply another weapon (little was known about its harmful radioactive side effects), and their immediate concerns were with how to end the war as quickly as possible.

In the final analysis, Truman and his advisors failed to comprehend that the bomb would add a grave new dimension to the morality of war and usher in a frightening nuclear age and they gave little thought to strategic considerations on how the event would impact upon relations with other countries and the long-term balance of power.

Fussell in his essay "Thank God for the Atom Bomb" forcefully introduced a new angle to the discussion of the atomic bombings. His essay has become part of the debate and is frequently included in anthologies or mentioned in books on the event and has fostered further discussion and debate. Whether one agrees or disagrees with his position, it should be acknowledged that it took some courage for him to publish it, especially at a time when historical revisionism was at its height. American academics are often politically liberal, and he would have undoubtedly received some pushback (probably some of it heated) from colleagues. Moreover, academicians are also generally quite reluctant to write outside their field and are suspicious of those who do. And being who he was, Fussell was unafraid to do so.

It is not unexpected that he took the stance he did, given the set of convictions we have seen that he held: a hardheaded empiricism in the British tradition, a privileging of combat experience when discussing war, a suspicion of rationalistic abstractions, a hatred of cant and dishonesty, the Orwell-inspired importance he placed on people facing unpleasant facts (especially about oneself and about others and their real motivations) and on individuals having a sophisticated but realistic moral imagination, and his own horrific experiences during the war. It is revealing that he later said his targets in the article were "pacifists, certain social scientists, international reformers.... One of my intentions was to strike back at the high-minded and unimaginative."[38] Publishing the article and reading the reactions to it must have delighted him because at this stage of his career he loved aggressively challenging conventional and mainstream beliefs.

Moreover, writing this essay must have also provided him again (both psychologically and intellectually) with an opportunity to deal with the war and to flesh out what its legacy meant for him. It also helped set the foundation, which began with *The Great War and Modern Memory*, for what would be a long-term, concerted effort on his part to disabuse people of romantic notions regarding the Second World War, specifically the widespread idea that it was a "good war," and about the real nature of war in general. This would come to fruition with his 1989 work, *Wartime: Understanding and Behavior in the Second World War*, his 1996 autobiography, *Doing Battle: The Making of a Skeptic,* and his final book, 2003's *The Boys' Crusade: The American Infantry in Northwestern Europe, 1944–1945.*

7

"A Touchy Subject"
Class in America

Paul Fussell's next book, 1983's *Class: A Guide Through the American Status System*, takes on what he called one of the dirty little secrets of contemporary American life: social class. At that time, many Americans preferred not to directly talk about the subject, in part because they did not consider it to be a major problem. As late as 1991, one survey revealed that 93 percent of Americans considered themselves members of the middle class.[1] Fussell first became interested in the subject while researching an essay on the Indianapolis 500 race for *Harper's* which was published in 1982. He expanded on the topic in the article "Notes on Class" for *The New Republic* which was also published the same year.

Fussell acknowledged that class can be defined in many ways. Scholars have commonly viewed it from the perspective of objective factors like economic background, education, occupation, income, race, and the amount of political power an individual has, and subjective characteristics like cultural and lifestyle traits such as leisure activities, religion, speech patterns, and cultural capital. Fussell's intention in *Class* is to focus not so much on economics but on easily observable qualities like habits, attitudes, status (tellingly, he prefers the term caste), and anxieties. Instead of relying upon the methodology used by social scientists like sociologists and anthropologists which depends on interviews, questionnaires, polling data, descriptive and inferential statistics, and other quantitative methods whose information is then fed into computers in an attempt to derive conclusions (an approach he finds too limited and incapable of revealing important insights), Fussell relies on simple perception and close observation. In *Class*, he is primarily interested in investigating the numerous complicated social markers and attitudes which characterize class in the U.S.

He agrees with George Orwell's position that economically there are only two classes, the rich and poor, but socially there is a complex hierarchy of classes, with differing traditions, manners, and attitudes that persist throughout the lifetime of an individual, and that it is very difficult for a person to escape from his class. Fussell also argues that class distinctions in the U.S. are extremely complex and subtle because of the fundamental tension that exists between the American creed of egalitarianism, the belief in self-invention, and the idea that everyone can succeed if they just try hard enough, and the natural human tendency to analyze things in a hierarchical manner with an emphasis on difference. Because the U.S. is a quickly changing society, these hierarchies change, and since class and status are intimately connected with self-identity, he holds Americans are constantly considering and sensitive to how they fit in, and are strongly driven by the need for respect, esteem, and recognition in order to stand out. Unfortunately, this need is often unsatisfied because when the creed meets reality and individuals encounter limits, disappointment, class envy, and resentments often occur. As he notes, "If you find an American who feels entirely class secure, stuff and exhibit him. He's a rare specimen."[2]

According to Fussell, there are nine classes in America: Top-out-of-sight, upper, upper middle, middle, high-proletarian, mid-proletarian, low proletarian, and finally, destitute and bottom out-of-sight. The first three classes roughly correspond to what is popularly known as the upper class, the next group, the middle class, and the final two, the lower class. He also maintains that wealth is not the only factor that determines which class a person belongs to, for "style and taste and awareness are as important as money."[3]

Most of *Class* consists of Fussell giving entertaining and astute descriptions of the various social or caste markers associated with class levels. Much of his analysis is based upon close observation (Fussell has a great eye for class displays, manners, and cultural tastes—little gets by him). He also relies upon the writings of a large number of renowned sociologists, social commentators, historians, and popular writers, including Thorstein Veblen, Max Weber, Alexis De Tocqueville, C. Wright Mills,

7. "A Touchy Subject"

Vance Packard, Walt Whitman, Alison Lurie, the American novelist John O'Hara, the British novelist Jilly Cooper, and even Lisa Birnbach's 1980 best seller *The Official Preppy Handbook*. In addition, the book is cleverly illustrated by Martim de Avillez's Hogarthian drawings of examples of various classes.

Fussell intended in this work, as he did with many of his books which were written for popular audiences, to make the reader uncomfortable, irritated, and get them to think, for he had long held that people are too easy on themselves and unquestioning. In *Class*, he forces readers to consider by implication how *they* fit into the class system. While he, at times, exaggerates and widely generalizes, mainly for effect (he would later somewhat disingenuously claim that the book was written with tongue firmly planted in cheek), he also accurately describes overlooked and revealing aspects of the American class system, and the differences both between and within status hierarchies.

One of the most conspicuous signals of class is the way people look, for as Fussell notes, appearance really does count. In chapter three, he explains why. Among the many points he makes is that good looks are most frequently a sign of the upper class due to natural selection reasons and the fact that if this class marries down, it is usually done for looks. Height and thinness are also indicators of the upper class (the top four classes aspire to be thin), largely because overweight individuals are usually found in the other classes. In terms of clothing, status can be assessed by factors like the type of fiber used (proles prefer synthetic, genuine members of the upper-middle class refuse to wear artificial fibers, and like cotton and other natural fibers), the color of your attire (if your raincoat is black, dark blue, or beige is an important class divider), whether you wear a hat (if you take hats seriously you descend in class), what your necktie looks like, whether your clothes are layered and understated (a symbol of the upper class), the kind of jewelry you wear, whether you own a tweed jacket (it implies country leisure and is an upper-middle class marker), and how neat and new your clothes are (the upper and upper middle like old clothes, too neat is lower class). Another important register concerns legible clothing, the general rule being that if words appears on your clothes, it is a sign of prole status, and "as you move up the classes and the understatement principle begins to operate, the words gradually disappear, to be replaced, in the middle and upper-middle classes, by mere emblems."[4] Fussell also interestingly claims that how closely you are supervised at work is a class indicator and that the more closely you are monitored, the lower the class.

Fussell suggests that what unites members of the leisure and the upper-middle class are their reverence for the dated and old (what the American economist and social scientist Thorstein Veblen famously called "the conservation of archaic truth" in his classic 1899 book *The Theory of the Leisure Class*). He perceptively notes that this veneration can be seen in these class's intense Anglophilia. "It is in part because Britain has seen better days that Anglophilia is so indispensable an element in upper-class taste in clothes, literature, allusion, manners, and ceremonies. The current irony of the Anglophilic class motive will not escape us. In the nineteenth century, with Britain commanding much of the world, it would seem natural for snobs to ape British usages. Snobs still do, but not because Britain is powerful but because Britain is feeble. To acquire and display British goods shows how archaic you are, and so validates upper-and upper-middle class standing."[5]

Fussell next turns his attention to the subject of what an individual's house says about their social class. He starts with the driveway, then moves to how the house's number is displayed, the garage, the lawn (the neglect of which is a major middle-class sin), and the items displayed on the lawn (high-proles like white urns or a statue of the Virgin Mary). Fussell also examines what the type of window in a dwelling and the type of automobile driven (and what is displayed on it) signify (he points out that the U.S. is the only nation in the world where people conspicuously demonstrate their class anxiety by displaying their college affiliations on their cars). But one of his most detailed descriptions concerns what a person's living room reveals about them. Among the many observations he makes is that upper-class living rooms have a high ceiling, and if wood is used on the walls (for this class, organic materials always trump man made), it is always dark. Hardwood floors with old oriental rugs are also popular with this class.

The middle class prefer imitation Tiffany lamps, wall-to-wall carpet, and "safe" pictures of ships, animals, and children, with the result being that the living room resembles a hotel room. The lower classes usually

7. "A Touchy Subject"

have in their living room an aquarium, thick plastic is used to cover the upholstery, the floor is made of linoleum, and there are also what interior decorators call "lots of "goop."[6] Another telling class marker that can be found in a house is where the television is placed. The upper class generally do not have one or it is hidden, while "down among the middles and the proles the set ceases to be an occasion of shame and becomes instead a specific glory of the family. Here you find sets flaunting their complicated technology."[7]

In chapter five, Fussell analyzes consumption and recreational class patterns. The chapter covers a large amount of material, from alcoholic beverages (scotch and water for the upper middle class, bourbon and ginger for the middle class, and for proles, beer in a legible container for special occasions or in a can for usual activities), the time one eats dinner (the middle class eat at 7–7:30, uppers at 8–9, and proles at 6), sport watching preferences and activities, travel practices (the upper classes often tour independently and the middle class like cruise ships), to class attitudes regarding mail-order catalogs (the middle class love them for the catalogs affirm their values and "supports their aspirations").[8]

Obviously, some of the examples Fussell uses and the broad statements he makes are done for humorous or satirical effect or to ruffle feathers. Others are now dated (for the book is more than 35 years old), but most of them do collectively add up to a general yet surprisingly revealing depiction of specific class attitudes, values, and aesthetic standards.

One of the book's most discerning chapters is "The Life of the Mind." In it, Fussell presents a brutally honest discussion of class implications embedded within the American higher education system. He points out from the start that because the U.S. does not have a hereditary system of titles, ranks, a landed gentry, or a tradition of a monarchy awarding honors, Americans have had to rely upon other institutions to perform this role. And one of the most important of these institutions is the higher education. He holds that the consequences of this reliance are immense, writing, "The psychological damage wrought by this incessant struggle for status is enormous just because of the extraordinary power of these institutions to confer prestige. The number of hopes blasted and hearts broken for class reasons is probably greater in the world of colleges and universities than anywhere else."[9]

American Gadfly

Fussell does not overstate his case. For many Americans, the topic of higher education is an area where class and status anxieties come to the fore. It is quite common for conversations among educated persons about colleges and universities they have attended (or wanted to attend) to eventually lead, in one way or another, to a disclosure of generally hidden and strongly held status and class related anxieties. These anxieties (and sometimes resentments) concern the ranking of schools, the respective prestige and the social capital these institutions carry, and deep worries over how one fits their educational background and current position into the class system. Moreover, the topic of schools is unduly sensitive because it is directly related to another extremely touchy subject, intelligence. As Fussell correctly notes, these apprehensions and aggrievements are long-lasting, and not surprisingly (especially among those who place a high premium on intelligence and educational background) often psychologically devastating and even debilitating. And, as Fussell notes, these feelings are not just applicable to a school's alumni or students but also professors, many of whom are haunted by feelings of inadequacy because they are not teaching at a better school or because of their own educational background.

Fussell also states that many American colleges and universities prey upon this widespread class anxiety about and search for status in education and fraudulently (and expensively) misrepresent the quality and status of their institutions in order to attract students, and as a consequence fail to adequately educate them. This misrepresentation takes the form of inflating the quality of faculty, facilities, location, and alumni, vigorously objecting to the school's national ranking, the unjustified upgrading the status of a school from that of a college to a university, making false promises about the job related value of attending the institution, the proliferation of questionable schools, and the creation of suspect majors. (The harsh reality of many of these schools can be seen in guides like the *The Insider's Guide to the Colleges by the Yale Daily News*.) In the end, Fussell finds it peculiar that Americans depend so heavily upon the higher education system as a way to channel class competitiveness, and that today a large number of them continue to be hoodwinked by the belief that a "'college degree' means something without the college's being specified ... even when confronted with the facts of the class system and its complicity with the hierarchies of the higher learning."[10]

7. "A Touchy Subject"

This chapter also describes class reading tastes. He contends that while the upper class display books, they seldom read them (except for the occasional business work or a mystery novel, they mainly read magazines), whereas high-proles like *Reader's Digest, TV Guide,* and tabloid newspapers, and the middle class love publications like *National Geographic, House and Garden,* and *The New Yorker*. But he also believes that the middle class is different from the upper and prole classes because they care about what you think of their reading. "The poor anxious middle class is the one that wants you to believe it 'reads the best literature,' and condemnatory expressions like trash or rubbish are often on their lips."[11] He provides a list of popular writers the middle class especially like and who exemplify to him the pretentious and undiscriminating taste of this class. On it are Pearl Buck, Lawrence Durrell, John Steinbeck, Irwin Shaw, Herman Wouk, and Will and Ariel Durant, all of whom he thinks are mediocre and affected.

But, Fussell believes that of all the many telling class signifiers he discusses the one that is the most visible is the way a person speaks. In chapter seven, he colorfully yet precisely lays out how an individual's vocabulary, pronunciation, diction, syllable multiplication, use of euphemisms (a major concern of the middle class), idioms, the objective case and the passive voice, the length of his utterances (minimal for the upper class), and the influence of advertising language, indicate his level. He concludes the chapter by insisting "that linguistic class lines are crossed only rarely and with great difficulty.... We're pretty well stuck with the class we're raised in."[12]

In chapter eight, Fussell describes a social phenomenon that has become even more prevalent since the publication of this book, namely what he calls "prole drift." He defines it as "the tendency in advanced industrialized societies for everything inexorably to become proletarianized. Prole drift seems an inevitable attendant of mass production, mass selling, mass communication, and mass education."[13] He maintains that it is easy to find this phenomenon, and that it can be seen in the decline in quality of newspapers, magazines, films, architecture, and even beer, in the current listing of bestselling books, and the way people behave in public areas.

But Fussell is not a complete pessimist. He ends the book by offering a way of opting out of the class system, by becoming a member of what he calls category X, which is not a class at all. He contends that "X" people are not born into this membership, as people are in the class system, but develop into a member. "You become an X person, or, to put it more bluntly, you earn X-personhood by a strenuous effort of discovery in which curiosity and originality are indispensable."[14] He believes that only by becoming an X person can one escape the class system.

For Fussell, X people are gifted. They can be but are not limited to intellectuals, but they also include musicians, actors, artists, journalists, and even sports stars. Many are self-employed, but all are "independent-minded, free of anxious regard for popular shibboleths, loose in carriage and demeanor. They adore the work they do.... X category is a sort of unmoneyed aristocracy."[15] Furthermore, they are easy to spot for they dress only for themselves, despise the usual forms of status display, watch much TV (but never "educational" programming), eat at home, are verbal, completely self-directed, intensely curious, read everything, and possess a good knowledge of languages, literature, history, and architecture. They also "adopt toward cultural objects the attitude of makers, and of course, critics ... [and] are impelled by insolence, intelligence, irony, and spirit."[16] Finally, they do not, as do most Americans, suffer from class anxiety.

The book also contains an appendix that has three parts. The first is a test in which the reader must ascertain the class of the person depicted in nine realistic situations. It is intended to instruct the reader on how to make class inferences. Next, is what Fussell calls a "living room scale," where the reader adds or subtracts points (starting with a score of 100) concerning items he has in his living room. The final score tells you what class you belong in. Finally, Fussell has a mail bag, where he answers a series of questions (many of them amusing but also pertinent) about the American class system.

Class: A Guide Through the American Class System is an intriguing, revealing, funny, and brutally honest introduction to what remains a touchy subject in the U.S. Moreover, Fussell is one of the few readers to directly address the topic of the meaning of status clues in America. While the book is short and decidedly unacademic, it is also based on close observation and contains pointed descriptions of many class markers that add up to a surprisingly good overview of the country's complex class system. The book also shows Fussell's great ability to take on a controversial subject

7. "A Touchy Subject"

and present something new. He would later claim that he wanted the book to offend everyone by making fun of Americans' fixation on status, and that he also intended it to be a satire on the jargon laden and overtly quantitative way social scientists have treated the topic. But as with all great satire, there is an underlying seriousness driving the mockery. Much of what Fussell says, beneath the bluster, the occasional *ad hoc* examples, and wild or odd generalization (like the upper class prefer dogs over cats as pets because they can be ordered about like lawyers and gardeners), and dated references to television programs and aspects of popular culture (the Internet, cable television, and social media did not exist when he wrote the book) remains accurate, so much so that some sociologists have cited the work.[17] Finally, his theory that there are nine classes is quite similar to theories that have been offered by several sociologists.[18]

Fussell would later return to and expand upon some of the points he makes in *Class*, especially those regarding the American higher education system, his idea of prole drift, and his attacks on aspects of popular culture, in his 1991 book, *BAD: Or, the Dumbing of America*.

The book received a great deal of attention when it was published and sold well. Reviews were mixed with many critics being confused or even deeply offended by it. The writer Alison Lurie, author of *The Language of Clothes* (which Fussell quotes from in *Class*), wrote, "As might be expected, Fussell is especially good at academic status systems, but his analysis of worlds far from academia is also impressive.... Mr. Fussell might inspire some of his readers to become X-people.... Most people, however, will simply enjoy the book as a shrewd and entertaining commentary on American mores today."[19] Margaret Manning in the *Boston Globe* wrote that much of the book is not surprising "because so much has been mined from other sources. Much will amuse.... Of course much of *Class* is obvious and could have been written with a paste-pot brush. But never mind, you'll laugh."[20]

Christopher Lehmann-Haupt in *The New York Times* spent much of his time in his snarky review getting personal by oddly critiquing Fussell's author photo, stating, "His visage seems a potentially humorous one completely abandoned to grouchiness, dyspepsia, contempt, disgust, suspicion, and barely suppressed rage."[21] He concluded that "maybe Fussell looks so bilious and ill-humored because his book isn't quite so clever as it needed

to be in order to justify yet another treatment of a slightly tired subject."²²
The Washington Post's Jonathan Yardley claimed that *Class* "is a provocative and frequently amusing little book. But it is also nasty and self-serving, loaded with unsupportable generalizations, snide asides and condescending sneers—all of them apparently designed to demonstrate nothing so much as the author's superiority to everything that passes before his unforgiving gaze."²³

In the *New England Review*, T. R. Hummer opined that "it would be pretty to think that readers were and are attracted to Fussell's *Class* by a genuine interest in the nature of class in America ... in fact, it appears more likely that many read it out of a sort of prurient interest in the 'tastelessness' of other people, and in order to establish their own superiority."²⁴ And the noted journalist James Fallows took Fussell to task, saying the book is "one long, mean-spirited sneer,"²⁵ pointing out that he avoided the topic of race in his analysis, cared little about getting facts right, did very sloppy research, and was unfair and just plain nasty about the prole class. Fallow's title for his review shows his major objection: "Why Paul Fussell Thinks He's Better Than You."

As with many of Fussell's popular writings, the strongest criticisms have often come from conservative commentators (who appear to believe that he is guilty of that most egregious of American sins: being anti–American). Mimi Kramer, in a long, scathing, and meandering review entitled "Whoring after Self-respect" in *The New Criterion* was dismayed by the book's style, "the effortful attempts at jocularity, the hyperbole unhampered by verbal agility, the too familiar quotation."²⁶ She also objected to Fussell's methodology, saying he "has no special knowledge to make his book worth the detour any more than he has the temperament to make such an excursion pleasant."²⁷ Finally, Kramer proclaimed that his theory regarding X-people smacked of reverse snobbery.

Judging from the harshness of some of these reviews, Fussell clearly accomplished his goal of offending people for he obviously did touch a collective nerve. The book also revealed that a startling number of book reviewers in the U.S. don't have much of a sense of humor, especially regarding the issue of class. The ferocity of some of their comments ironically reinforces Fussell's main point about the extreme sensitivity of the topic of class status in America, and the fact that people are threatened

7. "A Touchy Subject"

by and have deep insecurities about it, in large part because of the deeply held belief (especially by those who should know better) that America basically remains a classless society. (Of course, their opinions might be different today.) Fussell's observation that while we might be legally and politically equal, socially we are not, seems also to have been offensive to most reviewers.

As we can see by the reviews, the standard charge made against *Class* is that Fussell is an intolerant, elitist snob, a self-satisfied professor who is looking down on the rest of us. Some of this criticism is odd because he is almost just as hard on the upper class as he is on the other classes in the book. The philosopher Carlin Romano has humorously parodied the ferocity of some of this criticism of *Class*, writing, "The jabs suggest Fussell was a captious twit who probably took his own cloth napkin to McDonald's—a genteel ninny ready to wither others with a raised eyebrow, or to drop the news that someone's misshapen polyester sports jacket was a disgrace and their use of negatives a blot on mankind. Fussell, they implied, would have dumped Marie Antoinette if she'd ordered the wrong kind of cake."[28]

Fussell attempted to counter this accusation by explaining that he was not a snob because a snob is obsessed with birth and money, which he didn't place value on. But he did admit he was an elitist, saying in an interview, "I'd like to be called a cultural elitist—with the proviso that I want everyone to be a cultural elitist. A snob is happy at his superiority to others. I'm unhappy about it."[29] Critics often overlook that Fussell's X-people are characterized by their curiosity and independence and not by the amount of money they make or their birth. Moreover, although he believed that one cannot ultimately escape from one's class, membership in the X category, which is not a class (but rather what Fussell calls a parody aristocracy), is earned through self-cultivation and application.

Unfortunately, as with many of his works written for general audiences, some critics spent most of their time fixated on, and distracted by, the satirical and blustery tone of Fussell's writing (which they find offensive) and not enough time on what he is actually saying. He constantly stressed in interviews that much of the outrage he displayed was a comic pose that was rooted in irony and that his works were written "with due pathos."[30] He also complained that many of his critics have no sense of humor, and he deplored the fact that in these times "Satire [is having] a very hard time of it.... We are in a terrible era of earnestness and self-congratulation. Wit is hard to get away with, and irony has a hard, hard time of it."[31] (To be fair, there was undoubtedly also an iconoclastic component to his style, a subversive love of shaking things up just for the sake of doing so.)

An interesting side note to *Class* is the way it was presented and perceived in other countries. In England, the book was published by Heinemann under the title of *Caste Marks: Style and Status in the U.S.* In Germany, it bore the title of *Cashmere, Cocktail, Cadillac: Ein Wegweiser durch das Amerikanische Status system*. And the American journalist Evan Osnos has written that in China "in 1998, a local publisher translated *Class*.... In Chinese, the satire fell away, and the book sold briskly as a field guide to the new world. 'Just having money will not win you universal acclaim, respect or appreciation,' the translator wrote in the introduction, 'What your consumption reveals about you is the critical issue.'"[32] And Fussell said he heard reports that Japanese tourists had been spotted in the U.S. using the book as a travel guide.

Time has been good for the book. *Class* remains in print and is still sometimes referred to (now more positively). Recently, Dwight Garner, *The New York Times* literary critic, wrote a column defending the book, asserting, "The line between wit and cruelty is always a fine one, and that is especially true in *Class*. But it's not an insensitive book, sensitivity, in fact, is among its themes."[33] Yale law professor and author Amy Chua in 2018 has called *Class* a book that helps explain the current social and political environment in the U.S.[34] She makes a good point. For although Fussell does not directly discuss political matters, in this age in the U.S. of deep political tribalism, of "Red" and "Blue" states, status anxiety, and cultural and class divisions, he does reveal class trends that have become more apparent and how classes fundamentally differ in attitudes, life styles, tastes, and behavior.

What's more, according to a 2018 study of the 2016 presidential election done by a team of political scientists who mined reams of polling and voting data, and surveys of attitudes, it was issues of identity—race, religion, gender, ethnicity—and not economics that motivated people to vote the way they did.[35] While Fussell did not directly write about these topics,

7. "A Touchy Subject"

his emphasis on the close connection between class and identity and the importance and intensity of the quest for status for Americans is timely.[36] Although observers going back as far as Alexis de Tocqueville in his famous 1848 work *Democracy in America* had also made this connection, Fussell has done it in *Class* in an engaging and at times illuminating manner. Finally, it is also not unusual to find allusions to his theory of X-people in writings today.[37]

Class further put Fussell on the map as a public intellectual and critic, and its publication also unexpectedly led to a significant change in his personal life. By 1982, his books, essays, and book reviews had become sufficiently well known that *The Washington Post* sent a reporter to his small apartment in Princeton where he had been living since his divorce from Betty Fussell to write a long article about his life, beliefs, and the upcoming publication of *Class*. The published article, "A Class Critic Takes Aim at America: The Slings and Arrows of Paul Fussell," christened Fussell as "the nation's newest world-class curmudgeon taking aim at The American Experiment,"[38] and lumped him with Gore Vidal and William F. Buckley. In it, Fussell acknowledged that he was a strong Anglophile, but he also characterized himself as a dedicated American writer. He also stressed the importance of curiosity, lamented the loss of the class of general critics who were humanists and were willing to discuss lowbrow topics, and praised essayists, remarking that essays "aimed at educated people, whereas an article is essentially for people who don't know anything and have to be told … essayists add the new thing to a large tradition."[39] This tradition to him included writers such as H. L. Mencken, Mark Twain, Evelyn Waugh, and Fussell's model, George Orwell. Fussell also said in the interview that his main rule in writing "is Thou shalt not be boring. I learned that teaching at a state university where students are a little sleepy."[40]

One person who was delighted with Fussell's comments was a Virginia widow in her fifties, Harriette Behringer, who worked in the public relations department of the Xerox corporation. She wrote a fan letter to him, they corresponded, met, and then married in April 1987.

From this time on, Fussell would cultivate a public image of being an irascible malcontent in numerous interviews, so much so that it became part of his message. In interviews with publications ranging from *People* (which described him as "a wounded literary guerrilla shooting back at

American Gadfly

the 20th century,"[41] to *Psychology Today* (which labelled him "The last curmudgeon") and warned readers, "He'll rip off your rose-colored glasses because he's at war with simple-minded optimism. But ... he'll do it with class, taste, and style—all the things he writes about,"[42] to the British *Guardian* (which titled their article, "Hello to All of That"). In these interviews, Fussell exhibited the public persona he would be best known for: witty, outspoken, at times outrageous, thoroughly anti–PC, informed, sardonic, plain spoken, mixed with a bit of the bad boy. He clearly enjoyed playing this role and was quite good at drawing attention. But he also knew how to turn this side off in lectures, on television, and when he was talking about his war experiences.

But it should also be borne in mind that Fussell did not like this label of being the "newest' or "last" curmudgeon, insisting (ironically in an interview for a 1987 book called *The Portable Curmudgeon*), "I don't like the word curmudgeon. It implies that there's something wrong with social and cultural criticism, which is the obligation of every educated person. If every educated person is to be a curmudgeon, fine. Certain people have to *notice* things.... The curmudgeon annoys and amuses people in order to bring about social change. The so-called curmudgeon is really an idealist, perhaps even a romantic, sentimental idealist."[43] Fussell has a point—while he was many things, he was certainly not a social reformer. Instead, he placed value on intellectual honesty and a dogged respect for experience. A more accurate characterization of him would be that of a gadfly in the traditional sense of term—a person who persistently stimulates or annoys or criticizes others (often those in authority) in order to move them to action. Not social action, but individual and intellectual action: to think, to examine, to reconsider, to be critical and skeptical.

8

"The Real War Will Never Get in the Books"

Paul Fussell's next book, 1989's *Wartime: Understanding and Behavior in the Second World War*, was a long time in the making. Its roots went back 17 years earlier to *The Great War and Modern Memory*, but he felt that he was not ready to directly write about his war until this time, later saying that it usually takes 10 to 20 years for these matters to properly come together. *Wartime* is concerned with the American and British psychological, intellectual, and emotional culture during the Second World War. Fussell's purpose in the book is to describe the damage the war did, not just physically to bodies and buildings and things, but also the severe (and often overlooked) harm it did to "intellect, discrimination, honesty, individuality, complexity, ambiguity, and irony, not to mention privacy and wit."[1]

Fussell's target in *Wartime* is crystal clear: any attempt to sanitize, elevate, romanticize, or sentimentalize the war, and anyone who would insist that it was a "good war." He also insists that, because America still does not comprehend what this war was like, it has not been able "to use such understanding to re-interpret and re-define the national reality and to arrive at something like public maturity."[2] Fussell does this by systematically and often angrily stripping away common misconceptions and myths about this conflict until only the underlying brutal reality of it remains. His approach can be clearly seen in many of the frequently ironic chapter titles he chooses: "Precision Bombing Will Win the War," "Chickenshit, an Anatomy," "Someone Had Blundered," "Drinking Far Too Much, Copulating Too Little," "The Ideological Vacuum," "Accentuate the Positive," "High-mindedness," "Deprivation," "Type-casting," and "The Real War Will Never Get in the Books."

American Gadfly

As he did with *The Great War and Modern Memory*, Fussell also uses in this work a wide variety of source material from popular culture, including magazines like *Life, The Nation, Time, The New Republic, Horizon* and *The Saturday Evening Post*, popular songs, magazine advertisements, radio commercials, popular books, movies, and plays.

Wartime consists of 18 chapters. Fussell begins the book by evoking an image of a fast moving, trim, sparklingly new army jeep towing a 37-mm gun and gracefully and confidently bounding over a hillock. He writes that the picture "suggests the general Allied understanding of the war at its outset. Perhaps ('with God's help') quickness, dexterity, and style, a certain skill in feinting and dodging, would suffice to defeat pure force. Perhaps civilized restraint and New World decency would suffice to defeat brutality and evil."[3] The initial chapters show how this image became increasingly misleading over time because of the technological, self-perpetuating, and corrosive nature of modern widescale war, which is oblivious to the ideology which originally drove it.

Fussell argues that modern war (especially a war of the scale of World War II) sets into motion events and situations that are beyond the control of individuals and that, in order to achieve a victorious outcome, war forces people to perform acts which are inimical to the values they initially held. As a consequence, early military "ideas of finesse, accuracy, and subtlety had yielded to the demands of getting the job over at any cost."[4] He also goes on to show that accidents, blunders (mainly caused by fear), service errors, and brute incompetence, contrary to popular perception and Hollywood films, were so shockingly ordinary and widespread that they nearly constituted the essence of the conflict.

Fussell's discussion on the prevalent and pernicious nature in the military of what he calls "chickenshit" in chapter seven has received a great deal of attention (so much so that it is quoted in some detail in the massive 2009 reference work *A New Literary History of America*). He defines the crude term as "behavior that makes military life worse than it need be: petty harassment of the weak by the strong; open scrimmage for power and authority and prestige; sadism thinly disguised as necessary discipline; a constant 'paying off of old scores'; and insistence on the letter rather than the spirit of ordinances."[5] He cautions that the term does not mean the annoying inconveniences of daily life in the military like the boredom,

8. "The Real War Will Never Get in the Books"

absence of privacy, and monotonous food, but that chickenshit is "small-minded and ignoble and takes the trivial seriously."[6] Moreover, it contributes nothing to the goal of winning the war.

He supports this by citing numerous examples of chickenshit behavior in British and American memoirs and works of literature on the war, as well as in the actions of such famous individuals as Adolf Hitler and General George Patton. He quotes from authors including the American novelist Robert Lowry, the British writer Tristan Jones, the poet Timothy Corsellis, and gives special attention to several satirical short stories by noted English novelist Kingsley Amis, who was a friend of Fussell, and about whom he would later write a book. Examples of chickenshit includes unnecessary and anxiety producing training procedures like inspections (many of them spot) of weapons, military equipment, barracks, and personal appearance conducted by higher-ups under the guise of instilling discipline, obsessions with small matters like the precise length of hair and arrangement of soldier's kit, and public verbal humiliations by persons of higher rank for the purposes of revenge upon those they dislike or disagree with. As Fussell notes, chickenshit insidiously changes the focus from the import—i.e. reality—to appearance.

Chickenshit, which has been experienced in one form or another by anyone who has served in the military, appears to have been especially resented by American soldiers during this war. Historian Gerald F. Linderman has written that American troops understood that in order to win the war they would have to obey orders and that basic martial discipline and subordination was important. But they also experienced a deep-rooted hatred of an ethos of command that many believed was more concerned with humbling and degrading them instead of making them efficient warriors. As a consequence, Linderman claims, they "developed a resistance to military discipline that became a fundamental feature of the soldier's experience in World War Two."[7]

In the one of the book's most controversial chapters, "The Ideological Vacuum," Fussell advances the view that the Second World War "seemed so devoid of ideological content that little could be said about its positive aspects that made political or intellectual sense.... As the war went on and duty grew heavier, casualties more numerous, and Allied purposes more confused, there developed a sense that sheer pragmatic unverbalized action on behalf of the common cause would somehow substitute for formulations of purpose or meaning."[8] According to Fussell, U.S. combatants did not have a romantic view of war because cynicism was present from the start (in large part because of the influence of anti-war writers and memories of the catastrophic First World War). If they fought for anything, it was for each other and to punish the Japanese for Pearl Harbor. (In fact, the main reason the European theater was important was because Germany had declared war on the U.S., and as soon as they were defeated, full attention could be paid to Japan.) The war for them was not a crusade or a fight to defend and expand democratic values, but a nasty job they had to do, a job the sooner completed, the sooner they went home.

Because of this growing lack of a believable positive ideology during the war, the problem of how to motivate people at home became important and Allied governments became obsessed with devising ways of building and keeping up morale. Bad news was considered bad for morale, so it was censored or minimized. Home-front morale was maintained by what Fussell calls the skillful use of "optimistic prose."[9] This included employing euphemisms when describing unpleasant matters like military disasters (like "disengagement" for retreat) and stressing the positive whenever possible (thus, "V for Victory" campaign, with victory gardens, victory cigarettes, victory girls, victory red lipstick, and most notably, Churchill's famous "V" gesture).

To sustain soldiers' morale, the military employed public relation officers who focused on creating group pride by conferring credit on units and individual soldiers through the writing of laudatory songs and celebratory service communiques, and the feeding of positive information to and the strict controlling of war correspondents (who were in this war, generally propagandists who essentially worked for the Office of War Information). In addition, the military also relied upon the old standby of blatantly lying about setbacks and blunders. As Fussell observes, these fictive and fraudulent publicity generating activities ultimately worked because they occurred "in a society which had not just developed advertising to a high pitch but trained an immense audience to believe it—and enjoy it."[10]

Fussell also discusses how the war negatively impacted on other aspects of language, asserting that it is difficult to find among the writings

8. "The Real War Will Never Get in the Books"

that were published during the conflict examples of literary writings. By literary, he means "pointed, illuminating, witty, ironic, clever, or interesting."[11] Instead, what one discovers "is the gush, waffle, and cliché occasioned by high-mindedness, the impulse to sound portentous, and the slumbering of the critical spirit."[12] He attributes this decline in usage to the ubiquitous presence of optimistic prose, euphemisms, the relentless stress on seeing the war through the lens of elevated morality, high-mindedness, and self-righteousness, and the deep suspicion of any form of skepticism, analysis, or satire. He details how soldiers counteracted these tendencies by creatively employing language that was original, ironic, skeptical, precise, and subversive (obscene). Fussell gives numerous examples of this new type of language usage (he also believes that many of these wartime phrases have a certain poetic quality to them because they have a certain rhyme) and observes that the language used by Americans was considerably more mocking and negative than that of the British.

As in *The Great War and Modern Memory*, Fussell is good at discussing soldiers reading practices during the War. He notes the popularity of Henry James, Anthony Trollope, Paul Gallico's sentimental novel *The Snow Goose* about a quasi-supernatural bird, Victorian writers in general, Jane Austen, and E. M. Forster. Moreover, books from the famous Armed Services Editions, Pocket Books, and Penguin series gave soldiers access to cheap reprints of classic works (the U.S.'s Armed Services Editions alone had 1,322 titles).[13] In spite of this easy access to books, he points out that the preferred choice of soldiers of reading material in this war was the ever-present comic book.

Fussell also contrasts the American and British military book culture by showing how widely used anthologies in the respective countries greatly differed in material and tone. The American anthologies were often nationalistic, avoided the topics of pacifism and skepticism, and mainly contained works that portrayed Americans in an extremely positive vein as tolerant, kind, vigorous, courageous, and heroic. The British collections were more nuanced and honest about war and had selections from stoic philosophers and noted classical writers.

In the chapter "Compensation," Fussell describes how certain works of literature and publications helped provide needed relief from wartime deprivations and hardships. On the American side, he mentions Walter

American Gadfly

Benton's 43-page, erotic, free-verse work *This Is My Beloved* which provided solace for sexually deprived soldiers. On the British side, he focuses on three superb writers. The first is Cyril Connolly, who edited the famed monthly publication *Horizon: A Review of Literature and Art*. This journal, which ran throughout the war, contained first-rate poems, prose, and art reproductions by renowned authors such as George Orwell, Bertrand Russell, Aldous Huxley, E. M. Forster, W. Somerset Maugham, T. S. Eliot, Graham Greene, H. G. Wells, Stephen Spender, and many others. Connolly believed that *Horizon's* task was "to remind the country that the survival of its culture was threatened as much by philistines at home as by hostile arms overseas."[14] He shared Fussell's concern about the coarsening cultural and social effects of the war, writing in the wartime essay "Writers & Society, 1940–43" that "war shrinks everything. It means less time, less tolerance, less imagination, less curiosity, less play."[15] Although *Horizon* seldom sold more than 5,000 copies, it was popular and provided a sense of aesthetic compensation for many individuals who had been troubled by the war.

Another author that provided comfort was the novelist Evelyn Waugh, whose lush, romantic and highly evocative 1944 work about an upper-class Catholic family, *Brideshead Revisited*, was a major best seller. For many, the novel offered in contrast to the years of wartime deprivations "the inestimable relief of the baroque, with its benignly impertinent curves and surprises, and its joy in the counterfeit."[16] And finally there was the eccentric Osbert Sitwell and his rococo five-volume autobiography. Starting with *Left Hand, Right Hand*, the work provided an evocative, ornate, highly visual, and nostalgic look at Sitwell's life and illustrious family. The volumes were best sellers in both the U.S. and England. Philip Ziegler has stated that it was so popular that it could "be found in virtually every English house which bought books with any regularity; matching in popularity the Bible and Shakespeare, the histories of Arthur Bryant and the novels of Evelyn Waugh."[17] The autobiographical series strongly resonated with people because of their desperate need for escape to an innocent, lost, prewar time, and because of the compensation provided by Sitwell's luxurious and intricate prose.

Fussell holds that Walt Whitman was not only correct when, after viewing and talking with hundreds of badly wounded soldiers during the

8. "The Real War Will Never Get in the Books"

Civil War, he said that "the real war will never get in the books." He also holds that this statement is true of war in general, and of the Second World War in particular. *Wartime* shows that this was because of the massive gap between what actually happens in a war and what is expected, and because of the contingency and absurdity of combat and its lack of meaning that runs so counter to everyday life. It also demonstrates that the American public during the war had been so conditioned by positive publicity and nationalistic ideology, so hampered by a lack of truthful information owing to government censorship, and were so prone, as humans are, to impose order and blind optimism upon things that they could not really comprehend what was occurring on the battlefield. Because of this disconnect, combatants felt that their experiences had been so falsified that it was impossible for them to adequately communicate them to civilians.

Fussell also writes that soldiers were driven to fury over civilians' "innocence about the bizarre damage suffered by the human body in modern war,"[18] not just from weapons but also from disease and stress. They were further infuriated by the public's failure to comprehend certain unpalatable truths about human beings that the war had revealed. Among these truths were that it was not just cowards but, given enough time, anyone who will break down in battle, and "that no appeal to patriotism, manliness, or loyalty to the group will ultimately matter,"[19] that the Allies were more frequently than assumed not driven by an immensely higher sense of morality than the Axis powers, that war often does not bring out the best in men nor were most heroes, and that rules regarding "civilized" behavior during war are largely a myth. The war for them was ultimately about survival and to survive you must kill. No matter how necessary or how justified, it is always a crime. Wars are won by the side that is better at mass murder.[20]

Fussell believes that it is important to point out that it was only a small number of individuals who actually did the fighting and directly experienced these conditions; most were performing much less demanding and dangerous administrative, supply, or transportation duties. By the end of the war, the American Army had 11,000,000 men, but only 2,000,000 were in combat divisions, and less than 700,000 in the infantry.[21]

American Gadfly

Despite these numerous limitations preventing people on the home front from having accurate information about what the war was really like, Fussell does acknowledge that some of its reality has been captured by a handful of writers. He praises works like Norman Mailer's *The Naked and the Dead*, James Jones's *The Thin Red Line*, Evelyn Waugh's *Sword of Honor*, Olive Manning's *Balkan Trilogy* and *Levant Trilogy*, and Anthony Powell's *A Dance to the Music of Time*. But he is also skeptical of the idea that novels can accurately describe the irrationality of war because of plot and pace requirements, and because many stories written about war have characters that tend to sound like and act as if they were in a stock Hollywood war movie. He reserves his greatest praise for British memoirs like Neil McCallum's *Journey with a Pistol*, the poet Keith Douglas's *Alamein to Zem Zem*, and John Guest's *Broken Images*. He also devotes much attention to Eugene Sledge's 1981 masterpiece *With the Old Breed at Peleliu and Okinawa*, which powerfully describes Sledge's horrific experiences as a Marine fighting in two of the bloodiest battles of the Pacific War (more about this book later).

Wartime also contains chapters on topics normally not discussed about the war such as heavy drinking done by soldiers and the effects on them of sexual deprivation. One of the more interesting of these chapters is "School of the Soldier," in which Fussell explores the novel topic of how soldier's high school/college school experiences colored their impressions of the conflict. He states that most of the individuals who fought in the war were very young and had been attending school prior to enlisting. For them, military training was in several ways ironically reminiscent of their school days. "What had been liberal learning is now vocational training, and with a vengeance. And the more murderously vocational, the more irony, the more curious the parallels."[22] Academic assumptions and idioms from school became part of their combat experiences. Soldiers who were in fraternities before entering the war and had recently undergone hazing viewed the chickenshit they had to undergo as being suggestive of their college indoctrination process.

Fussell also finds a surprising difference between the war writing of the Second World War and that of the First in that the famous Great War poets rarely made allusions to school, while some of the great poets of World War II did refer to schools and schooling. It is odd that Fussell

8. "The Real War Will Never Get in the Books"

overlooks in his discussion of schools a work that he praises in *Wartime* that does present an explicit and highly ironic connection between school and the military, namely *The Sword of Honor* trilogy by Evelyn Waugh. The books recount the military misadventures and comic travails of well-intended British army Captain Guy Crouchback. In the first book of the trilogy, *Men at Arms*, Crouchback is shipped to a former British public school for officer training. The school's classrooms which now serve as officer's bedrooms retain their original names which were based upon famous Great War battles like Loos and Anzac. Crouchback's room is tellingly called Passchendaele, which was one of the most infamous, bloody, and controversial battles fought by the British during the First World War. Moreover, Waugh draws a close connection between the officer's training and school, noting that its "curriculum followed the textbooks, lesson by lesson, exercise by exercise, and the Preparatory School of Life was completely recreated. They were to stay there until Easter—a whole term."[23]

In *Wartime*, Fussell provides a much-needed curative to popular misconceptions about World War II that have sanitized, prettified, sanctified, and idealized the ghastly reality of the conflict, and that have proclaimed that it was a "good war." He brilliantly and forcefully details not just what the war did to everyday soldiers, civilians, and language, but also the immense intellectual, moral, and psychological toll it took on American and British societies. He also candidly discusses unpleasant aspects of the war that have been avoided or minimized.

While *Wartime* is not as focused and rigorous as *The Great War and Modern Memory*, it is more personal, expansive, empirically grounded, and satirical in tone and substance. The differences and similarities between the works can also be seen in the pictures that Fussell selected for each book's cover. The one for *The Great War and Modern Memory* depicts a discouraged infantryman complete with helmet, uniform, and mud splattered waders, his arms shoved deeply into his pockets, staring at what appears to be an overwhelming task that needs to be done. The cover for *Wartime* is also of an infantryman, but this time he is under attack, lying in a shallow indentation in the ground, his body tense and closely drawn together. He is protectively pulling his helmet low to protect himself, and his rifle is lying on his knee. While the disheartened Great

American Gadfly

War soldier still has some agency left but will probably be long haunted by what has occurred if he survives, the second infantryman is passive and appears to be overwhelmed by what he is enduring. The photographs drive home his contention that the First World War was relatively civil when compared to the Second and heavily ironic, while the Second World War was almost incomprehensible in terms of its magnitude and savagery. Both pictures also illustrate Fussell's point about the utter madness of war, the impossibility of fully conveying to others what it is like, and graphically show the impact of combat on a soldier's mind.

It is important to understand that *Wartime* is also deeply informed by the 18th century British Augustan tradition that significantly made up his worldview. As the historian Samuel Hynes has observed, when Fussell writes about the damage the war did to "intellect, discrimination, honesty, individuality, complexity, ambiguity, and irony, not to mention privacy and wit,"[24] most of these terms are "from the vocabulary of Fussell's Augustans. Swift and Pope who would have shared his concern for discrimination, irony, and wit.... Certainly Fussell sees the war as the enemy of those values and of that style."[25]

Reactions to *Wartime* were varied but even most of his strongest critics acknowledged the power of the book. It was popular, selling 36,000 copies during the first week of its publication. The famed novelist and *Catch 22* author Joseph Heller, gave it superlative praise in a blurb for the book, stating, "Paul Fussell has written the best book I know of about World War I. Now he has written the best book I know about the Second World War. No novel I have read surpasses its depiction of the awful human cost to all sides of modern warfare. I don't think I'm exaggerating when I say it is unforgettable."

Samuel Hynes wrote in *The New Republic* that while *Wartime* is a politically flawed book, and Fussell's attempt to attack the idea that the war was a "pure moral act against an absolute evil ... doesn't, perhaps, exactly "balance the scales," it [is still] a useful corrective. Nobody who reads it will come away thinking about the war complacently."[26] Jack Fuller in the *Chicago Tribute* admired Fussell's attempt to provide an honest examination of what war is really like. He concluded that "the point of *Wartime* is similar to the one my father was trying to make as I contemplated what seemed to be the uniquely awful aspects of Vietnam: that war

8. "The Real War Will Never Get in the Books"

is ghastly, whether its ends are noble or base, and only history can know what purpose has been served. The lesson was too mature for me then, and it is difficult to take even now. But innocence is worse."[27]

The Washington Post's Nina King said that although *Wartime* lacks a grand theme like *The Great War and Modern Memory*, "Fussell is a wonderful writer—at once elegant and earthy. He gives us much to ponder in this volume, and despite the grimness of the subject, considerable pleasure. There are even moments in which the curmudgeonly Fussell shows just a trace of wartime nostalgia."[28] Hillel Schwartz in the *Los Angeles Times* was not very impressed (but liked the chapter "The Ideological Vacuum"). Schwartz opined that "*Wartime* is essentially an afterthought conditioned by the images we now have of a war without glory [Vietnam]. Like good graffiti, the book will shock some people, will linger for a time on walls and shelves, then fade beneath other bolder strokes."[29] And strangely, Robert Wilson in *USA Today*, while praising much of the book, accused Fussell of being a snob, writing that his "tone in this and other of his books is unapologetically snobbish. He is one of those U.S academics who praise all things British (and upper class) and denigrates all things American (and middle class). For much of the book made me root against him."[30]

But some of the strongest criticism came again from the military historians Robin Prior and Trevor Wilson, who had savaged *The Great War and Modern Memory*. They argued that for Fussell "no cause can be worth serving, and no object worth attaining, if it requires the caste-ridden, power abusing, chickenshit worshipping British and US armies to accomplish it…. The assertion is enticing. But it can only be sustained by the device of very large omissions. There is no context to Fussell's Second World War."[31] They also claim that Fussell never really discusses why the war occurred and what would have happened if the Germans and Japanese had been allowed to expand. Furthermore, Prior and Wilson contend that Fussell brings to this book the same attitude they disliked in *The Great War and Modern Memory*," namely that "wars are entered into for no good purpose. Combat achieves nothing. Military institutions are about the abuse of power…. Wars are appallingly destructive events which do grievous damage to the worthwhile qualities of English-speaking societies."[32]

American Gadfly

The most scathing criticism of *Wartime* came from the historian Jonathan Marwil. In a long, blistering, and at times, mean-spirited article, Marwil attacked Fussell's methodology, asserting that he "has every right to 'my war,' and as memory his war is dramatic, deeply felt, and self-revealing—qualities admirable in a memoir. But *Wartime* is not a memoir, despite its autobiographical aroma. As a deliberate work of criticism, historical and literary, it has to be judged by other standards: namely the use of evidence and the quality of argument. By those standards, the book carries little authority."[33] Marwil also attacks the sources Fussell uses, arguing that he misquotes authors, fails to reference proper witnesses, and that the anecdotes he uses to buttress his position do not constitute adequate proof.

Moreover, Marwil condescendingly blames the book's limitations on the fact that Fussell had a terrible time during the war, writing, "If we ask about insight, the question of value, we find, especially in *Wartime*, much less than what has been admired. The book's method—of discovery and discourse—is to blame; but so, and perhaps more importantly, is the fact that Paul Fussell had a bad war." (To underscore the force of this criticism, Marwil both starts and ends his article with the sentence "Paul Fussell had a bad war.")

There is no evidence that Fussell ever read or responded to Marwil's critique. But if he had, he would have probably first of all noted that Marwil had clearly never been in the military nor experienced combat, and that since he was born in 1940, he would have been too young to have remembered many of the home-front conditions discussed in the book. Moreover, Fussell would have pointed out that because Marwil was trained as a historian, he appears oblivious to what can be considered evidence in literary discussions. To be fair, it is true that Fussell got some of his historical facts wrong (as he did in *The Great War and Modern Memory*), sometimes overexaggerates his claims, and uses his own terrible war experiences to generalize about all the war experiences of those who fought in the conflict. The question is whether he got them so wrong that it significantly impacts upon the central points that have been cited that he makes in his preface to the book. Marwil does not show this conclusively to be the case.

Nor are Fussell's errors and misquoting as "regular" and "systematic"

8. "The Real War Will Never Get in the Books"

as Marwil would have us to believe. In fact, what makes his overreaching criticisms disingenuous is that he is fully aware of why Fussell wrote the book in the form he did. In the review, he writes that "Fussell, and others may smile at this list of errors [that he argues Fussell makes] and dismiss it as pedantry. *Wartime*, like *The Great War*, is not intended to be a sober work of scholarship, they may argue, but a passionate and provoking essay in cultural forms and memory. As such it should not be held to the standards of conventional scholarly histories.... An essay, after all, is an attempt at a subject; it sets out to discuss, suggest, and incite."[34] Marwil fails to show this defense to be wrong.

Furthermore, Marwil appears oblivious, as were Prior and Wilson in their critique of *The Great War and Modern Memory*, of the literary and humanistic tradition Fussell was operating from and ignores his important remarks on the devasting damage the war did to language, intellect, honesty, irony and wit (as did many other reviewers of the book).

One of the major criticisms of *Wartime* by reviewers was that it ignored the political setting of the War, and that Fussell claimed that the conflict had no meaning. First, it should be pointed out that, in spite of his strong anti-war remarks, Fussell did not consider himself a pacifist, but rather a person who held a narrow view of what constituted America's national interest. In an interview conducted with *The New York Times* in October 1989, Fussell responded to this criticism by acknowledging that the Second World War "was both necessary and awful. The war was necessary and just and it caused a mess of intellectual and moral ruin.... What I'm getting at in the book is the irony of the pursuit of good—that of the defeat of Nazism—by evil means. And anyone who senses both those poles cannot come away from the experience without a sense of irony and moral complexity."[35] He also said that his goals in *Wartime* were to introduce a feeling of moral complexity into discussions about this war which he strongly felt had been depicted as being far too Manichaean, and to inform young people about what war was really like. He also mentioned that he had received letters from veterans who told him that he had accurately described their feeling and experiences.

In an interview conducted by the historian Roger J. Spiller, Fussell was asked to respond to another frequently expressed criticism that he had gone too far in the book in his negativity about the war. He replied,

"No. It would be impossible to go too far in the other direction ... one must never forget the war *was* a war, and therefore stupid, destructive, opposed to every decent and civilized understanding of what life was like. So I don't think I went far enough. I didn't go farther because you want to revolt the reader only up to a certain degree; otherwise you wipe out the effect you want to create."[36]

9

The BADness of American Culture

Paul Fussell always had an intensely ambivalent and frequently negative attitude towards American popular culture and society. He wrote in his autobiography *Doing Battle* that during the 1950s he felt the country to be "more than ever bellicose, ignorant, selfish, and greedy, shot through with quasi-religious fraud and hypocrisy."[1] As a result, he felt impelled when he could get a break from teaching to travel overseas (usually to Europe). During the 1960s, he became convinced that there was something fundamentally wrong with the U.S. because of the country's widespread violence, anti-rationalism and rebellious attitude of college students, and the intellectual classes' obsession with scientific and mechanistic methodologies. Because of these societal changes, he sadly came to the conclusion that his longstanding hope that he had held since he was a student that the widespread appreciation of literature and the ideas that literature carries would serve to counter the parochial character of American society, was now wrong-headed. Consequently, he began to increasingly stress in his university courses writers who were critical of America like Walt Whitman and Ezra Pound. During the 1970s and 1980s, he became increasingly dismayed by what he perceived to be the overall banality of American culture and most American movies, the declining educational standards and rise of illiteracy rates, and the poor quality of public discourse in newspapers, magazines, and on television.

Although Fussell had previously published several critical essays on aspects of American cultural along with his sociological study of class, it was not until his next book, *BAD: Or, the Dumbing of America*, which was published in 1991, that he launched a scorching and wide-ranging assault on what he considered to be the explosion of pretentious, phony, and vacuous taste in American life, the loss of civility, and the overall dumbing down of the

American Gadfly

country. He had also long been appalled by the pernicious influence of the advertising industry upon American culture, especially since the end of the Second World War. When he was a college senior, he had read Frederic Wakeman's famous polemic against the industry, *The Hucksters*, which he found extremely disturbing. Moreover, given his fascination with the topics of the difference between actuality and representation, modernity, and irony, and his conviction that Americans as a group are chronically incapable of facing unpleasant facts, it was inevitable that he would eventually write a book on this subject.

BAD rests upon a distinction Fussell draws in the first chapter of the book between the terms *bad* and *BAD*. He defines bad as "something like … a failing grade, or a case of scarlet fever—something no one ever said was good. BAD is different. It is something phony, clumsy, witless, untalented, vacant, or boring that many Americans can be persuaded is genuine, graceful, bright or fascinating…. For a thing to be really BAD, it must exhibit elements of the pretentious, the overwrought, or the fraudulent. Bathroom faucet handles that cut your fingers are bad. If gold-plated, they are BAD. Dismal food is bad. Dismal food pretentiously associated with the word *gourmet* is BAD."[2] He maintains that "the larger the distance … between the touted grand appearance and the commonplace actuality, a distance perhaps perceivable by the disillusioned customer after buying the item but never before … the greater the BAD."[3]

Fussell would later state in an interview that it took him three to four years to write this book, and during this period he kept "a file of things … that annoyed me, or things I thought I could be funny about shooting down."[4] The file would eventually consist of 30 categories of BADness and form the chapter headings for the book. These categories, which are listed alphabetically in the work, run the gamut from BAD advertising, architecture, behavior, colleges and universities, conversation, food, hotels, ideas, language, to BAD magazines, movies, people, poetry, restaurants, signs, and television.

The noted historian Michael Kammen has pointed out "that two crucial factors (or variables) shaping and reconfiguring mass culture are technology and advertising…. These are not discrete phenomena. They are intimately connected in complex ways."[5] Fussell chiefly focuses on the connection between advertising and BAD, arguing, "Advertising is the *sine qua non* of BAD … for BAD depends upon and arises only out of it."[6]

BAD: Or, the Dumbing of America, is, on one level, a continuation and expansion of Fussell's book *Class*. It too posits that Americans, because of

9. The BADness of American Culture

the supposed egalitarian nature of the country, suffer from status anxiety, an anxiety which is translated into an endless quest for individual social importance, approval, and respect, and a deep fear of insignificance. But *BAD* examines how this anxiety has impacted upon popular culture and society, and describes how the banality, uniformity, and lack of meaning of actual American life and its sharp disconnection from tradition created the condition for BAD to occur.

Fussell frequently uses caustic exaggeration, sarcasm, and wild generalizations in the book to satirically make his points, and as was true of *Class*, some of his remarks were obviously written for humorous effect and not to be taken seriously. Some of the harshness of his criticisms is leavened by his sharp humor, but his purpose is serious, for there is little doubt that he is attacking aspects of American life that he has long felt to be deeply troubling. The sardonic and curmudgeonly influence of Fussell's undergraduate hero, the American writer H. L. Mencken, is clearly stylistically present throughout the book. In his autobiography, Fussell admitted that Mencken's use of exaggeration "became a stigma of my own style."[7] In *BAD*, he references Mencken, describing him as a person who was "secure enough in his standards, contemptuous of money, fraud, and uncowed by pretense"[8] and says these are times when we desperately need him.[9]

Fussell's purpose in publishing this book, like most of his writings for popular audiences, is didactic. The bulk of *BAD* is diagnostic; he wants to identify what he believes are the major problems of American society and culture. But it is also prescriptive; he wants, as he did in all of his books, to get his readers to be critical, aesthetically discriminating, aware of nuance, and sensitive to the differences between good from bad and BAD, as well as on their guard against deceiving themselves about these matters. His approach dovetails with H. L Mencken's view that "the capital defect in the culture of these States is the lack of a civilized aristocracy, secure in its position, animated by an intelligent curiosity, skeptical of all facile generalizations, superior to the sentimentality of the mob, and delighting in the battle of ideas for its own sake. The word I use, despite the qualifying adjective, has got a meaning, of course, that I by no means intend to convey."[10] In short. as Fussell concisely states at the end of *BAD*, his goal is to convince educated people that criticism and disinterested skeptical analysis should be their main business in life, for he thinks this is the best way to counter the harmful effects of BADness.

Among the more noteworthy chapters in the book are his remarks on BAD beliefs. He describes a puzzling American epistemological phenomenon (a conundrum that has become even more pronounced since the appearance of *BAD*). It concerns the question: How is it possible that in an age of universal education, an era where science has made its greatest strides, when more factual information is easily available to individuals than ever before, when everyone has access to a computer, Americans believe the arrant nonsense that they do? Specifically, Fussell points to commonly held beliefs in astrology, UFOs and alien abductions, the prophecies of Nostradamus, soothsayers, ghosts, psychic pets, Bigfoot, lucky numbers, parapsychology, the lost continent of Atlantis, life after death, creation science, and the idea that God answers prayers. He is careful to state that simply believing in such things, as problematic and indefensible as it is, is just bad. For Fussell, it becomes BAD when a person becomes self-satisfied and proselytizes their belief. He attributes these erroneous ideas to "the widespread current inability to bring evidence and skepticism to the idea of causality,"[11] and suggests that they serve as a recompense for the disappointments people suffer when living in a country that promises happiness and just rewards but fails to deliver. He also squarely blames much of America's current intellectual and cultural difficulties and the progressive dumbing down of the country on the deleterious effects of television viewing (along with the invention of the laugh track) and the breakdown of the public education system.

Fussell's comments on America's higher education system are both insightful and bitingly funny. The chapter on this topic is one of the longest in the book. Some of the points he makes were previously raised in *Class*. He depicts how the purpose of education shifted from the laudable principles of liberal learning based upon reasoning, logic, analysis, informed skepticism, and evidence, to that of crass and strictly utilitarian concerns. Fussell maintains that this occurred "because it was soon discovered that real education was of little value in the American life of action, ambition, acquisitiveness and getting-on ... [and] an actual impediment to enthusiasm and good fellowship."[12] He then proceeds to mock the wide gulf between the pretentious ways many colleges present themselves and their reality, and describes how these institutions have become corporatized (as "costly sports centers and health spas"[13]) in an attempt to attract students, thereby turning schools into just training centers. He also shows, as he did in *Class*, how some colleges, in a transparent effort to raise their status and project intellectual distinction, have unjustifiably awarded themselves the title of universities, and hilariously chronicles those schools that have done so. For Fussell, this bogus transformation is a striking example of BADness because of the "pretense that these

9. The BADness of American Culture

institutions are real universities, honorable, learned, incorruptible, somehow a beacon because of their pursuit of disinterested scholarship. Real BAD."[14]

Fussell's criticisms of the American higher education system have become even truer today than when he first wrote them. Nowadays, the business model has an even greater influence over the running and organization of many colleges. This can be easily seen in the recent proliferation of highly paid administrators, the overt catering to virtually every non-academic need of students, the nearly total gutting of the tenure system, the great rise in number of poorly paid and treated adjuncts, the dumbing down of the curriculum, and rampant grade inflation. In addition, the goal of higher education has in many institutions become highly politicized and strayed even farther than ever from the original purpose Fussell described. Examples of this devolution in educational philosophy can be easily found today. One recently published book on higher education has the author seriously declaring, "Yes, colleges and universities need to equip students to productively enter the workforce, but they should also teach students to 'contest workplace inequality, imagine democratic forms of work, and identify and challenge those injustices that contradict and undercut the most fundamental principles of freedom, equality, and respect for all people who constitute the global public sphere.'"[15] It is not difficult to image what Fussell would have thought of this string of cliché-ridden goals and the cant used to support them.

Another chapter from *BAD* worth mentioning concerns what Fussell calls BAD conversation. Here he asserts, half in jest, that the U.S. is probably the home of BAD conversation, in part because Americans constantly interrupt each other while talking because of the supposed egalitarian belief that everyone is always entitled to loudly express his opinion. As Fussell puts it, "for most people, it's a pleasure—they have so little opportunity to assert themselves and thus achieve a bit of selfhood and some illusion of power."[16] He also humorously but accurately describes several stock casual conversational strategies that Americans commonly employ to keep informal interactions with strangers or acquaintances tame and bland. He concludes the chapter by positing that BAD American conversation focuses primarily "on personal desires and images, and for all its offensiveness, is really an unvoiced call for help."[17]

Fussell's section on BAD television remains timely because what he says about local TV news is equally applicable to today's cable news programs. He severely criticizes programs that contain panel discussions because they create the illusion that the conversation will be just as open and free as that in a seminar or among educated friends. But in reality, "an inflexible set of personality clichés and *ad hominem* ideological conventions determines that nothing new or unsuperficial can take place."[18] He also observes that today everything in the news business must be made into some sort of story, and nothing is presumed to be real unless some form of commentary is attached to it. As a result, presentation constantly trumps substance. Continuing along these lines, his remarks on BAD newspapers during that time contains criticisms—of their frequent use of non-newsworthy fillers, their giving precedence to showy and technically pleasing surface appearances over content, overt simplification of issues, focus on entertaining readers instead of informing them, constant use of screaming headlines and breaking news items, and the ubiquitous presence of dubious looking advertisements—that could be easily applied to the journalistic practices that govern today's Internet news websites and cable news outlets.

Despite his harsh criticisms, Fussell was not a complete pessimist about the state of the U.S. He does concede in *BAD* that the country has several good points and that a modicum of good taste and culture exists in the country. He praises its open borders, the First Amendment, the instilled American conviction that Americans are free, their ability to travel the world, and the country's acknowledgment that the Vietnam War was a disgrace.

BAD ends with a chapter entitled "The Future of BAD." His prognosis is dark for he feels that the march of BAD is insurmountable, concluding, "BAD has gotten such a head start that nothing can slow it down much."[19] He does finish the book with a list of recommendations of what he thinks can be done to slightly slow its growth in the areas of education and society. They include putting Latin back into the curriculum in high schools, teaching the young to treat advertising with scorn, emphasizing the importance of writing English with style and sensitivity, making intelligent movies, ending grade inflation, doing away with intercollegiate sports and teachers colleges, nationalizing the airlines, cultivating a sense of national humility, and restraining the national instinct to brag and cover up.[20] He concedes that these recommendations are probably not likely to be implemented, so the only recourse for an individual "is to laugh at BAD. If you don't, you're going to have to cry."[21]

Other noteworthy targets are BAD behavior, advertising, restaurants, and objects and collectibles. A handful of the examples he uses in the book are now dated (especially in the chapters on BAD movies, movie actors, television, and people), but given the tenor of his comments, they can be easily updated to include contemporary examples.

9. The BADness of American Culture

Many of the criticisms Fussell makes have also been offered by other American writers and foreign observers. As far back as 1851, Alexis De Tocqueville noted, in a chapter called "Why the Americans Are Often so Restless in the Midst of Their Prosperity" in *Democracy in America,* that "when men are more or less equal and are following the same path, it is very difficult for any of them to walk faster and get out beyond the uniform crowd surrounding and hemming them in. This constant strife between the desires inspired by equality and the means to satisfy them harasses and wearies the mind.... In democratic times enjoyments are more lively than in times of the aristocracy, and more especially, immeasurably greater numbers taste them. But, on the other hand, one must admit that hopes and desires are much more often disappointed, minds are more anxious and on edge, and trouble is felt more keenly."[22]

Henry Adams, Mark Twain, and Thorstein Veblen famously offered trenchant takes on American society and culture. More recently, several books discussed topics like the increasing power and influence of the advertising business and the ignorance of many Americans that Fussell rails about in *BAD*. For example, Richard Hofstadter in his classic 1963 work *Anti-Intellectualism in American Life* demonstrated how anti-intellectualism and utilitarianism are part of the legacy of the U.S. Daniel J. Boorstin in the 1961 book *The Image: A Guide to Pseudo-Events in America* showed how the fabricated, the cult of celebrity, pseudo-events, and the theatrical have replaced the genuine, authentic, and real. Joe McGinniss in his 1969 work *The Selling of the President 1968* documented how image makers created the "new Nixon" and greatly helped Richard Nixon win the presidency in 1968.

Around the time Fussell was researching and writing *BAD*, there was a plethora of books appearing that took a hard and critical look at the state of American society, criticizing the country's materialism, obsession with self and fads, and the perceived intellectual poverty of American higher education. In 1976, the sociologist Daniel Bell published his influential work *The Cultural Contradictions of Capitalism* in which he argued that the unrelenting drive of modern capitalism and the culture it makes has resulted in a destructive search by people for personal self-satisfaction which is undermining the moral foundations of the traditional Protestant work ethic in America and other Western liberal capitalist societies. The historian Christopher Lasch published in 1979 a lacerating attack on American values in his bestselling book *The Culture of Narcissism: American Life in an Age of Diminishing Expectations.* In it, Lasch grimly argued that life in America had become emotionally shallow, banally obsessed with pseudo self-awareness, and narcissistic. This was the same year President Jimmy Carter gave his infamous "malaise" speech decrying the vapid consumerism, materialism, and impulsive self-interest of the country. In 1981, the journalist Tom Wolfe presented a damning indictment of modern American architecture in *From Bauhaus to Our House*, insisting, "Has there ever been a place on earth where so many people of wealth and power have paid for so much architecture they detested? I doubt it."[23]

In 1987, the philosopher and classicist Allan Bloom came out with his bestselling critique of the American higher education system, *The Closing of the American Mind: How Higher Education Has Failed Democracy and Impoverished the Souls of Today's Students*. Bloom maintained that colleges have failed to properly expose students to the great Western humanistic tradition of philosophy and literature and instead subjected them to vulgarized and nihilistic Continental ideas, and the cant of "liberation." One historian, Philip Jenkins, has gone so far as to state that the period from 1975 to 1986, when Fussell was thinking about social trends in the U.S., writing *Class* and researching *BAD*, were watershed years in the country's history, a period when people perceived that America's security was under threat both internally and externally. Jenkins calls this time the "decade of nightmares."[24] Fussell's thinking fits into this mindset, but he would argue that the threat to the country was primarily internal and cultural and had been building up since the end of the Second World War.

The year that *BAD* appeared saw the publication of *Voltaire's Bastards* by John Ralston Saul. Saul contended that many of today's intellectual, economic, and political problems have been caused by the modern science of administration as informed by the rationalism of the Enlightenment, the West's quest for ultimate efficiency, and obsession with pure reason, systems analysis, and experts. He takes aim at some of the targets of *BAD*, including the destructive influence of the business model on education, the rise of the highly paid techno-administrators, the vacuousness of popular culture, and the intellectual poverty of current literary criticism. Saul ends the book with a strong defense of the importance of the values Fussell cherished: doubt, skepticism, and the use of simple, clear, and honest language.

This is of course not to claim that *BAD* is of the same caliber of most of these works, nor did Fussell intend it to be. It is a short work, not scholarly, and written for a popular audience. It is certainly not one of his better works. But he does raise numerous pertinent cultural and moral issues similar to

9. The BADness of American Culture

what many of these writers have broached, and he does this in an engaging and wickedly funny polemical fashion. Fussell clearly had a lot on his mind about the American condition and had been keeping a little list. While the book does dangerously border at times on being a screed, he also communicates some truths that a sizeable number of people felt at the time and continue to feel.

Not surprisingly, *BAD* received mixed reviews. The harshest reviews came from several conservative academics who again raised the specter of Fussell being anti–American. The noted historian Gertrude Himmelfarb, in a review entitled "The BAD-mouthing of America," was especially critical. In it, she strangely argues that the book is "a primer in SC (Social Correctness) to complement PC (Political Correctness)."[25] Himmelfarb charges Fussell with hypocrisy and of not realizing that many of his criticisms of the American middle class are in fact examples of BADness and affectation. She concludes the review by heatedly writing that the book is an example of "'BAD faith,' recognizing the pretentiousness of others but not of oneself, elevating social gaffes into spiritual failings and lapses of tastes into moral evils, and compounding the banality of a radical-chic PC with the snobbery of a Tory-chic SC."[26]

In *The American Scholar*, a doctoral student in history called *BAD* "a vicious, overdrawn, humorless rant.... Its tone is sour and off-putting, and its analysis is disfigured by an odd intensity of emotion. Equally disfiguring is the obvious contempt Mr. Fussell feels for practically *every* aspect of the country he has been forced by birth to inhabit."[27]

Academics can be a rather humorless lot and prone to take themselves too seriously. This was clearly the case with these two reviewers who treated *BAD* literally and ignored the book's satirical and moral thrust. They appear either oblivious to, or unable to understand, the two traditions Fussell was operating from: the rich American critical tradition of mocking sacred cows, and the British tradition of caustic moral satire as exemplified by such writers as Alexander Pope and Jonathan Swift who used their satirical swords to mock the coarsening and corruption of public life. Like them, Fussell held that the modern commemoration of pretense, glamour, ostentatious style, and "presentation" was emblematic of an important change in society's moral awareness. For Fussell, this change started in the 18th century and accelerated after World War II. The responses of these conservative reviewers are more reflective of their narrow conceptions of what America is than of what Fussell thought of the country.

American Gadfly

Other reviewers were more sympathetic. *The Chicago Tribune* called *BAD* a "dictionary of the hilariously dismal.... Fussell [is] perhaps the most eagle-eyed American curmudgeon since Thorsten Veblen ... he's good at connecting the attitudes, idiocies, and artifacts of popular culture with the ethos of an event or people at a certain time."[28] *The Wall Street Journal* was more guarded in its praise, stating, "A gifted stylist, Mr. Fussell hits his targets with amazing accuracy, when he hits them.... *BAD* is a vastly entertaining collection of crotchets, but it is not much more than that."[29] Moreover, the conservative publication not surprisingly objected to Fussell's negative comments about President Reagan and argument for stronger gun control laws and curiously stated that *BAD*'s "stink of the reformer is overwhelming."[30] Humorist Christopher Buckley described the book as Fussell's "summa contra America.... He has seen the future and it is broken. [Fussell writes that] 'The new Goddess of Dullness is in the saddle, attended by her outriders Greed, Ignorance, and Publicity.' You can say that again, bub. America in the late 20th century ain't no place for an 18th century man."[31] Finally, noted critic Jonathan Yardley of *The Washington Post* wrote that while *BAD* is not a BAD or even a bad book, it is too spotty in analysis "when what is needed is a careful, thorough examination of how—and if it is possible to say why—America has lost whatever sense of excellence it may once have possessed and now wallows merely in the mainly meretricious and shoddy."[32]

Yardley is correct that the book would have been much better if Fussell had explained in greater detail how BADness became so much a part of the American fabric (but it can also be argued that some of it had been present in the country from the start, and that, as de Tocqueville observed, it was the product of a society that ideologically put a strong emphasis on egalitarianism). Finally, *BAD* nicely complements Fussell's previous study on class—together they offer a unique and at times revealing take on American society.[33]

10

The War Continues
An Anthology, Introduction and Lectures

The early 1990s was a busy time for Paul Fussell. In addition to being the Donald T. Regan Professor of English Literature at the University of Pennsylvania, he also taught at King's College London in 1990–92, and in 1992, gave the John Coffin Memorial Lecture at the University of London on the topic of "Poetic Form and the Lyric Subject." In 1991, his book *BAD* was published. But Fussell thoughts also remained fixated on the topic of war. He now viewed himself as a cultural or social historian, and when invited to lecture or to attend conferences, the invitation he received came from history and not English departments.

In 1990, Fussell wrote a short introduction to an anthology of poems about the Second World War. In it, he provided further details on how the literature of this war differed from that of the Great War, noting that in World War II, unlike World War I, American poets produced verse that was of the same quality as that of the British, and that American poets were generally more original in their compositions than the English. He also contended that the poetry of this war displayed "a general skepticism about the former languages of glory and sacrifice and patriotism. Sick of the inflated idiom of official morale-boosting tub-thumping and all the slyness of wartime publicity and advertising, the poets now preferred to speak in wry understatement, glancing less at the center of the topic that at its edges, proceeding by hints and indirection rather than open, straightforward declaration."[1]

In 1991, Fussell published a large anthology of modern war writings

American Gadfly

which he had edited for W.W. Norton & Company entitled *The Norton Book of Modern War*. The collection was comprehensive and contained poems, essays, works of fiction and journalism, and excerpts from memoirs, on the Great War, the Spanish Civil War, the Second World War, and what Fussell calls "The Wars in Asia" (Korean, Vietnam). The compilation of an anthology involves much more work than is commonly assumed. It is also a personal and humbling endeavor. As he states in a later book, "paying attention to other's music is an effective antidote for egoism and self-absorption.... So is making anthologies ... the way an anthology reveals its maker [is] almost as forceful as a written confession or testimony."[2] In addition, the anthologist "has the opportunity to exercise values that used to be regarded by universities as their business, notably intellectual curiosity and taste, as well as accuracy, textual responsibility, and the conveyance of non-utilitarian knowledge."[3]

Fussell's purpose in compiling this anthology can be seen in the title selected for its publication in England, *The Bloody Game*, which comes from the Siegfried Sassoon's 1919 poem "Aftermath." In it, Sassoon writes:

> Have you forgotten yet?...
> For the world's events have rumbled on since those gagged days,
> Like traffic checked while at the crossing of city-ways:
> And the haunted gap in your mind has filled with thoughts that flow
> Like clouds in the lit heaven of life; and you're a man reprieved to go,
> Taking your peaceful share of Time, with joy to spare.
> But the past is just the same—and War's a bloody game...
> Have you forgotten yet?...
> Look down, and swear by the slain of the War that you'll never forget.[4]

Fussell clearly spent a considerable amount of time researching and compiling material for this collection for it contains an impressive amount of material and is much larger (825 pages) than the usual war anthology. It has works by 97 writers covering all aspects of modern war and includes selections from such famous writers and historical figures as Rupert Brooke, Vera Brittain, John Dos Passos, Ernest Hemingway, John Fitzgerald Kennedy, Erich Maria Remarque, Marguerite Duras, Studs Terkel, General Douglas MacArthur, and contemporary authors such as Tim O'Brien, Seymour Hersh, Truong Nhu Tang, and Ron Kovic. To his credit, Fussell also includes a generous helping of intriguing but lesser known

10. The War Continues

persons as the minor poet Wilfred Gibson, Great War privates Daniel J. Sweeney and Frank Richards, and poignant family letters from Second World War soldiers like American Corporal Harry Towe and Second Lieutenant Kermit Steward.

Each chapter has an introduction which historically situates the conflict under discussion. The entire work illustrates and reinforces his themes of how technological developments have increasingly exacerbated the horror of modern war, the ubiquity of armed conflict in the 20th century, how modern war has been one of the causes of cultural modernism, and how modern warfare has greatly differed from traditional warfare in the past. He concludes in typical Fussellian fashion in the book's introduction that "what people learn from wars seems to be this: the techniques for making each increasingly efficient—that is destructive and vicious. Or one learns merely what the cartoonist Bill Mauldin has learned, who says: 'One of the startling things you learn in wars is how much blood can come from a human body.' But those are adept students of war who learn what Ernest Hemingway learned from his lifetime of observing men at war: 'Never think that war, no matter how necessary, nor how justified, is not a crime.'"[5]

All in all, *The Norton Book of Modern War* is an excellent and wide-ranging collection of writings on numerous aspects of modern 20th century warfare. Fussell would state after its publication that he found the writing of the book depressing and that he was tired of discussing mass murder and wanted to move on to something more pleasant (his next book would be on his friend the British author Kingsley Amis). But he would soon turn his attention yet again to the topic of war.

In 1994, Fussell gave two conference lectures that are worth examining because they sharpened some of his ideas concerning both World Wars. The first talk, "The Culture of War," was delivered at the Mises Institute in Atlanta in May 1994. In it, Fussell attempts to describe the special characteristics that constitute the culture of war. For the term culture, he relied upon the definition T. S. Eliot formulated in his 1948 book *Notes Towards a Definition of Culture*. In this work, Eliot construed culture to mean not just artistic or elevated activities, but also "the general forms and usages and techniques of a given society including military society."[6]

American Gadfly

Fussell was trying in this lecture on one level to concretely explain why he gave such importance in his writings to the experiences of soldiers who have been in combat over those of non-combatants and civilians. He begins his discussion by noting, as he did in *Wartime*, that only a very small number of people really know about war, and that among the soldiers who served in the military during a conflict like the Second World War, most were involved in providing support for combat troops by driving trucks, cooking, or transporting supplies, and few actually fought with weapons.

He considers it impossible for civilians to understand what war is like because they "occupy a world, thank God, which is in large part rational and predicable, a world that makes sense in an old-fashioned way."[7] To illustrate this point, he tells about a phone conversation he once had with a New York lawyer who was teaching a class at West Point on the connection between language and violence. The lawyer wanted information about problems Fussell had encountered during the War when using normal language while writing after action reports. As the conversation continued, Fussell says that he found himself becoming more and more angry. He eventually asked the lawyer if he had ever been in a war and then emphatically tells him that he never wrote an after action report because there was no time to compose one because of the demands of combat and the immediate problems associated with dealing with its after-effects like caring for the wounded and prisoners, and repositioning soldiers. He testily ends the conversation by informing the lawyer "that producing an after-action report is the privilege of leaders who are non-combatants and are useful only in works of fiction."[8]

Fussell uses this story to make the point of how "a very representative human being, suffered from an extreme naivete about the facts of war. One would expect a lawyer, in New York City, especially, to be quite sophisticated about the facts of life, but here is one who imagined that the conduct of the war was rational."[9]

This would be a good place to examine in greater detail why Fussell so fiercely believed in privileging the experience of military combatants (including his own) over that of those who were not, an assumption which as we have seen has received a good amount of criticism by commentators, especially regarding his works *The Great War and Modern Memory*, *Wartime*, and his essay on the atomic bombings of Japan.

10. The War Continues

Fussell's tone when discussing these matters can be off-putting, and does in fact come off, at times, as self-righteous, and with an "I-alone-can-understand" gist that distracts from his message. Moreover, his tone sometimes smacks of the stridency mocked in the old joke about the Vietnam war: How many Vietnam vets does it take to change a light bulb? You wouldn't know, you weren't there.

He was aware of this criticism and said that his intention was to deliberately provoke readers, to rub their nose in the nastiness of war, and that his ironical and black take on the subject was "a form of revenge. Indeed, the careful reader will have discerned in all my [writings] a speaker who is really a pissed-off infantryman, disguised as a literary and cultural commentator.... I embraced it with a special vigor once I found out how it annoyed people who had not fought at close quarters in terrible weather and shot people to death and been hit by a shell from a German gun.... Whenever I deliver this unhappy view of war, especially when I try to pass it through a protective screen of irony, I hear from outraged readers."[10]

But it can be argued in his defense that his point goes deeper than that. Although Fussell would maintain it was ultimately impossible for noncombatants and civilians to fully comprehend the unique nature of war as experienced by soldiers, he would also acknowledge that the epistemic/empirical gap between the two could be narrowed through the skillful and honest use of several methods.

The first is through personal acquaintance with the effects of war, physical and/or psychological. This can be done by the method of conducting detailed and honest discussions with combat veterans who are willing to talk about their war experiences. Moreover, medical professionals who deal with veterans can also obtain some understanding as well as family members of those who served.

The second method is through an act of imaginative sympathy or commiseration, which entails a person attempting to empathetically put themselves in the shoes of others who have fought and imagining what they must have undergone. An example of this can be found in Vera Brittain's acclaimed 1933 memoir of the First World War, *Testament of Youth*. Brittain, who lost her fiancé, brother, and two close male friends in the conflict, and had directly experienced the effects of war as a nurse, graphically describes in the book the time when she encounters the uniform her fiancé was killed in which had been returned to his family: "the tunic torn back and front by the bullet, a khaki vest dark and stiff with blood, and a pair of blood-stained breeches slit open at the top by someone obviously in a violent hurry. Those gruesome rags made me realize, as I had never realized before, all that France really meant. Eighteen months afterwards the smell of Etaples village [where Roland died], though fainter and more diffused, brought back to me the memory of those poor remnants of patriotism."[11]

She would later write to her brother Edward about this experience, saying, "Everything was damp and worn and simply caked with mud. And I am glad that neither you nor Victor nor anyone who may some day go to the front was there to see. If you had seen, you would have been overwhelmed by the horror of war without its glory. For though he had only worn the things when living, the smell of those clothes was the smell of graveyards and the Dead.... There was his cap he wore rakishly on the back of his head—with the badge thickly coated with mud. He must have fallen on top of it, or perhaps one of the people who fetched him in trampled on it."[12]

Another way to narrow the experiential gap is by a close reading of realistic writings on war—well-informed memoirs, diaries, works of fiction, poetry, and well researched military histories—that are based on the actual experiences of soldiers. Fussell claimed that good war literature enables those who never experienced it to see "what a number of extraordinarily intelligent, sensitive, and articulate observers made of it all."[13] He felt that poetry was especially conducive to revealing truths about warfare because of its directness, sparseness, concision, and because it carries a strong sense of immediacy.

Nonetheless, Fussell also strongly felt that these methods were limited and that while they could decrease the epistemic and empirical divide, they fail to close it. For him, war is literally and figuratively another world and is governed by "rules" that are completely removed from everyday life. It is a realm where people you do not know and who do not know you are actively trying to kill you, and you are attempting to kill them, and where people you do know are killed right next to you. To be a successful soldier means you must know how to effectively kill, and to do so entails

10. The War Continues

acting upon impulses that have been strongly and long suppressed by civilization and the socialization process. Few things in life, if any, are experientially comparable. Research has shown that learning to kill is not an easy matter, for there exists "a powerful, innate human resistance to killing one's own species."[14] As a consequence, armies have had to develop psychological training techniques to counter this resistance.

Fussell contends in his lecture that the lawyer he had the heated conversation with was "a victim of what I call 'inappropriate rationalism,' mixed in with a bit of inappropriate optimism as well.... The culture of war, in short, is not like the culture of ordinary peace-time life. It is a culture dominated by fear, blood, and sadism, by irrational actions and preposterous (and often ironic) results. It has more relation to science fiction or to absurdist theater than to actual life, and that makes it hard to describe."[15]

Fussell also noted throughout *Wartime* that there is a natural human propensity to project order, reason, strict causality, and meaning upon one's experiences. But in wartime situations, this tendency becomes completely upended by the horrific nature, irrationality, and sheer contingency of combat, where people are frequently killed or grievously wounded by the chanciest of events. Freud famously observed that it is impossible for people to imagine their own death because whenever they try to do so, they can only conceive of it when they are still present as an observer, and that we all unconsciously believe that we are immortal. According to many individuals who have fought in prolonged and intense battle conditions, one can get under those circumstances an inkling of what one's demise would be like.[16]

Furthermore, as Dave Grossman, a former American army lieutenant colonel, has pointed out in his groundbreaking 1995 book *On Killing: The Psychological Cost of Learning to Kill in War and Society*, it is impossible to communicate to others what occurs in a soldier's mind in combat—the constant fear, the heavy weight of physical exhaustion, "the impact of memory and the role of guilt,"[17] the deep psychological burden associated with killing, and the massive toll all of these physical and psychological factors take on an individual's senses. Again, very few people in life have ever been placed in a situation in which they had to experience these stresses.

American Gadfly

One reason Fussell was so attracted to the war poetry of Wilfred Owen was that he completely shared Owen's deep anger over the fact that what soldiers had witnessed during a war could never even be conceived of by civilians, especially those who think they understand it. This fury is clearly expressed in Owen's most famous poem, "Dulce et Decorum Est":

> If in some smothering dreams, you too could pace
> Behind the wagon that we flung him in,
> And watch the white eyes writhing in his face,
> His hanging face, like a devil's sick of sin;
> If you could hear, at every jolt, the blood
> Come gargling from the froth-corrupted lungs,
> Obscene as cancer, bitter as the cud
> Of vile, incurable sores on innocent tongues,—
> My friend, you would not tell with such high zest
> To children ardent for some desperate glory,
> The old Lie: *Dulce et decorum est*
> *Pro patria mori.*[18]

Hence, for Fussell, because of these unique factors associated with war and because it is so radically different from normal experience, it is ultimately impossible for a non-combatant to really know what it is to be in combat. At first glance, this might appear to be the same sort of defense that a defender of religious or a mystical experience would offer to a skeptic. But his point is different in that a genuine combat experience is capable (under the right conditions) of being empirically checked and even verified, and its veracity need not be based simply upon faith.

In the field of the philosophy of science, there is an important concept called commensurability. It maintains that two scientific theories are commensurable, and scientists can critically discuss and compare them if and only if the theories refer to a common body of data and they share the same nomenclature or system of terms and names and rules governing them. Theories are incommensurable if they are based in vastly differing conceptual frameworks or sets of concepts and ideas whose language do not sufficiently agree or meet for them to be compared. For Fussell, because of the nature of the culture of war the world of the combatant is ultimately incommensurable with that of the non-combatant.

Fussell's position was also the product of his empirically based epis-

10. The War Continues

temology. Knowledge claims for him concerning war had a high probability of being true only if they were grounded in what individuals have directly experienced during combat, and the closer one was to combat, the greater the chance the claim is true. While the claims of non-combatants, like those of certain war correspondents, medical personnel, and people who had served but had not directly been in battle were not unimportant (his writings reference some of them as does his war anthology), he felt the greatest epistemic import should be assigned to combat veterans. Moreover, his perspective was also influenced by the humanistic tradition he operates from, where personal experience is the supreme source of authority and meaning.

This is not to say that he categorically claims that if a veteran says something about a war, it therefore is automatically true. He would admit that memories can be or become flawed or even fabricated, and that when pen is set to paper, as Robert Graves observed, inaccuracies and distortions can and do occur.

Returning to the topic of the methods individuals have used in attempts to comprehend the reality of war, there are several additional problems. One method, direct personal acquaintance, could run into the obvious problem that many veterans are reluctant to talk about their experiences, and those who are not, often find it difficult to precisely articulate the unique nature of war for the reasons just described. A second method, the process of imaginative sympathy, is a much more complicated process than commonly assumed. It involves first doing extensive research and becoming informed about the topic of war, and then not merely envisioning what it would have been like to have undergone the experiences of a soldier in a battle, but also honestly and realistically projecting and assessing how *you* would have physically and morally acted and thought in comparable circumstances, sit-uations of which you have no experience. Unfortunately, this carries with it the danger that doing this could easily result in imagining playacting at war. In short, to successfully carry out this act could be quite difficult.[19]

Finally, regarding a third method, close reading of well-written works on war, the poet Edmund Blunden has noted the limitations of war memoirs for readers who were never soldiers, writing in the preface to his own account of the war, the widely acclaimed *Undertones of War*, "I know that the experience to be sketched in it is very local, limited, incoherent; that it is almost useless, in the sense that no one will read it who is not already aware of all the intimations and discoveries in it, and many more, by reason of having gone the same journey. No one? Some, I am sure; but not many. *Neither will they understand*—that will not be all my fault."[20] As Fussell would say in a later interview, "there's an immense gulf—it's unbridgeable, philosophically—between the experience of the senses and the rendering of that experience in black marks on a white page. They're totally different things. And the success of a writer of a memoir is measured by the degree to which he or she had managed to bridge that unbridgeable distance."[21]

Again, Fussell would still insist that these methods are worth pursuing (he has used all of them in his writings himself) but he also maintained that at best they can provide only an inkling of wartime experience. Fussell's critics have argued that there exists a contradiction with this line of thinking. They point out that, on the one hand, his longstanding mission was to educate people through his books, articles, and lectures about the reality of war, but that he at the same time vehemently insisted that it was ultimately impossible to adequately capture in mere words its reality and attacked those who thought you could. In his defense, Fussell would have argued that we simply must do the best we can with the tools we have available, as limited as they are. Furthermore, the fact that an event cannot be completely described and understood does not mean that one should therefore give up the attempt to comprehend an important subject like war as well as one can.

It is legitimate to raise the question, as some critics have, of whether Fussell's highly negative opinion of the war, which was based on his own terrible experiences and wounding, was representative of most of the other U.S. soldiers or a careless overgeneralization. Veterans can vastly differ in the way they react to a war after the guns have fallen silent and reflection sets in. As we shall see in chapter twelve where Fussell's memoir is discussed and compared to other famous memoirs of the war, while his experiences seemed similar to the experiences of other soldiers, the dark conclusions and intense feelings of disillusionment he took away from the conflict were in several ways different from those of many other accounts. Other combat veterans have tended to find some ultimate meaning or

10. The War Continues

value in the midst of the carnage, and positively described the intense and comforting feelings of group solidarity, comradeship, and acts of courage and leadership they chronicled.

Fussell never directly addressed this difference in view, but he would have maintained that on a fundamental, experiential basis his reaction was representative, and this was shown by the fact that he received many letters from fellow veterans thanking him for expressing what they had thought and experienced. Moreover, he had won the respect of noted individuals who wrote their own accounts of the war such as Samuel Hynes and E. B. Sledge. He did write that he believed that those who fought on the front lines "constituted an in-group forever separate from those who did not, [and possessed] a special empirical knowledge, a feeling of a mysterious shared ironic awareness manifesting itself in an instinctive skepticism about pretense, publicly enunciated truths, the vanities of learning, and the pomp of authority. Those who fought know a secret about themselves, and it's not very nice."[22] Fussell's thinking appears to have been that those who have experienced the brute reality of war shared a strong commonality of understanding or knowledge regarding its basic nature and the implications it holds. But he would have probably also added the caveat that whether these individuals would ultimately find any additional or ultimate meaning in their war experience was another question (he did not) and that the answer depended upon the person and factors like their background, religious beliefs, the branch of the military they served in, the relationships they had in the unit they served in, etc.

In the second lecture, "The Great War and Cultural Modernism," delivered in September at a conference on the Great War, Fussell spoke about the relationship between this war and Modernism. He starts the talk by pointing out that there are two opposing views regarding this connection. The traditional approach contends "the war was an important cause of modernism, or powerfully advanced it. But it is also possible to consider the war as just another expression of modernism, like the Bauhaus, Picasso, the Empire State Building, the melodramatic rejection of the recent past, and the convention of sexual outspokenness."[23]

Fussell spends some time during the lecture discussing the influential book, *Rites of Spring: The Great War and the Birth of the Modern Age* by Modris Eksteins, which claims that the war itself was a modernistic work.

American Gadfly

Eksteins thinks that our modern obsession "with speed, newness, transience, and inwardness—with life lived, as the jargon puts it, 'in the fast lane'—to have taken hold, an entire scale of values and beliefs had to yield pride of place, and the Great War was ... the single most significant event in that development."[24] He also asserts that by the beginning of the 20th century, "fundamental conflicts were surfacing in virtually all areas of human endeavor and behavior [on the continent]: in the arts, in fashion, in sexual mores, between generations, in politics. The whole motif of liberation, which has become so central to our century—be it the emancipation of women, homosexuals, proletariat, youth, appetites, peoples—comes into view [then]."[25]

Rites of Spring was published in 1989, nine years after the appearance of *The Great War and Modern Memory*. Fussell appears willing in the lecture to make some slight modification to his defense of the traditional view in it. At one point in the talk, he states, "Whether we hold with Eksteins ... or agree with a more traditional view that the war was largely the cause of the consolidation of modernism in the 1920s and 30s, we'd have to notice that outcrops of something very like modernism had been appearing since 1855, when Whitman set forth the terms of his quarrel with the past, and in his free verse and novel diction showed how that quarrel could be conducted and finally won by poets of the future."[26]

Fussell also remarks that the modernistic adversary stance toward the past grew increasingly stronger by 1907 and can clearly be seen in such works as Joseph Conrad's *The Secret Agent* and Edmund Gosse's popular memoir *Father and Son*. He points out that because "these modernistic elements were not caused by the Great War but were already there well before it, perhaps the soundest thing to say about the relation between the war and modernism is that the war accelerated prewar modernist impulses, provided them with telling examples, and strengthened them, making them fit to be passed on uncompromised. It is clear regardless that the adversarial posture of modernism owes much to the realities of the trench warfare."[27] But Fussell also continues to insist as he did in *The Great War and Modern Memory* that the war contributed to the modernistic stress on irony.

He ends the talk with a useful warning about the dangers of finding

10. The War Continues

in the First World War "only what we are looking for, using our yardstick to measure only ourselves while imagining that we are measuring external reality and all of contemporary history. Only superhuman humility and skepticism about our own interpretative techniques and habits will save us from making a fatal confusion between what we see and what we are."[28]

11

Defending "Not a Very Nice Fellow"

Fussell's choice of subject for this next book, a study of the 20th century English writer Kingsley Amis, is easy to understand. He had been an admirer of the author since the 1950s because he felt that Amis's writings exemplified important critical values like skepticism, moral satire, intellectual and moral honesty, devotion to language, and a dogged willingness to take on received views and a willingness to discuss topics concerning popular culture—all values that Fussell held dear. He also thought Amis a writer who both significantly resurrected and was strongly committed to these virtues. Writing on Amis also enabled Fussell to indulge in his "devotion to British literary journalism and non-academic critical prose."[1]

Moreover, Fussell was a friend of Amis and had known him since 1958 when they met in the U.S. while Amis was teaching creative writing at Princeton University and still basking in the acclaim for his famous first novel *Lucky Jim* which had been published four years earlier. They often saw each other in the 1960s when Fussell was writing a book in London, and he became part of a group of reactionary friends Amis would meet with weekly at Bertorelli's restaurant for what they called "fascists" lunches. During these long, alcohol fueled meetings, gossip would be exchanged, and politics argued. Fussell found the political discussions strange but the nonpolitical conversations fascinating, later writing, "Sometimes I stared in wonder at the quasi-paranoid turn these conversations took, but the talk was so good, so passionate, so inventive and energetic that I demurred only once or twice."[2] Fussell and Amis also spent a summer together with their families in 1968 on Rhodes. Both took

11. Defending "Not a Very Nice Fellow"

delight in playing word games together but disagreed over politics. In later years, if he was visiting London, Fussell would meet Amis at his favorite drinking spot, the Queen's Public House, and was present in 1992 at the writer's 70th birthday party.

For his part, Amis enjoyed Fussell's wry sense of humor and thought highly of his book on class. In an August 1984 letter to him, Amis notes that he has written "a rave review of it [*Class*] for the *Daily Telegraph* ... a bloody funny book. I should love to go through it with you page by page pointing out how the Brits differ but much more how we are just the same."[3] Amis also favorably mentions the book in his autobiography. Moreover, the critic Terry Teachout has written that he thinks that Fussell was "the model for a character in Amis's 1988 novel *Difficulties with Girls*."[4]

Both men had quite similar personalities. They were, at times, difficult and complex individuals, known for their curmudgeonly behavior, outrageous pronouncements, and adversarial stance towards cultural orthodoxies and the mores of their respective countries. They both loved a hard-fought disagreement, were extremely well read and articulate, were culturally conservative, and were very good at drawing attention to themselves. But, underneath all their bluster, they both considered themselves primarily moral satirists.

Fussell's main argument in *The Anti-Egoist: Kingsley Amis, Man of Letters*, which was published in 1994, is that too much attention has been paid to Amis's novels and that the focus needs to be redirected to his other great achievements, namely "his performance as a critic, a learned anthologist, a memoirist, a teacher and a poet ... a writer conspicuous for complex literary knowledge and subtle taste as well as for vigorous views on politics and society."[5] In short, Fussell contends that Amis, because of his wide interests, huge output, and serious criticism, should be viewed as a man of letters in the traditional sense of the term.

The Anti-Egoist is divided into ten short chapters and discusses Amis's writings on language use, food, poetry, his book reviewing, social criticism, and his work as an anthologist. It also briefly touches on Amis's life, covering his education, time in the army, and years working as a college teacher. Fussell tries to show that a deep moral sense consistently informed both his fiction and nonfiction, and that Amis was a first-rate moral satirist.

American Gadfly

Fussell begins the book by immediately defending Amis from the widespread charge that he was "not a very nice fellow."[6] He argues that this criticism has largely prevented many people from viewing Amis as an important literary figure. Fussell thinks this belief is based on several misconceptions. The first, he says, is that Amis was politically seen as a conservative reactionary because of his behavior and some inflammatory remarks he made during the Cold War. Fussell defends Amis by explaining that his political beliefs were heartfelt, and that he really believed that the Soviet Union during this period posed an immediate threat to the West, a threat that Amis felt was connected to the expansion of British universities in the 1960s and the drop in academic standards, the power of the Labor Party, the rise of the social sciences, and the dramatic decline of intellectual life and the arts in London.[7]

Fussell also discusses the uproar over Amis's controversial 1991 autobiography, *Memoirs*. Many people were offended by the book because they felt Amis was mean-spirited and unfair in his depictions of individuals like the American author Leo Rosten, the English academic Lord David Cecil, the British writers Malcolm Muggeridge and Philip Toynbee, and the British philosopher A. J. Ayer. Fussell agrees that Amis is frequently impolite, rude, and outspoken in the work, but he also argues that it is done for the purposes of moral satire, and that Amis was actually trying to expose "numerous phonies and pretenders to high culture."[8] He also holds that most readers of the work completely overlook Amis's "implicit celebration of modesty, taste, learning, and genuine rather than publicized, literary achievement."[9]

Fussell is correct in arguing that *Memoirs* has some good points. It is considerably more humorous than many autobiographies (most are not), in a very dry way. Amis is pleasingly honest when writing about himself and is usually modest. The chapters on his experiences in the army and his time teaching for a semester at Vanderbilt University in 1967–68 where he encountered rampant southern racism among the faculty and others, are good examples of Amis using moral satire to great effect. Being British, Amis manages to also put in some obligatory sharp digs against American culture and literature, at one point writing in the book, "I think most American literature is a disaster.... Americans as a whole do not really care for poems or novels or plays as such, as individual works of art, each

11. Defending "Not a Very Nice Fellow"

of which is to a certain extent self-contained and autonomous. They like the generalizations that can be drawn from them, the messages, the bits of uplift, or downpush, the statements, the long imponderables reached as soon and as directly as possible without niggling, limiting, specializing details (seen in things like character, story, setting, motivation, etc.) and proclaimed as loudly and eye-catchingly as possible."[10] Amis also inexplicably blames Edgar Allan Poe for starting this American proclivity.[11]

But Fussell goes so far as to claim that certain chapters of the autobiography (like the one on Leo Rosten) puts Amis on a par with such great moral satirists (and heroes of Fussell) as Pope, Swift, Twain, and even H. L. Mencken.[12] This, however, seems quite a stretch. Critics have noted that some of the depictions in the book were either fabricated or completely misrepresented.[13] Ultimately, Amis's negative depictions of individuals in *Memoirs* simply come off as being both petty and mean-spirited, and his positive pieces affectionate and kind. To remotely equate some scattered semi-satirical passages in the book with Pope and Mencken and other great practitioners of moral satire does seem an exaggeration.[14]

In this chapter, Fussell also insists, based upon Amis's fictional writings, that his favorite targets were the arrogant and the pretentious, and that he constantly displays in his fiction an acute "sensitivity to daily cruelty ... [a] concern with social generosity when meanness or stinginess is in evidence."[15] This statement seems to be true of Amis's novels and short stories, but Fussell also states that Amis displayed these qualities in his personal life, which is questionable. He does not appear to seriously consider the idea in the book that a writer might exhibit great moral sensitivity and concern in their writing, but at the same time be very unpleasant and not a sympathetic person in real life. Numerous cases of such apparent divided personalities abound throughout literary history. Unfortunately, this also appears to have often been the case with Amis, especially during his later years (and around the time Fussell was writing *The Anti-Egoist*). While Amis was personally capable of a great deal of charm, his authorized biographer Zachary Leader has noted that "once Amis got into the habit of behaving badly, even old friends were fair game, especially friends who challenged or patronized him.... 'The price you had to pay for his company got higher,' [the British novelist Julian] Barnes explains. 'Every meeting would involve at least one remark, riff at what you thought, well, I'm not going to rise to that.'"[16] According to Leader, this rudeness was even more pronounced towards those who were part of Amis's circle.

These frequent bouts of prickliness and bad temper that Amis's British friends had to put up with were also directed at Fussell. This can be seen for example in a letter Amis wrote to him in June 1993 in response to some inquiries Fussell was making for *The Anti-Egoist*. In it, Amis roundly criticizes Fussell for his "trendy use of *perception*. When Sam J [Samuel Johnson] said of whomsoever, "Sir, I perceive that you are a vile Whig,' he meant not "My view of you is that you are a v.W.' but 'I see through to the truth, which is that you are a v.W.' There used to be only one true perception, now there are as many as the people doing the perceiving. One more tiny but revealing example of the lefty movement to dethrone absolute or objective truth and institute a republic of equally 'valid' relative truths. So watch it, Jack."[17]

The chapter on Amis's experiences in a British army signal unit during the Second World War is revealing for our purposes because it shows that Amis's attitude towards the military was like Fussell's. Although Amis was never in combat, his experiences in the army also irrevocably changed him, both psychologically and educationally. It also gave him a basis for understanding literature and made him skeptical of institutions in general and sensitive to the moral costs of lives lived under these organizations. In his autobiography, Amis states that the army is very similar to the type of society encountered in science fiction stories, explaining that it is "a world much like our own in general appearance but with some of rules changed or removed, a logic only partly coinciding with that of our world, and some unpredictable areas where logic seems missing altogether or to point opposite ways at once.... One of the things the army does for you is to enlarge your concept of human nature and what is possible."[18] Needless to say, Fussell emphatically concurs. He also praises the realism of three short stories that Amis wrote ("I Spy Stranger," "Court of Inquiry," and "My Enemies' Enemy") which describe the pettiness of army life. (Fussell also discussed these stories in *Wartime*.)

Fussell makes a convincing argument for the importance of Amis as an essayist and book reviewer. As he says, Amis's criticism was influential mainly because he "was reintroducing the archaic critical virtues of skepticism and honesty as a counterweight to publicity, cant, critical affection

11. Defending "Not a Very Nice Fellow"

and cultural orthodoxies. He was also bringing to non-academic criticism a refreshing focus on literature itself as the subject of interest—rather than on literature as an auxiliary to politics, ideology, or manners."[19] Characteristics, as we have seen, that Fussell greatly prized.

To support this claim, Fussell turns to articles Amis wrote on Jane Austen, Evelyn Waugh, Dylan Thomas, Vladimir Nabokov's *Lolita*, Max Beerbohm, Amis's close friend the poet Philip Larkin, Ian Flemings's James Bond spy classics (about which Amis wrote two books—one a study of the novels and the other a novel involving Bond). These essays have been collected in the books *What Became of Jane Austen and Other Questions* and *The Amis Collection: Selected Non-Fiction, 1954–1990*.

Fussell also shows that Amis was a talented anthologist of poetry, noting that his *The Oxford Book of Light Verse* and *The Amis Anthology* demonstrate "scholarly values that used to be regarded by universities as their business, notably, intellectual curiosity and taste, as well as accuracy, textual responsibility, and the conveyance of non-utilitarian knowledge."[20] Fussell also has some flattering things to say about Amis's poetry, his skill as a restaurant and drink critic, and his strong criticisms of current English language usage (which was also a pet peeve of Fussell).[21]

The Anti-Egoist generally received favorable reviews. The famed critic and biographer Terry Teachout wrote in *The New York Times*, "There are really no weak moments in the *Anti-Egoist*, whose pages are packed with good things. The literary world would be a pleasanter place if more writers followed Paul Fussell's elegant example and wrote short books about their favorite artists."[22] The noted literary scholar William H. Pritchard said "the claims Fussell makes about Amis' contribution as a man of letters are eminently valid and presented with documentation—admittedly in the brief span of this short book—that strikes me as undeniable."[23] Brian Murray in *First Things: A Monthly Journal of Religion and Public Life*, stated that Fussell "demonstrates that Amis is a very thoughtful and literary man, devoted to the sane and sound study of literature at a time when much criticism reveals more the desire to obfuscate than delight."[24] And William Laskowski in his book on Amis for the Twayne author series, called it a "sound but ultimately unsatisfactory depiction of Amis as a complete writer,"[25] largely because he thought Fussell's close friendship with Amis hindered his objectivity.

American Gadfly

Fussell's *Anti-Egoist* provides an informative and succinct introduction to Kingsley Amis's prolific writings. It also offers a different focus on publications by Amis that have not received much attention and makes a good case that he should be viewed as a man of letters. In addition, he intersperses among his discussions of Amis interesting information on the history and development of British literary journalism, critical prose, and literary Modernism. The book, though, is occasionally marred by Fussell's tendency to be overprotective of Amis and too defensive about his flaws (one hopes that he intended the book's title to be ironic and not descriptive, but this looks not to be the case). His attempt to soften and explain some of Amis's controversial comments and behavior is not wholly successful. As William Pritchard has observed, "There are moments when Fussell sounds a little too eager to attest to his friend's sterling moral qualities."[26] This defensive impulse is partly because Fussell was a close friend, but chiefly because the values he ascribes to Amis were, as we have seen, values that formed much of Fussell's own mental set.

12

The Autobiography of a Natural Warrior

In 1996, Paul Fussell, at the age of 72 published his autobiography, *Doing Battle: The Making of a Skeptic.* Although the book presents itself as a comprehensive intellectual autobiography (the Library of Congress classification for the work is "English Teachers—U.S.—Biography," "Critics–U.S.–Biography"), it is clearly primarily a war memoir. The book is 316 pages long and 172 pages are devoted to his war experiences. Fussell later remarked that he wrote it in large part to validate on a personal level the points he had made in *Wartime*. It also served as another part of his long-standing mission, starting with *The Great War and Modern Memory* and continuing with essays, reviews, lectures, *Wartime*, and his war anthology, to educate people about the realities of war in general and to desentimentalize and provide a corrective to widespread misconceptions about the Second World War in particular. He also used the memoir to trace his intellectual development and explain why he placed such an importance on the values of skepticism, informed criticism, and his belief that tragic irony was the proper way of viewing life. Finally, the memoir gave Fussell the opportunity to get in some well-aimed jabs at American culture and institutions, and what he considered the country's fatuous optimism.

Fussell once said that combat veterans have to live through their war experience, and if they survive, they live with it for the rest of their lives. *Doing Battle* is in one way an account of how he was able to do this himself. Lest readers have any doubt about this, Fussell opens the book with a special note to them which states: "Late in the afternoon of March 15, 1945, in a small woods in southeastern France, Boy Fussell, aged twenty, was ill treated by members of the German Wehrmacht. His attackers have never been identified or brought to justice. How a young person so innocent was damaged this way and what happened as a result is the subject of this book."[1]

The book opens with a riveting eight-page account of the day Fussell was severely wounded in 1945. In the remainder of the chapter and the next several chapters, he presents a warm and nostalgic but also critical account of his privileged, exceedingly happy, and remarkably innocent upbringing in Pasadena, California. He describes sun-filled summering at Balboa, the books he read, hobbies he pursued, crushes (both male and female) felt, his gift for the language arts, concerns over his growing weight problem and hatred of physical education classes, and memorable teachers. He also describes his memorable firsts: his first haircut, exposure to poetry, and even his first orgasm. He is particularly good at describing slices of adolescent taste, smell, and sound memories. As he says, for boys these senses serve as a key way to know the world. Fussell evokes the smell of Mennen Brushless Shave Cream, the special taste of tennis racket strings, wood, and the tar on newly paved roads, and songs that marked memorable moments in his upbringing. He also acknowledges the at times suffocating Midwestern moralism and philistinism of Pasadena and Pomona College.

Doing Battle next briskly takes the reader from Fussell's induction into the army in 1943, his long months of training in California, Georgia, Texas, and New York, to his landing in France four months after the Normandy invasion in November 1944, the months of tough fighting in the Alsace region and Western Germany, the increasing disillusionment he felt about the army, and finally his discharge in June 1946. He also details his daily life at the front, the appalling conditions, and relates stories about his fellow soldiers, including accounts of individuals who had redeemed themselves by performing heroic actions, and the "great turkey shoot" where several dozen German soldiers who had surrendered were killed in a crater by American infantrymen. Throughout his account, Fussell is modest, painfully honest, self-disparaging, and occasionally wry.

The uniqueness of Fussell's memoir can be seen when it is compared with three popular and widely acclaimed memoirs of the war, namely, William Manchester's 1979 *Goodbye Darkness: A Memoir of the Pacific*

12. The Autobiography of a Natural Warrior

War, 1981's *With the Old Breed: At Peleliu and Okinawa* by E. B. Sledge, and George MacDonald Fraser's 1992 *Quartered Safe Out Here: A Recollection of the War in Burma*. All three works deal with the fighting in Asia, and according to the historian John Keegan, they are the greatest war memoirs of the Second World War.

William Manchester, in the first chapter of his memoir, which is revealingly entitled "Blood That Never Dries," states that the book's composition was sparked by a series of recurrent nightmares he had had in the 1970s involving two men meeting at the crest of a mountain. One of the men is a cocky young Marine Corps sergeant wearing muddy battle dungarees from 1945 who bears his name, the other is the Manchester of today—overweight, Brooks Brothers clad, and elderly. In the dream, the older man appeared uncertain of himself as the sergeant loudly demands from him an explanation regarding "what had happened in the third of a century since he laid down arms.... The sergeant felt betrayed. He hadn't anticipated that his country would be transformed into what it had become, nor his generation into docile old men who greedily follow the Dow-Jones average and carry their wife's pocketbooks around Europe."[2] After waking up, Manchester wonders which person was right, "the uncompromising Sergeant or the compromiser he had become. Here was the ultimate generation gap: a man divided against his own youth. Troubled, I saw no way to heal the split."[3]

After much thought, Manchester decided that the only way to resolve this split was to return to the Pacific, visit major battlefield sites, retrace his war experiences, and try to discover "what I had lost out there and retrieve it."[4] *Goodbye Darkness's* organization is unusual because it is bifurcated. Each chapter gives background histories of the battlefield sites he visits and the countries they are in, and the toll these battles took. These descriptions are contrasted with the often-rampant commercialism and materialism of these locations today. Manchester discovered, much to his chagrin, that Japanese companies now have a strong economic influence in many of these areas. The jarring contrasts between the past and the present serve to reinforce Manchester's central point in the book that although the war was horrific, brutal, and not worthy of being glorified, there were still traditional values (self-restraint, respect, discipline, loyalty) that he was educated with, that were at times exemplified in the conflict, and that these values are quickly disappearing today and worthy of respect and preservation. The book ends on a positive note with another dream that Manchester had at a Hong Kong hotel. In this dream, the older man ascends Sugar Loaf Hill in Okinawa where Manchester was wounded in 1945. When he reaches the summit and looks down on the reverse slope, the man strangely hears nothing. He then suddenly understands why "embers would never glow in the ashes of his memory. His sergeant would never come again. He turned away, blinded by tears."[5]

E. B. Sledge's account follows the traditional pattern of war memoirs, starting with boot camp, proceeding through his combat experiences, and ending with his discharge. But the work is distinguished by its extremely graphic, honest, yet compassionate depiction of the terrible fighting by the U.S. Marines on the islands of Peleliu and Okinawa in the Pacific. The book is simply and modestly written. Sledge does not pull any punches regarding the types of sadistic acts men are capable of performing when they are fighting for their survival under terrible conditions. Like Manchester, he is also very proud of having served in the Marines and appreciates the values it taught him. And as with Manchester, Sledge believes that there were certain virtues and ideals, like honor, loyalty, responsibility, and courage, that were displayed during this war and should be maintained. Although the atrocities committed by some soldiers, both Japanese and American, drove Sledge to moments of deep despair, he did not believe that they were caused by man's flawed nature, but were rather the result of the savage conditions under which soldiers had to fight.

Sledge concludes *With the Old Breed* by writing, "Combat leaves an indelible mark on those who are forced to endure it. The only redeeming factors were my comrade's incredible bravery and their devotion to each other. Marine Corps training taught us to kill efficiently and to try to survive. But it also taught us loyalty to each other—and love. That esprit de corps sustained us. Until the millennium arrives and countries cease to enslave others, it will be necessary to accept one's responsibilities and to be willing to make sacrifice for one's country—as my comrades did. As the troops used to say, 'If the country is good enough to live in, it's good enough to fight for.' With privilege goes responsibility."[6]

George MacDonald Fraser's *Quartered Safe Out Here* is the story of his experiences as a 19 year old serving in the Border Regiment in Burma

12. The Autobiography of a Natural Warrior

from late 1944–45. Fraser, who was the author of the splendid Flashman series of novels, comes off in the book as a beefy, no-nonsense John Bullish sort of fellow. He is a traditionalist and a robust defender of British traditional values. Fraser says he wrote the memoir not to cleanse his "demons" about the war, but to depict his own experiences, to show what war is really like, and to honor his comrades. He has a definite gift for dialogue (much of the book consists of darkly humorous conversations by his fellow Cumbrian Borderers in Cambrian dialect with footnotes to it when necessary) and for realistically describing front-line action. He is unapologetically proud of his service, and has no regrets, maintaining, "Glad I was there: I wouldn't have missed it for anything. A good thing to have done, and to have been, as Samuel Johnson so wisely observed. No regrets about it, and much gratitude."[7] Fraser also claims that the best commentary ever written on infantry warfare can be found in several lines from a poem by Rudyard Kipling which states, "When first under fire and you're wishful to duck/ Don't look nor take heed at the man that is struck/ Be thankful you're living, and trust to your luck/ And march to your front like a soldier."[8] Far more than Manchester and Sledge, Fraser regrets what he considered the passing of traditional British values that helped sustain soldiers during the war. For him, these values included a concealment of emotions and a stiff upper lip no matter how difficult the situation, and a well-developed sense of public spirit, duty, self-discipline, and personal responsibility. In the memoir, Fraser also makes some strongly worded attacks on the British media, revisionist historians, and what he calls the "fashionable attitudes" of Modern Britain.

Interestingly, Fraser also launches in *Quartered Safe Out Here's* introduction an attack on Fussell's book *Wartime*. His criticisms are written in response to a book review of *Wartime* Fraser had read in which the reviewer summarizes Fussell's main points. Fraser writes "to start with, anyone who writes of 'unacceptable reality' [of the war] simply does not know what he is talking about; the reality of the Second World War was acceptable and accepted, and no 'rationalizations and euphemisms' were required. This may well be required by a modern writer looking back; he may not understand that the rhetoric and propaganda of newspapers, broadcasts, and newsreels were recognized as such, at the time."[9] He also says, "Whatever damage the war inflicted on intelligence, honesty, etc.,

American Gadfly

cannot be measured, let alone proved, even by a modern academic. I doubt it had any special effect on anyone's intelligence or honesty; how you can inflict damage on complexity, ambiguity, and irony, is not clear to me, or, I suggest, to anyone who prefers plain English to jargon."[10] Fraser clearly did not know Fussell's army background and that his remarks were about the American media during the war. (To be fair, Fraser does acknowledge he had not read *Wartime* and knew nothing about the writer's background, but it is rather indefensible that he did not take the time to do some research before putting his criticisms in a book.)

Although Manchester's and Sledge's memoirs have both traditional and critical elements, all three men strongly believed that some meaning can be extracted from the war, and elevated traditional values like loyalty, discipline, self-sacrifice, courage, and honor over the brutality of the conflict. They were also very proud of their service, the units they served in, and what they accomplished. All of them had faith in their respective societies and institutions that supported them, and each deeply lamented what they believed was the decline of societal values they believed had enabled them to endure the war. Although they had appalling war experiences, they felt gratitude for what the war taught them and for their experiences of comradeship.

Fussell's memoir is different from Manchester's, Sledge's, and Fraser's accounts. His portrayal is considerably less traditional and much more critical in substance and tone. While he had also encountered individuals who had displayed some of the values these three veterans have extolled, he did not share in their attempt to exalt these ethical principles over the horrors of the war. He strongly felt that there was ultimately nothing in infantry warfare that was uplifting, and that the psychological and physical damage that the war had done to participants far outweighed any individual acts of virtuous behavior and attempts to impose overriding meaning. Moreover, as John Bodnar has observed, Fussell also spurns in *Doing Battle* "the aspirations of traditionalists like Manchester and Sledge [and Fraser] to a restoration in faith in self-sacrifice and an older set of moral values because he has come to resent how they could be placed into the service of warfare."[11]

As we have seen in a previous chapter, Fussell was not especially pleased with serving in the infantry during the war and had a much more

12. The Autobiography of a Natural Warrior

negative view of the performance of American infantry units than Manchester or Sledge. What's more, though he admitted there were some good things associated with his boot camp and OTC training, he was not impressed by it as Manchester and Sledge were and grew to despise its redundancy and dehumanizing chickenshit character. Fussell was also considerably more critical of the competency of the military staff and American society and institutions at the time, which he believed had become corrupted by the war and U.S. government propaganda.

Although Fussell was a great admirer of Sledge's book (so much so, as earlier noted, that he wrote an introduction to a reissue of the work), he differed from him in that he had a more negative view of human nature and a much narrower view regarding a citizen's responsibilities to the government. He would have agreed with these writers that the war was a formative experience in his life and that he was also in some ways grateful to the army for what it had taught him. But Fussell also states in *Doing Battle* that his education was primarily of a negative nature, and that he had spent his time after the war attempting to live a life that was intellectually diametrically opposed to the tenets and values of the military, a life which would, as he puts it, "illustrate a theory of antithesis and compensation."[12] Unlike the other memoirists, he remained forever angry about the war, how it was conducted, and what it did to him, and was never able to fully reconcile himself to the psychological damage it had caused, insisting that it forever destroyed his belief in optimism and American innocence.

Did Fussell have a more difficult experience during the conflict than Manchester, Sledge, or even Fraser? Clearly not. But his perspective on it does not fit the pattern of standard war memoirs of the period. The final and perhaps most revealing difference between his account and those of Manchester's, Sledge's, and Fraser's is that it is impossible to conceive of any of these authors subtitling their memoirs as Fussell did, "The Making of a Skeptic."

Doing Battle has been compared by some critics to Robert Graves's *Goodbye to All That*. There are some similarities in that both writers were very critical of the war they fought in and the way it was managed. They were both tough-minded individuals who greatly appreciated and used the techniques of irony and satire, but their memoirs are otherwise different. Although Fussell was a great admirer of Graves's work, it is not evident in the way *Doing Battle* was written and organized (even though he did say that *Goodbye to All That* was one of his models). Furthermore, *Goodbye to All That* is considerably more satirical than *Doing Battle* and critical of society. Graves also employs (as Fussell has noted) subversion, the techniques of the Renaissance dramatist Ben Johnson, and the British music hall tradition of caricature, melodrama, and comedy to great effect in the book, and admittedly fabricated aspects of his story, while Fussell did not. Finally, Graves remained very proud of his service with the Royal Welch Fusiliers throughout his life and was not as adamantly anti-war as Fussell was.

Doing Battle can perhaps best be thematically compared to a not well known and now out of print British memoir which Fussell called one of the best chronicles of the war. *Journey with a Pistol: A Diary of War* by Neil McCallum was published in 1959. The book is based on notebooks and letters that McCallum wrote when he was a junior infantry officer in the British Eighth Army. It covers the period of July 1942–July 1943, when he saw action at the Battle of El Alamein in Egypt, and in Libya, Tunisia, Malta, and Sicily. Fussell loved the book because it is drenched in dark humor, highly literate, and eccentric. It consists of 159 pages and episodically describes McCallum's war experiences, but it also contains numerous brief but intriguing philosophical speculations on, and poses question about, warfare, fate, and democracy. McCallum expresses views on war, the army, the reality of combat, martial values, and the idea that the Second World War was a crusade that are quite similar to Fussell's own beliefs and aligned with his subversive and skeptical sensibility. McCallum's memoir is generally more literary than Fussell's and more introspective.

Among the remarks McCallum makes that could have easily come from Fussell himself or which he would have heartily agreed with are the following: "When you look straight into a rifle barrel you look into the black nothingness which is war: the absolute denial of all living values.... Military discipline reaches into the heart of the individual to corrupt that self-sufficiency, the self-respect and integrity that makes a man. All so that people may lie dead with a hole in their heads, or their legs blown off, or their guts spilled and fly covered. For military discipline is not self-discipline. Military discipline destroys the living sensitive thinking man before it finally kills him. It annihilates all that it touches. Death is only one of its objects."[13]

12. The Autobiography of a Natural Warrior

McCallum also has a keen awareness of the way war corrupts and cheapens language and the disingenuous ways in which people evoke martial values. Writing about the American writer Stephen Crane, he notes, "Crane saw through the martial values with which barbarism cloaks itself. If he did not entirely destroy the cloak he at least lifted it so that one could see something of the real hero inside, the normal vacillating hero-coward, the ordinary man of flesh and blood."[14] He also devotes much time, like Fussell, to trying to explain what makes combat so unique and so hard to adequately describe. "It is terrifying to know that from a few hundred yards to a few miles there are people trying to kill you. Let me put this as accurately as I can. The terror is not as in a cloak-and-dagger thriller. There is nothing of that. I do not believe it is entirely personal, either, the fear of personal death. It lies in the fact that this killing is quite impartial; it has the cold indifference of a great organization, it is an impersonal routine, a job. There is always a taint of lunacy in our life here."[15]

Finally, McCallum shares Fussell's disdain for the argument that the Second World War was a "good war," an ideologically pure war, as well as Fussell's dark view of modern man. "'We fight not for glory, nor gain, nor riches, but for that true liberty which no good man will lay down except with his life.' Has war ever presented itself so simply? One is hemmed in by group loyalties, group interests, group traditions. Whatever the American tank-manufacturer is fighting for is not what I am interested in. Nor would my war aims be resolved into language that Churchill would care for. Is the cohesion of the allied armies merely purely *ad hoc*—to win a victory of blood because men must fight?"[16] Watching fellow soldiers rummaging in the hold of a British merchant ship in Tripoli carrying clothes, food, cigarettes, "all the ordinary things of ordinary life, but seared with the slime of murder,"[17] he nightmarishly sees the soldiers as "madmen crawling in the labyrinths of an insane world. There was concentrated here, swaying on the dark sea, the fulfillment of millions of years of evolution, of painfully learned skills, of laborious centuries of experiment and failure and success. It had been brought to a specific physical position in place and time off the coast of Africa. All the wonderful genius of man was here, directed to bring death and misery and pain."[18] This is a book that could have also been subtitled "The Making of a Skeptic."

American Gadfly

The final section of *Doing Battle* concerns Fussell's education, and career after the War. It is an account of his intellectual odyssey and describes why he turned into a sceptic, and details his battles against pretense and dishonesty, and how he found his mental template in the Augustan humanists and other writers. Consequently, he devotes much space to writing about teachers and authors that influenced him and provides interesting background information on and his motivations for writing his books.

The American higher education system and teaching in general also figure prominently in these chapters. After his discharge from the army, Fussell promised himself that he would never be under anyone's orders again. As a result, he was drawn to colleges and universities because they were a type of social organization that was in theory diametrically opposite to that of the military. He clearly enjoyed the freedom (when compared to most other jobs) that academic life and teaching offered as well as the sabbaticals, generous research grants, and the chance to teach material he was interested in. (Fussell was luckily employed during the heyday of college education in the U.S.; his opinion probably would be vastly different today.) But he also disparagingly writes about the mediocrity and apathy of many of his students, the drudgery of grading papers (especially for composition classes), the intrusiveness of student protests during the 1960s, the decline of the importance of English literature in the curriculum, the rise of literary theory and political correctness, administrative blunders, and the ignorance of many of his colleagues. He appears never to have been really satisfied with his situation until he got to the University of Pennsylvania, and even there, he grew to hate the power of the business school, which he considered a sellout to monied interests. *Doing Battle* also gives the impression that he was a strict and quite demanding teacher.

But there is also some contrary evidence. John C. Brereton, who was a graduate student at Rutgers when Fussell was teaching there, discloses in his review of *Doing Battle* that when he was "pacing the Rutgers English Department offices an hour early for my PhD. orals, Fussell, ready to be my examiner, noted my nervousness and invited me out to lunch. After a pleasant hour and a fortifying glass of beer I returned, nervousness gone, and passed without trouble. It was a simple act of kindness that I've not forgotten."[19] In addition, the autobiography has a detailed scene where

12. The Autobiography of a Natural Warrior

Fussell movingly describes a sentimental visit he took shortly before he left for Penn to all the classrooms he had taught in at Rutgers during his 28-year stint at the school. He stopped "in each classroom to recall favorite students and moments of intellectual and psychological pleasure,"[20] and reflects on "the melancholy thought that when deserted by students, classrooms are dead in a way no other public spaces are."[21] Fussell then gives a meditative riff on the passage of time, the swift passing of youth, the fading of hopes, and death.

John Keegan observed in a review of *Doing Battle* that while Fussell's depiction of infantry fighting in the book "is acerbic and self-deprecating, there is a touch of the natural warrior about him. He claims to have been more frightened of the Germans than they of him, but I wonder. Let loose on the academic world, he took departmental warfare seriously. The Harvard professors were snooty, his colleagues at Connecticut College for Women were dim, the management of Rutgers were drearily bureaucratic. He wanted to teach at Princeton. Perhaps he should have been given the chance."[22]

Keegan's point, though cheekily expressed, is astute. Fussell frequently comes off in *Doing Battle* as if he was on permanent war footing against large swathes of 20th century American society and popular culture. As he shows, the war had hardened him, as it did many soldiers, reinforced his prewar contentious and satirical side, and while his long simmering fury over it was genuine and even at times almost debilitating, there is also little doubt that he had become intellectually a fighter and armed with a warrior-like attitude when expressing his opinions (nevertheless while employing an elegant writing style). Fussell was a complicated individual, and as *Doing Battle* (as well as many of his other writings) demonstrates, highly ambitious and driven, at times conflicted between his modern and traditional impulses, torn between his anti-war impulses and deep anger over his own war experiences and his obsession with warfare and the military. While he was sensitive and thoughtful, he was also equipped with a strongly subversive sensibility, and was probably at his happiest shaking things up and poking sticks at orthodoxy. As we have seen, he had long insisted that people were far too easy on themselves in terms of their beliefs, and that criticism was the central job of a thinking person, and as he notes in *Doing Battle*, curiosity was the handmaiden of criticism.

American Gadfly

The book ends on a plaintive note with Fussell telling a story that illustrates the human fallout from the Second World War. In the late 1940s, when he was a student at Harvard, he was eating alone at a restaurant in Cambridge and noticed that a middle-aged woman was staring at him. He naturally wondered if he knew or had meet her before. Suddenly the woman started to uncontrollably cry and Fussell asked himself, "Did I remind her of her dead son? Had she been angry for a long time too?"[23]

Doing Battle is just that, a well-written account of one man's long fight to psychologically and intellectually deal with the effects of war and carve out an identity for himself as a skeptical, secular humanist. In addition to being an account of an intellectual odyssey, the book is also a unique war memoir which sharply goes against the grain of standard memoirs of the Second World War and the idea that the conflict was ultimately virtuous, meaningful, and a "good war." Engrossing, funny, self-effacing, painfully honest, barbed and bitter, it is also an elegy about the passing of innocence and the learning of hard truths.

Reviews of the book were generally quite positive, although some critics were slightly put off by what they thought to be Fussell's sometimes preachy tone. Poet Anthony Hecht in *The Washington Post* was thoroughly impressed, writing, "This is an extraordinary memoir. Genuinely modest, candid about foibles and failures, it refuses to posture or boast, it is self-deprecating and honest, and in retrospect, more cheerful than any reader would be entitled to expect. It must be immediately added that it is an outraged, embattled, and blistering indictment of the standard pieties of the world. Reading it has won my perfect consent."[24] *The New York Times'* Richard Bernstein stated that it "is elegant, witty, caustic and moving, a frank and at the same time discreet summing up of a well-lived life…. Mr. Fussell writes with breezy charm, and he has a distanced, quizzical unheroic view of himself. The image reflected in this work is of a man unafraid to show us what he is really like."[25] But he also took issue with what he considered Fussell's crankiness, and too pious dislike of the U.S. and praise of Europe.

The noted military historian Russell Weigley believed that *Doing Battle* helps correct many false misconceptions about the Second World War, but he takes Fussell to task for presenting "a distorted history of what World War Two signifies; that we ought to feel a certain national

12. The Autobiography of a Natural Warrior

satisfaction over what our country did to rid the world of various monstrosities."[26]

John C. Brereton pointed out what he believes is a contradiction in *Doing Battle* and some of Fussell's other works between Fussell's presentation of himself as a traditionalist and skeptic concerning literary studies and the approach he takes in these books, noting, "this carefully constructed stance seems to blind him to the decidedly untraditional nature of his best accomplishments. He's rightly proud of the books everyone knows him for.... But each of those books is a breakthrough in ways a traditionalist might detest.... *The Great War and Modern Memory* and *Abroad* led the way towards expanding the purview of literary scholarship to texts that were not, by the standards Fussell had promulgated, literature. He was doing something akin to literary studies."[27]

Brereton goes on to contend that "Fussell's pronouncements throughout *Doing Battle* lead one to believe that literature and scholarship are truly worthy enterprises, while nonliterary works and teaching are much lower in the value scale. But Fussell's actual career belies his profession: his best and most characteristic work was either conceived and originally marked as a textbook, or, like *Abroad*, *The Great War and Modern Memory*, or *Wartime*, is brilliantly anti-canonical."[28]

Brereton's remarks are baffling since Fussell has explicitly stated that he had a much more expansive definition of what constitutes literature, a definition wider than what Brereton claims. To be fair, Fussell was a traditionalist in the way he viewed literature, he firmly believed in the central importance of the Western Canon, and was distrustful of the use of literary theory and of attempts to politicize literary texts. But he also broadly held (following his hero George Orwell), as we saw in his introduction to *The Boy Scout Handbook and Other Observations*, that "a thing is literature if it's worth reading more than a couple of times for illumination or pleasure."[29] Furthermore, in his writings (especially in his book on Kingsley Amis), he often deplored critics for not making more use of popular works in their studies.

Doing Battle also contained glowing blurbs from famous writers and historians, including again the novelist Joseph Heller who called it "an engrossing work of genuine literature that transcends the immediate experience of the author and radiates dramatically with truth, suspenseful action, and intelligent conversation," the military historian Martin Gilbert who said, "I invite the reader to enter Paul Fussell's world and to become entranced by it as I was," and even the controversial historian Stephen Ambrose (with whom Fussell would later have some disagreements) who stated, "I've never read so sensitive or thoughtful an account of the effect of the war on an individual."

13

A Book about Appearances and Belonging

In 2002, Paul Fussell published his 21st book, *Uniforms: Why We Are What We Wear.* He wrote the book for several reasons. First, he had been long intrigued by uniforms, in large part because he said much of his youth was spent in uniforms: when he was very young, his mother dressed him in a little sailor suit, then he playacted being a soldier wearing his father's Great War uniform, later on he joined the Boy Scouts, after that he was a member of his college ROTC, and finally, after the U.S. entered the Second World War, he enlisted in the army. As a result, he became fascinated by the universal predicament uniforms pose, namely that "everyone must wear a uniform, but everyone must deny wearing one, lest one's invaluable personality and unique identity be compromised."[1] The book also gave him the opportunity to return to some topics that had interested him in *Class* and *BAD*, for instance, the American obsession with status, what can be inferred by what a person wears, and "the comfort and vanity of belonging, which everyone has experienced."[2] Finally, a study of uniforms also enabled him to write further about one of his major interests: the culture of the military.

Fussell writes that *Uniforms* is "unashamedly a book about appearance. I have long despaired of discovering what's really going on in people's insides (like their brains).... Despairing, I deepened my curiosity about what's happening on their outsides—what can be inferred from their looks, figures, clothing, speech, gesture and the like.... This is also a book about the comfort and vanity of belonging, which everyone has experienced. Every soldier knows its pleasures, as does every person who has put on any kind or uniform or black and white formal clothes."[3]

He also states that his analysis in the book is "implicitly guided"[4] by the sociologist Erving Goffman's highly influential 1956 book *The Presentation of Self in Everyday Life*. Goffman famously contended that there is a close connection between how people behave in everyday life and theatrical performances, maintaining that when we interact with others, we are constantly attempting to discern and control what people think about us by adjusting our manner and appearance. Goffman believes that in our face to face social interactions people are like an actor. "When in the presence of others, the individual typically infuses his activity with signs which dramatically highlight and portray confirmatory facts that might otherwise remain unapparent or obscure. For if the individual's activity is to become significant to others, he must mobilize his activity so that it will express *during the interaction* what he wishes to convey.... A status, a position, a social place is not a material thing, to be possessed, and then displayed; it is a pattern of appropriate conduct, coherent, embellished, and well-articulated."[5]

Goffman suggests that people, like an actor, operate in two contexts. The first is on a stage or in public, where we are in front of an audience, and we try to display our positive aspects through the way we dress, look, and present ourselves through role playing. The second is the backstage, the area behind the public stage, where the public is not allowed, and where we prepare for the role we are going to play and the props we will use, and plan for the goals we want to accomplish when we return to the stage. As a consequence, the clothes or uniform we wear, like those of an actor's, are an important component in the way the self is defined and presented.

Fussell starts the discussion by drawing an important distinction between uniforms and costumes, noting that uniforms desire to be taken seriously, are obligatory, implicitly regulated, and imply expertise and competence (airline pilots, senior chefs, white lab coat clad doctors), virtue (members of the clergy, robed judges), courage, (police, firemen, and military members), obedience (college and high school band uniforms, the Ku Klux Klan), and hygiene and sanitation (hospital workers, ice cream vendors). Moreover, a uniform generally dignifies in some way the wearer, says he has a job, and therefore is associated with a form of success. In contrast, costumes are playful, inauthentic, theatrical, and temporary.[6]

13. A Book about Appearances and Belonging

Uniforms has short chapters covering several types of uniforms and the cultures behind them, including Russian, Japanese, German, Italian, as well as the uniforms of religious groups like the Salvation Army, Jewish Hasidim, Krishna Society, Knights of Columbus, and the Amish. He also examines the apparel of postal workers, the police, college and high school bands, doormen, bellhops, brides, Amtrak conductors, bus drivers, delivery men, the KKK, baseball and football players, nurses, Boy and Girl Scouts, Civil War reenactors, and of course, the military.

Among the book's more interesting chapters are those on the history and symbolic value of blue jeans, the influence of naval uniforms on the design of uniforms, the eroticism of uniforms, and the uniformity of dress in America by students in higher education. Fussell notes that while blue jeans were once worn as a symbol of rebellion and anti-fashion, virtually everyone now has a pair and they have obtained the status of a "square" uniform. As a result, he says, today they are comparable to a dark suit, thereby proving the rule that "a device for flaunting an anti-fashion stance, with appropriate political and intellectual implications, ends as an obligatory style. We can reason that there is finally no escape."[7] In another chapter, Fussell touches on the curious phenomenon of traditional naval dress directly influencing a wide range of other uniforms, including that of airline and dirigible pilots, American and British blue police officer's uniforms, and the little sailor suits worn by children.

He also maintains in the book that further study is needed to explain the strange effects uniforms exert on both audiences and wearers. For example, he observes that certain uniforms like those of the military, uniforms that have military style elements in nonmilitary dressings, and even those of UPS deliverymen have been documented to have exerted an implicit sexual appeal, especially among females. In a chapter called "Uniformity in American Higher Learning," he discusses how the forces of conformity have impacted on the rapidly changing clothing that college students wear. Fussell holds this is because Americans 18–21 years old are deadly afraid of getting criticism from peers and being humiliated, so they are very careful that the way they dress conforms with the fashionable styles of their classmates and try not to sartorially stand out (he does concede that females are generally allowed more inventive variations in clothing than males). He also attributes this behavior to the fact that college students are in a setting in which their future is probably going to be determined and their main goal is to be successful. As a result, "They often speak in a way that seems to celebrate individuality, but they almost never venture to practice it. Too risky. Once they have grown up and been beaten about by life a bit, they may feel safer in practicing some singularity, even if loneliness develops. But please, not yet."[8]

Fussell believes that what makes uniforms so interesting is the paradox they pose, "each person senses the psychological imperative to dress uniformly and recognizably like others, while responding at the same time to the opposite tug, the impulse to secretly treasure and exhibit occasionally a singular identity or 'personality.' It is something like 'anxiety' that propels both urges: the one towards hiding safely among the masses, thereby avoiding disapproval; the other fear of nonentity or insignificance. Which to choose?"[9]

He argues that Americans in particular suffer from this dilemma because of status anxiety and the longstanding tension between American's "pride at resisting outside pressure and nervousness lest one's freedom" elicit disapproval."[10] One way, Fussell maintains, that some Americans have solved this paradox is through the wearing of a uniform. He insists that, contrary to popular opinion, most people take pride in wearing their uniforms (even those, he says, who work in low paying jobs). He ascribes this pride to the intense societal pressure on individuals to follow the crowd and people's fear of loneliness. Because of this pressure, persons naturally gravitate to ways of standing out by becoming a member of something, and uniforms provide a conspicuous way to do this.

He also addresses the frequently expressed criticism that uniforms ultimately enslave people and prevent them from being an individual. He finds this objection too simplistic, and in a response that would have pleased Erving Goffman, says that for uniform wearers "the language tone, and gestures of irony and disbelief are always available and often employed.... A uniform says a great deal that you don't have to say yourself, and, indeed, one of its functions is to let you assume a character not your own. Sentimental imputations of sincerity are wide of the mark."[11]

Uniforms also contains many amusing vignettes on the eccentric dress of famous military figures such as George S. Patton, Douglas MacArthur, Field Marshal Bernard Law Montgomery, and Dwight D. Eisenhower, as

13. A Book about Appearances and Belonging

well as President Richard Nixon's infamous and ill-fated attempt to replace the garb of the White House police with a uniform that was patterned on the grandiose apparel worn by European palace guards which had greatly impressed him on a presidential trip, and a scathing aside on Ernest Hemingway's disgraceful attempt to exaggerate his record as a war correspondent and become a "uniformed hero."

The book ends with a chapter entitled "Notes Toward the Reader's Own Theory of Uniforms," where Fussell briefly discusses such varied uniform related topics as military nostalgia, trade uniforms, jacket vents and blazers, shoulder knots, the connection between insignia and shame, the hazards associated with uniforms, how military uniforms have influenced civilian male fashion, and bagpiper's dress, Mark Twain's reasons for wearing his famous white suit, and even the history of the famous white solar topee. He finishes the chapter with a sardonic take on the American Legion's formal uniform, concluding, "But it is doubtless unfair to ridicule an institution whose beer brings pleasure to so many."[12]

Uniforms offers a short, informal, and leisurely (but sometimes digressive) sociological tour of the odd world of uniforms, what they symbolize, changing beliefs about them, the often-surprising history behind them, and why they are still frequently admired and even prized. Fussell is also good at showing how strong societal pressures to conform constantly impose conventions that are translated into uniforms. Like most of his popular writings, his observational skills are acute; he presents intriguing, new information; and his tone is humorous but pointed.

Reviewers were generally not very impressed with the book. Michiko Kakutani of *The New York Times* complained about Fussell's "tendency to write only in the shallowest, most descriptive of terms, consistently ignoring or aestheticizing the social and cultural implications of his subject. The result is a highly superficial work, a glib magazine article inflated into a book."[13] Kakutani also grumbled that *Uniforms* failed to adequately explain why we are what we wear, and that Fussell offers no original thesis as he did in *The Great War and Modern Memory*, but instead only a series of obvious statements.

Conservative political satirist and journalist P. J. O'Rourke found the book to be "not a book about uniforms, it's the notes for a book on uniforms—the contents of a file folder of clippings and jotted thoughts on the subject ... a ditty bag of off-duty observations and *apercus*."[14] O'Rourke also took issue with Fussell's contention that there is a fundamental tension between the traditional love of uniforms and today's modern emphasis on individualism, writing, "Bare nonsense. A uniform invests my invaluable personality with the power of a respected and disciplined group."[15]

Kakutani's criticism that Fussell fails to elucidate what he means by the subtitle of the book is puzzling given that he spends time specifically explaining why people have been attracted to uniforms and what this says about the way we view ourselves. She is correct that *Uniforms* presents no strikingly original thesis (to demand that he produce one that was comparable to what he offered in *The Great War and Modern Memory* sets a very high bar). But Fussell does raise some important questions regarding the connection between uniforms, personal identity, class, conformity, and democracy that bear further examination. Undoubtedly, the book would have been more focused and better if he had incorporated some of the insights and techniques he so cleverly employed in *Class* regarding status and class anxieties, which are the driving forces in the way people view uniforms. O'Rourke's casual dismissal of the tension induced by uniforms appears to be based on the idea, to a certain extent, that popular attitudes towards uniforms have not changed, especially since the social upheavals of the 1960s and the more recent pushback against the increasing power of large companies. Fussell would have agreed with him regarding the virtues associated with uniforms (he notes it in the book), but he would have also claimed that there still exists, certainly among sizeable parts of the U.S., a strong ambivalence towards certain types of explicit uniforms, and that the U.S., especially when compared to countries like Germany, Italy, and Japan, has long had an anti-uniform bent.

The noted fashion and style historian Anne Hollander, author of *Seeing Through Clothes* (which Fussell references in *Uniforms*), in a sympathetic review, ultimately got it right when she perceptively wrote that the book is a "modest entertainment intended as a meditation, a familiar essay, an old-fashioned literary sort of book, expounding the author's crotchets through anecdote, sardonic observation, and mild polemic. There is neither index nor bibliography, nor illustrations—it faintly suggests Carlyle's *Sartor Resartus* (quoted at the onset), but it is really more like several discursive short works on dress written in the first half of the last century:

13. A Book about Appearances and Belonging

The Eternal Masquerade by H. Dennis Bradley (1923) or Quentin Bell's *on Human Finery* (1947). Fussell ponders the fact that we all want to look the same, but each wants to look entirely individual as these and other writers have pondered before him."[16]

A side note: late in his life, Fussell seriously considered writing a book on the famed U.S. General George Patton. He had long been fascinated by the general and in 1995 had written a detailed review of the movie *Patton*.[17] The book would have dealt with the general question of whether the personal characteristics and behavior Patton was notorious for—relentless showmanship, bullying, flagrant eccentricity, and avid self-regard—are requisite for obtaining high military office or whether the position of military high command, which requires the ability to creatively come up with the most efficient and effective ways to kill people, produce these characteristics. He never wrote this book, but he does briefly deal with the question in *Uniforms* by examining Field Marshal Montgomery, who was in many ways temperamentally like Patton. Fussell comes to no firm conclusion but seems to lean towards the position that those personal characteristics are requisite for success, but that the nature of the military and the irrational character of war exacerbated them.[18]

14

A Final Look at the "Good War"

It is somehow fitting that Paul Fussell would return again to his war experiences for his last book, 2003's *The Boys' Crusade: The American Infantry in Northwestern Europe, 1944–45*. The book was part of the Modern Library Chronicles series in which distinguished historians and critics write short books on famous topics. The authors in this series included such respected writers as Ian Buruma, Frank Kermode, Alistair Horne, Gordon Wood, and Alan Brinkley. Fussell was 79 years old when it was published, a stage in life when the thoughts of many men increasingly turn to the past and they contemplate events which had a major influence upon their lives. For Fussell, it was of course the Second World War. But he was also motivated to write *The Boys' Crusade* because of two things that were occurring in the U.S. at the time.

Books on America's participation in the Second World War had long been popular in the U.S. This was especially true since the later 1990s when a slew of them appeared sparking further interest in the war. Best sellers like 1998's *The Greatest Generation* by Tom Brokaw, and works by Stephen Ambrose like 1997's *Citizen Soldiers: The U.S. Army from the Normandy Beaches to the Bulge to the Surrender of Germany, June 7, 1944–May 7, 1945*, and others, as well as films like *Band of Brothers* and *Saving Private Ryan*, and History Channel and PBS documentaries, have celebrated America's contribution to this war and insisted that it was a "Good War" fought by the "Greatest Generation" (hereafter referred to as GW/GG). These books and films insist that the war was necessary and that its just cause trumped the ugliness and the amount of blood that was spent in the conflict. They also have greatly extolled the special American

14. A Final Look at the "Good War"

virtues of the U.S. soldiers who fought in it, emphasizing that the war brought out their best qualities. They frequently refer to these participants as "citizen soldiers," characterize them as high-minded and idealistic "soldiers for democracy," and claim they were fighting for personal and political freedom. These publications and films also praise the society that produced these soldiers and the democratic institutions that supported them, while minimizing the contribution of other countries (like the Soviet Union) to winning the conflict.[1]

A more expansive spinoff of the Good War myth has been advanced by the popular military historian and Fox News commentator Victor Davis Hanson, author of such books as *Carnage and Culture: Landmark Battles in the Rise of Western Power* and *The Soul of Battle: From Ancient Times to the Present Day, How Three Great Liberators Vanquished Tyranny*. Hanson, who was trained as a classist, has argued for a concept he calls "the soul of battle" and is fond of phrases like the "Western epic marches for freedom."[2] He is interested in the ethical character of democracies when they are at war and contends that "when a free and consensual society feels its existence threatened, when it has been attacked, when its citizens at last understand an enemy at odds with the very morality of its culture, when a genius at war leads an army to do what he wishes, when it is to march at a set place at a set time, then free men can muster, they can fight back well, and they can make war brutally and lethally beyond the wildest nightmares of the brutal military culture they seek to destroy."[3]

According to Hanson, the "soul of battle" occurs "when free men march unabashedly toward the heartland of their enemy in hopes of saving the doomed, when their vast armies are aimed at salvation and liberation, not conquest and enslavement. Only then does battle take on a spiritual dimension, one that defines a culture, teaches it what civic militarism is, and how it is properly used."[4] Hanson believes that armies cannot be divorced from culture, and that democracies are capable of producing the most murderous and superior armies because they are inspired by spiritual and not just the material values, and are informed by Western values and culture. His heroes (he calls them liberators) are the Theban general Epaminondas and the American generals William Tecumseh Sherman and George Patton.

American Gadfly

Fussell wrote *The Boys' Crusade* in large part because he was worried that the GW/GG view had begun to define how most Americans viewed the conflict and because he felt obliged to set the record straight yet again about what the Second World War was really like. As he notes in the book's preface, "Now, almost 60 years after the horror, there has been a return, especially in popular culture, to military romanticism, which, if not implying that war is really good for you, does suggest that it contains desirable elements—pride, companionship, and the consciousness of virtue enforced by deadly weapons. In this book I have occasionally tried to confront this view with realistic details.... There is nothing in infantry warfare to raise the spirits at all, and anyone who imagines a military 'victory' gratifying is mistaken."[5]

A final factor that almost certainly influenced Fussell's decision to write this book was the Iraq invasion that occurred the year the work was published. He was a very strong critic of the war (later stating in an interview that "if you don't get angry about this war you don't deserve to be alive"[6]) and no doubt felt that the invasion was further verification of his longstanding contention that since Americans have never had a good understanding of what war (especially the Second World War) was really like and the terrible cost it inflicts on individuals and societies, the country will continue to stumble into unnecessary wars, and that romanticizing a war is one of the easiest ways of drumming up support for another.

Fussell had written on several elements of the GW/GG perspective before in *Wartime* and *Doing Battle*. In 1998, he took on the movie *Saving Private Ryan*, stating that he liked the realism of the first half-hour of the film which depicted the D-Day landing, and applauded "its authenticity about blood and noise, and about the tendency of both sides to shoot prisoners with pleasure,"[7] but he thought the rest of the movie had a typical "boy-adventure-story plot,"[8] and objected to the film's neglect of the common problem of the open cowardice of troops as well as the refusal of the Hollywood industry to really capture the entire truth of anything because of the profit motive, concluding that "honorable as it is in places: *Saving Private Ryan* does not mark a new moment in Hollywood history. Hollywood's purpose is profit, and it has learned that violence sells."[9]

In *The Boys' Crusade*, Fussell scrutinizes the war from an angle that is different from the way he had previously viewed it. The book describes

14. A Final Look at the "Good War"

the experiences of the U.S. infantry in Northwest Europe during an 11-month period from the D-Day invasion on June 6, 1944, to the surrender of Germany on May 7, 1945. Fussell drives home throughout the book a factor that many people are not aware of about the War: the youthfulness of these soldiers, most of whom were 17, 18, and 19 (hence the word boy in the book's title), and the fact that of the millions of soldiers the U.S. sent to Europe, 14 percent of them were infantrymen who suffered 70 percent of the casualties. *The Boys' Crusade* begins with a list of the personal characteristics and shared beliefs of these "men-children ... [who] weren't children, weren't quite men either, even if their officers addressed groups of them as such."[10] These men-children had a strong sense of optimism that the war would have to end, and they would not be wounded or killed. They had a talent for feigning courage no matter the circumstances, prized black humor and irony, were adept at gathering small objects, and had good eyesight and physical stamina.

Because these boy soldiers had similar personal convictions, they were generally able to get along with each other. These beliefs included that the U.S. was the greatest country in the world, a leader in technology, and that the American army, despite its drawbacks, was tops in the material support it provided its soldiers. Concurrent with these convictions were some shared hatreds: officers, the French, people who received exemptions from the war because of ailments like high blood pressure, flat feet, etc., individuals that occupied a combat position that was behind the infantry, engineers (except combat), and of course higher-ups who were too frightened to visit the front lines.[11]

Tellingly, when the British edition of *The Boys' Crusade* was published in 2004, the book's subtitle was changed to "American GI's in Europe, Chaos and Fear in World War 2." This is a fair summary of what Fussell is trying to capture in the book, for his focus is on the terrible conditions under which these men-children fought, what they were exposed to during combat, and how they reacted to, and felt about, it. As a result, he devotes much time on the savagery of the fighting, and the many human errors, military blunders, and failures of the campaign. Some of the material he presents he had previously discussed in *Wartime*, but Fussell also provides further details, new stories and material. His purpose in taking this approach is to undercut the claims of the GW/GG view and to show that it fails to adequately discuss the real conditions of this conflict, and either minimizes, understates, or simply ignores what the War actually involved.

Among the eye-opening facts Fussell reveals is that self-inflicted wounds to get out of combat were so common among front-line infantry (the little finger being a popular target) that hospitals established special wards and a designation SIW (self-inflicted wounds) for it. Regarding desertions, he points out that in the European theater, the numbers were higher than commonly stated. There, 19,000 American soldiers deserted, and only 9,000 had been captured by 1948. The massive black market in Paris alone was run by more than 2,000 U.S. army deserters. Most deserters were not cowards and left out of overwhelming fear and some over genuine disgust over the behavior of fellow soldiers or the war itself.[12] In addition, the ill treatment and even the killing of surrendering German soldiers (especially towards the end of the war) was a common practice. And contrary to popular perception, the French had contempt for American troops because of their arrogant behavior, cultural insularity, the fact that they were there because France had been defeated, and for their carelessness about French lives during attacks. The British attitude was more complicated. British troops and male civilians were resentful of American soldiers' higher pay scales and their ability to attract English girls, looked down on their comparative lack of military experience, and hated having to serve under American command. In general, they considered the Americans to be crude and ignorant. Moreover, the British population in general was appalled by the American military's segregation policy regarding black soldiers.

There is still a great deal of controversy over the strategy the Allies used during the campaign and whether Eisenhower's broad front strategy had really shortened the war. But one of the biggest problems Fussell notes concerned the American army's infantry replacement system, which was mentioned in the first chapter. Because combat casualty rates were considerably higher than expected, inept long-range planning by the War Department, and the massive outbreak of trench foot disease among soldiers, there was a large shortage of American soldiers (especially of rifleman and officers). To fill this need, drafted, poorly trained and equipped, green replacement troops were rushed into depleted rifle companies where they knew no one and had not established important group bonding con-

14. A Final Look at the "Good War"

nections. As Fussell bluntly puts it, "unless military planning and training is almost as brutal and cynical as battle itself in attending to the nature of man, unless replacement troops are trained rigorously and prepared psychologically, disaster is likely to happen."[13] And according to him, disasters frequently did occur, and morale, discipline, and combat performance became a major problem. As a consequence, the quality of the American ground forces deteriorated over time.

Fussell also draws attention, as he did in *Wartime*, to the numerous cases of friendly fire mistakes, intelligence failures, and incompetent staff tactical decisions which resulted in major mishaps and which were covered up or "spun" by the military, with the acquiesce of war correspondents. Incredibly, Stephen Ambrose claims that "the American press corps covering ETO ... did an outstanding job."[14] Fussell has shown in *Wartime* and *The Boys' Crusade* that this was in the main not the case due to strict military censorship, the restricted movements of journalists, and the vast and draconian power of the military's public relations department.[15]

The Boys' Crusade has several short chapters describing infamous battlefield calamities which occurred, including the infamous Cobra operation where U.S. troops were bombed on several occasions by their own air corps because of faulty service coordination, the notorious incident of the Falaise Pocket where 40,000 German soldiers were allowed to escape due to Allied mistakes, the battle of the Hurtgen Forest which was fought according to a ludicrous plan created by General Courtney Hodges that resulted in 33,000 American casualties, and the Battle of the Bulge which Fussell says was initially "a rare theater of disgrace."[16]

Throughout the book, Fussell employs the "Boo-Hoo Brigade" approach to military history as practiced by the British historian Martin Gilbert, which intersplices discussions of military tactics and strategy with short human stories about participants to remind readers of war's moral dimension and the terrible cost and suffering it inflicts. Fussell's sensitivity to this fact can be seen on *The Boys' Crusade* dedication page, which is "To those who suffered on both sides." Another way he shows this cost is the chapter "One Small-Unit Action" which tells the tragic story of how a unit of the 104th infantry lost most of its members in a bloody and unwarranted attack due to poor platoon leadership and bickering among officers.

American Gadfly

One of the cornerstones of the GW/GG take on the war concerns what motivated American GIs to fight the war. Ambrose has written that "in general, in assessing the motivation of these GIs, there is agreement that patriotism or any other form of idealism had little if anything to do with it. The GIs fought because they had to. What held them together was not country or flag, but unit cohesion. It has been my experience through four-decades of interviewing ex-GIs, that such generalizations are true enough."[17] So far so good, Fussell makes the same point in *Wartime, Doing Battle*, and *The Boys' Crusade*.

But Ambrose goes on to contend that "there is something more.... As much as the Civil War soldiers, the GIs believed in their cause. They knew that they were fighting for decency and democracy and they were proud of it and motivated by it.... At the core, the American citizen soldiers knew the difference between right and wrong, and they didn't want to live in a world in which wrong prevailed.... They just didn't talk or write about it."[18] (This of course leads to the obvious question of how Ambrose would know this to be true?)

Needless to say, Fussell is dismissive of this type of thinking. As we have seen in *Wartime*, he argues that the motivating factor for soldiers was to get revenge for Pearl Harbor, and that soldiers fought for each other, had disdain for any appeals to abstract terms like freedom or democracy, and were deathly afraid of bringing dishonor to themselves by letting others down. Fussell's position has been supported by comprehensive government studies on the subject and by many historians. William L. O'Neil in 1993's *A Democracy at War: America's Fight at Home and Abroad in World War II* has concluded that "easily the most striking thing about the GI was how well he fought considering his truly remarkable lack of abstract motivation. Thanks to extensive studies made at the time by social scientists, we know more about the GIs than we do about the soldiers in any other war ... [they] make abundantly clear that most GIs had little interest in war aims and cared only about getting it over with."[19] Furthermore, O'Neil points out that "all accepted that having been attacked the United States must defend itself and they owed the nation a duty. However, for most winning the war was not the primary goal but rather a means to their real end to be discharged from the army.... This low level of interest in the war's purpose might seem odd today, considering that it is remem-

14. A Final Look at the "Good War"

bered as the one all Americans believed in. Yet, it could not have been otherwise, given the strength of isolationism earlier and the fact that America seemed to have so little at stake as far as most citizens were concerned."[20]

In *The Boys' Crusade* Fussell expands upon the position he stakes out in his other books regarding soldier's motivation, writing that "because the vast majority of the Boy Crusaders were unenthusiastic conscripts, their attitude toward the army and all its works was, in one degree or another hostile.... Ninety-nine percent would have escaped if there had been any non-shameful way out. It was only the buddy system, every soldier's audience of familiar moral acquaintances, that kept the boys, in this respect at least, honorable."[21] But he also admits that after soldiers were exposed to or heard of the German death camps during the final weeks of the War, moral attitudes changed, and the war for them became a crusade when it had not been viewed as one before.

Another mainstay of the GW/GG perspective is that American soldiers possessed special virtues that distinguished them as the "Greatest Generation" not just in American history but in all of history, and that these virtues enabled them to win the War. The journalist Tom Brokaw is the most noted purveyor and panjandrum of this view. In his widely popular, highly patriotic book *The Greatest Generation* and its follow up, 1999's *The Greatest Generation Speaks*, Brokaw effusively characterizes the men-children soldiers as selfless, self-reliant, grateful, modest, and citizen heroes, who had "pride in all they've accomplished for themselves, their families, and their country."[22] He contends that they gave fresh meaning to the old virtues of courage, honor, and sacrifice, and then returned home from the war "to resume lives enriched by the values they had defended,"[23] and even though they gave so much, they asked very little in return. The books contain many personal stories of individuals from this generation (including ordinary citizens and community leaders) whom Brokaw claims illustrate his thesis.

Fussell makes few direct allusions in *The Boys' Crusade* to this perspective. In one, he sarcastically refers to "all the chatter about the Good War and the suggestions of special virtue among the boyish citizen soldiers."[24] In the suggestions for further reading section, he remarks that "the troops' memoirs in my listing of sources will be found rewarding, especially to readers interested in exploring the fact that what has been celebrated as the Greatest Generation included among the troops and their officers plenty of criminals, psychopaths, cowards, and dolts."[25] As *The Boys' Crusade* indicates, most American infantrymen in the European theater were in reality just ordinary very young males who acted as most males have done in previous wars, and possessed like most people of that age no outstanding or special virtues. They were frequently afraid but tried to hide it, but at times, overwhelmed by events. They desperately tried to learn the ropes of survival, constantly complained but had the self-control not to cry, and were not ideologically driven. They possessed a sense of obligation to their immediate brother soldiers, did not like the army and its chickenshit, but they did what they could under terrible circumstances, and only wanted what they viewed as a nasty job to be over and to go home.[26]

Brokaw also asserts that "World War II and what came after was the result of a nation united, not a nation divided."[27] According to Fussell, another mistake committed by proponents of the GW/GG view was their complete avoidance of the subject of how the war had degraded and hardened American society, language, institutions, and ideas of individuality and criticism. Brokaw does not seem aware that the years immediately following the war were not a golden age of collective unity. In fact, after all the joyous celebrations and parades, it was a period of anxiety with a loss of the sense of wartime national unity, and deep worries about the economy over whether there would be another depression because the country was making a massive transition from being a wartime economy to a peacetime one, and concerns over whether it could absorb the millions of returning soldiers. There were also deep hostilities between workers and management which resulted in the biggest wave of strikes in American history, a growing uneasiness about the Soviet Union and its influence in Europe, the rise of demagogic anti-communism political rhetoric, an increase in the power of the media and advertising to determine what is real, and the development of the National Security State. It was also the time when the psychological fallout from the war, which had been long repressed, was coming to the fore, and of mourning for the 400,000 American dead. On top of that, 15 million veterans were making very difficult readjustments to civilian life and trying to find jobs. The darkness and

14. A Final Look at the "Good War"

fears being felt by veterans and others was expressed in popular culture, especially movies and in the development of film noir, as well as in literature.

In the final analysis, Fussell alleges that advocates of the GW/GG camp on the Second World War are ultimately glorifying and trying to "normalize" the conflict by greatly simplifying what really had occurred, and avoiding the irony, tragedy, and moral ambiguity of warfare. Moreover, he also believes that this perspective avoids the bigger moral picture. As we have seen, Fussell always had his eye on the butcher's bill and the brute fact that war is always about the killing and maiming of human beings. At most, he would have agreed with the British historian Max Hastings who concluded at the end of his massive history, *Inferno: The World at War, 1939–1945*, that "almost all those who participated, nations and individuals alike, made moral compromises. It is impossible to dignify the struggle as an unalloyed contest between good and evil, or rationally to celebrate an experience, and even an outcome, which impressed such misery upon so many.... All that seems certain is that Allied victory saved the world from a much worse fate that would have followed the triumph of Germany and Japan. With this knowledge, seekers after virtue must be content."[28] In *Wartime*, Fussell held that during the conflict, Americans at home were not told even 10 percent of the horrors of the war. Today, he would have argued that thanks in large part to the strong influence and widespread popularity of the GW/GG version of the war, the number of those who still don't know remains indefensibly high.

In terms of Hanson's thesis, while Fussell never commented on it, it is easy to surmise what he would have thought of it. He would have pointed out that Hanson's analysis fails to factor in the numerous costly errors that democratic governments made in the Second World War (and in other wars like Vietnam and Iraq), the problematic quality of U.S. soldiers in the European theater of operations, and the bald fact that the Germans held the upper hand throughout most of the war and without the help of the undemocratic Russians would have not been defeated. (It has been estimated by some historians that by the end of the war, four out of every five Germans killed in combat were killed by the Soviet Army.)

Fussell would also have considered Hanson's thesis that Western cultural values, like discipline, the belief in dissent, the concept of citizenship, freedom and flexibility, have consistently produced great armies and that free societies always have the advantage during a war, to be another flawed version of the special virtues argument touted by defenders of the GW/MM school of military history, and he would have affirmed that weapons were really the decisive advantage these armies have had. Moreover, Fussell would have thought Hanson's attempt to spiritualize war laughable, historically inaccurate, and dangerous, and that it represented yet another facile attempt by individuals to elevate or romanticize war. He would have also probably asserted that this type of thinking leads to disasters like Vietnam and the Iraq War (a war which Fussell would have noted Hanson was a big supporter of, as well as his being an advisor to former Vice President Dick Cheney). Finally, characteristically, Fussell might have also observed that Hanson had never been in combat and therefore had no real understanding of what motivates soldiers to fight and how they behave in wartime.

The Boys' Crusade provides a compact, straightforward, informative, and easy introduction to the realities of infantry combat in Europe during the Second World War and helps to dispel some misconceptions that have been fostered by some recent American movies and popular celebratory historical accounts. It is a necessary corrective to works like Stephen Ambrose's *Citizen Soldiers* which covers the same time period (in fairness, Ambrose's book, though marred by his overt piety, does contain some good information). In addition, the book also contains three pages of useful suggestions for further reading.

The Boys' Crusade received good reviews. *The New York Times* called it a riveting and unflinching look at the Americans who fought in the European theater that "allows for heroism, but dwells more on what went wrong."[29] Screenwriter Clancy Sigal, who fought as an infantryman in Europe during the War, wrote in the *Los Angeles Times* that "it should be mandatory reading for future military leaders at West Point. The unbearable fear, systematic screw-ups, and mangled corpses, that are the daily ration of any infantry combat soldier are so vividly and personally drawn that it might give pause to any glory lovers among the cadets who dream of conquest without blood."[30]

The Guardian found it "a curious piece of work, its horrors made the more shocking by the visceral intimacy with which they are told. But for

14. A Final Look at the "Good War"

such a short book it feels oddly fragmented."[31] *The Sewanee Review* stated that "by showing us the boys we sent to do the job, Fussell goes a long way towards giving them back to us the way they really were; and, in so doing, he uncovers their sound moral dimension."[32] And Benjamin Schwartz in *The Atlantic Monthly*, in a review that must have pleased Fussell, said that he had successfully "confronted the sanctimonious 'military romanticism' of Messrs. Ambrose, Brokaw, and Spielberg ... his book is the smartest, most concise, and mostly briskly written introduction to its subject. It would make an excellent high school text."[33]

Paul Fussell died from the effects of dementia and Parkinson's nine years after the publication of *The Boys' Crusade* at a long-term care facility in Medford, Oregon on May 23, 2012. He was 88 years old. In the final years of his life, he walked with a pronounced limp which he did not have before because old age had exacerbated the pain of his war wound. In 1994, he retired from the University of Pennsylvania and later moved to Rochester, New York. In 2007, he participated in Ken Burns's popular documentary on the Second World War entitled *The War*, where he emotionally discussed his combat experiences.

In 2011, one year before his death, Fussell was interviewed by English professor Paula Marantz Cohen for a cable television show. She would later write it was the most memorable interview of her career, stating, "Fussell arrived at the interview clutching his cane and looking feeble and confused. The first few minutes of the interview were halting; he seemed to have a hard time comprehending the questions and keeping on track. But as we continued, he got his bearings and began to answer with the cogency that I associate with his writing. He spoke about his harrowing experiences in World War II, when, as a young lieutenant, he relied heavily on the guidance of an experienced older sergeant. That man was later blown to bits next to him during a mortar attack—an event, he said, that would have a shaping effect on the rest his life. He spoke about his father and his upbringing, about eighteenth-century poetry, about academic conferences and academic pretension, about ocean liners vs. airplanes, and travel vs. tourism. It was a wonderful, wide-ranging interview, full of the wit, heart, and crankiness of a larger-than-life personality."[34]

Fussell was survived by his second wife, Harriette Behringer, and two children from his previous marriage, Rosalind "Tucky" Fussell, a visual artist and visual arts teacher who has taught in Paraguay, Kuwait, and the Philippines, and Samuel Wilson Fussell, who lives in Montana and works as a rescue, recovery, and salvage scuba diver.

Samuel is also the author of the widely acclaimed 1991 book, *Muscle: Confessions of an Unlikely Bodybuilder*, which was praised by such critics as Camille Paglia. The work describes his experiences after graduating from Oxford University as a bodybuilder and his four-year quest to develop the perfect body. In the book, he describes the shocked reaction of his father on the phone to news that he would not be attending graduate school at Yale but pursuing bodybuilding instead. "My father's voice broke through. "Son, have you ever given any thought to what your peers will be in this seamy enterprise?" For five full minutes I defended my action.... I thought he would understand. He didn't. He was even more disgusted than usual."[35] Later in the book Samuel writes, "To him, I wasn't an agent provocateur or even a grotesquerie, but a derelict, plain and simple. 'I understand the urge to spit,' he wrote to his son, the muscle stooge, 'but does it have to be facing the wind?' He had sent me but one communication since then, enclosing the heavily underlined Frost poem, 'The Road Not Taken,' and the University of Pennsylvania Law School Application."[36]

Fussell's importance and influence can be seen in the large amount of attention his death received and the fact that many noted newspapers and magazines published detailed obituaries.[37] *The Washington Post* called him "a curmudgeonly essayist and scholar who bridged the gap between academia and popular culture with his trenchant studies of the cultural effects of war, travel and social class."[38] *The New York Times* said, "Mr. Fussell brought an erudition, a gift for readable prose, a willingness to offend and as many critics noted, a whiff of snobbery to subjects."[39] Harvard historian Drew Gilpin Faust praised Fussell's scholarship and surmised the deep anger that characterized his life may have been "derived from discovering that innocence is born again and again. He made it his lifework to deploy the force of language and ideas to destroy that innocence before it led yet another generation of young soldiers to confront the horror he endured on March 15, 1945."[40]

The Guardian noted that Fussell "was the classic public intellectual ... he had the intellectual confidence to tackle any subject that interested him.... All too often, Fussell was described as sardonic when, in fact, he

14. A Final Look at the "Good War"

was a deeply caring critic who wanted the world he lived in after the Second World War to avoid the wartime chaos and violence he saw firsthand."[41] *The Economist* called him a "warrior against war.... In interviews he was amiable, even sentimental; he laughed readily until, like a bear's, the gaze set and the broad claw swiped at something he abominated."[42] In an article published by the *Associated Press*, Fussell's old friend John Scanlan, a professor of 18th century literature, said, "Samuel Johnson was his great hero ... he loved to insert himself into everyday American life. Being around Paul was a tonic."[43] And Eric Randall in *The Atlantic Monthly* simply wrote, "You were quite stinging to us, Paul, but we imagine America will miss you nonetheless."[44]

But perhaps the best obituary was penned by Fussell's friend, the distinguished Yale University Great War cultural historian Jay Winter, who gave in *The Chronicle of Higher Education* both a professional and personal assessment of Fussell. "When he published *The Great War and Modern Memory* he set in motion what is now an avalanche of studies of all kinds on the First World War. He created the field in which I have worked for the last four decades.... He remained a survivor, with a sense of the fragility of life. It also made him intolerant of civilians gung-ho about war.... Paul was both an angry and a witty man. He was drawn to the poets and novelists of the Great War in Britain in part because they were, like him, truth-tellers about war. But his earlier work on Augustan poets of the 18th century predisposed him to the delights of irony, and the savagery of words usefully applied to the cruel masters of the world."[45] Winter also tells a revealing story about Fussell. When the two were travelling by car to an academic conference in Germany, Winter noticed that every time they passed a hill or came to a crossroad, Fussell would always quickly but thoroughly scan the horizon. When Winter eventually asked him why, Fussell replied that this "was a reflex from his army duty he still could not change. Whenever he passed a point of interest, he scanned the landscape for the best place to place an antitank gun."[46] This was, Fussell further explained, yet another way he remained stuck in the War that had never really ended for him.

15

The Power of Facing Unpleasant Truths

It is not difficult to predict what Fussell would have thought of the current state of the U.S. He would have of course been appalled, but also not surprised for he had long been pessimistic about cultural, social, intellectual, and political trends in the country. In fact, he had noticed, commented on, and warned in the 1980s and 1990s in books like *Abroad, Class, BAD,* and *Uniforms*, essays and reviews, as well as interviews, about much of what is now happening. For example: the increasingly pernicious influence of the digital world and people's obsession with and addiction to electronic devices; the deepening vulgarization of American popular culture and public discourse; the progressive "dumbing down" of the population; the increasing dominance of the business model not just in higher education but all aspects of American life; the ubiquitous presence and impact of advertising; the country's insular preoccupation with self and rampant anti-intellectualism; the increasing importance of class in America and the ever-widening class divide; the coarsening of public discourse and debate (especially on network and cable television and the Internet); the awful standardization and sterility of the tourism and airline industry; the decreasing importance of the humanities in the college curriculum and the rise of STEM and business majors (today 25 percent of degrees in top liberal arts colleges are in the humanities, in 2011 it was 33 percent); the corrupting intellectual influence of post-structuralist literary theory; the decline in literacy rates; the ideological absurdity of the gun lobby; and the rise of political correctness[1] and identity politics on college campuses and in the media.

Nor would Fussell have been surprised about how epistemically chal-

15. The Power of Facing Unpleasant Truths

lenged large swathes of the country had become. He never had a high opinion of the intelligence and knowledge base of Americans and had expressed concerns about this before (in *BAD*, he states "the stupidity and ignorance of Americans has long been a topic of hilarity in Europe. Instead of the Greening of America, we can now speak of the Dumbing of America"[2]). But he might have been taken aback about how quickly it has accelerated and reached the level it has at today. Fussell would have considered it highly ironic, as he also did in *BAD*, that in an age where more factual information is available at the fingertips of an individual on a personal computer than ever before, intense disagreements exist over basic historical, scientific, or political facts. He had long thought that Americans' obsession with electronic devices was more about appearing fashionable, asserting status claims, and bending to the power of conformism, and much less about their actual usefulness, and he would have considered the Internet and social media as another way people avoided questioning their beliefs and asking hard social and cultural questions.

Contrary to common belief, Fussell was not an unrepentant snob nor was he a class elitist, but he was definitely a cultural elitist (which sometimes bothered him). He had high expectations for people and insisted that they had an ethical responsibility or moral duty if they aspired to be educated, cultured, and humane, to demand more of themselves, to ferret out the facts, to be skeptical, to assess and evaluate, even if the process leads to disagreeable truths. And criticism was the heart of this enterprise, for "criticism implies not so much carping or faultfinding as analysis, leading to assessment and valuation. Once you've learned, from experiencing literature or music or art, to criticize in the full sense, you can do it pretty well with anything."[3] For Fussell, critical thinking stimulates us to revise, improve, and clarify our ideas and our conduct. It entails more than just criticizing, for it is a method, and an essential part of a style of thinking and of a way to view man.

Moreover, he would have agreed with the American philosopher Roderick Chisholm who maintained that if an individual wanted to be considered a rational and thinking person, then he must obey two epistemological rules when considering any serious proposition: "(1) he should try his best to bring it about that if that a proposition is true that he believe it; and (2) he should try to bring it about that if a proposition is false that he not believe it.... One might say that this is the person's responsibility or duty *qua* intellectual being."[4]

For Fussell, it is not so much the conclusions that you come to that are important but rather how you think and arrive at them. And if you thought well, honestly, and clearly, and closely and sharply observed things, then, he felt, you could avoid committing the three moral sins he most despised: cant, hypocrisy, and ignorance.

There are however two aspects of contemporary American life he would have found troubling. The first is the country's current glorification of the military, which for many can do no wrong, and the concurrent cult of military heroism. In his 1994 lecture, "The Culture of War," Fussell had strongly cautioned that "if you are trained to be uncritical of government and authority, and even to be uncritical of all established and received institutions. The ultimate result is the death of mind, the transformation of the higher learning and independent scholarship into a cheering section for whatever popular notions and superstitions prevail at the moment."[5]

He would have considered this blind veneration very unhealthy and agreed with the American historian and retired army officer, Andrew Bacevich, who has argued that things like the military ceremonies before sporting events constitute acts of what the German theologian Dietrich Bonhoeffer called "cheap grace," which is "the grace we bestow on ourselves" which is unearned, redemption without contrition, and designed to make ourselves feel better without having to sacrifice anything in our daily lives or serving.[6] Fussell would also shake his head over the fact that the "good war" and "greatest generation" myths about the Second World War still hold sway, thereby reinforcing his point that the U.S. will never grow up about war and will continue to make the same mistakes until it understands what it involves.

The second is the election of Donald Trump as president which would have been a major shock for him. He would have considered it even worse than the election of Ronald Reagan, whom he considered a national joke. Fussell actually discussed Trump in *BAD* and *Class*, stating that Trump was a perfect example of the rule that there is no connection between having great wealth and possessing taste, style, and class, for these characteristics can only be developed through acts of character.

In terms of Fussell's legacy, six of his works will continue to endure.

15. The Power of Facing Unpleasant Truths

He will remain best known for his writings on war, which are still widely cited. *Wartime* and *The Boys' Crusade* remain excellent sourcebooks on the Second World War because of their honesty and because they provide a useful corrective to still common misunderstandings about that conflict. *The Great War and Modern Memory*, though now somewhat dated and limited, will forever stand as the most influential and precedent establishing work on the subject, and a model on how to do engaging and first-rate cultural history. In addition, it is a study that will always have to be considered when discussing the effects of this war. *Doing Battle* remains a highly unusual and revealing war memoir and offers an unconventional take on the war. His essay "Thank God for the Atom Bomb" continues to provoke thought and offers a different take on the controversy. Of his non-war related writings, *Class*, while in need of some updating, is still an insightful, surprisingly accurate, and humorous guide to a topic of increasing importance. *Abroad* is still cited in studies of travel literature, and several of the pieces from his essay collections still entertain and inform. These writings all lay bare and squarely face certain unpleasant facts, thus meeting George Orwell's essential requirement for being an honest thinker.

But it is Fussell's distinctive and highly readable style (which he claimed was that of an essayist) and critical attitude that continue to attract, illuminate, and educate. Although he was an academician throughout most of his life, he wrote clearly, honestly, and free of jargon, was distrustful of fashionable systems of belief, conventional orthodoxies, and the powers that be, and loved using irony and satire to drive a point home. His roving curiosity (he once stated that it was curiosity that made life worth living), ability to cut across various fields, wide reading, and willingness to take seriously "lowbrow" subjects that made his books intellectual feasts that provided a valuable education. Fussell had the great ability, as has been stressed throughout this book, to take on subjects that had never been examined before or of offering new angles on old controversies, a talent that is far rarer than commonly assumed, as a quick inspection of the books being published today will reveal.

Fussell was a gadfly, but a gadfly with a serious message. Beneath all his skepticism, provocation, polemics, and hard analysis was a deeply secular and humanistic seriousness, and frequently a sense of despair. His fascination with and frequent use of irony and satire in his writings were intended not simply to entertain, vex, and compel people to think, but also to illustrate and underscore the tragedy inherent in the human condition and man's inescapable limitations.

Fussell's writings also had some drawbacks. Occasionally his anger would get the best of him and cloud his judgement and he could come off as preachy, self-righteous and self-congratulatory. He was capable of overgeneralizing from his own experiences and being intolerant of the experiences of others. Nonetheless, these occasional failings did not negatively impact upon most of the main points he raised. Through it all, he presented human nature in an interesting way, which according to the 18th century English poet, Alexander Pope, one of Fussell's Augustan period heroes, was the mark of human wit. Which is another reason why Paul Fussell matters.

Chapter Notes

Preface

1. W. D. Ehrhart. "Paul Fussell: A Remembrance," *War, Literature, and the Arts*, 24.1–2 (2012): 3.

Chapter 1

1. Paul Fussell, "My War: How I Got Irony in the Infantry," *Harper's*, January 1982: 44.
2. Ibid., 44.
3. Rick Atkinson, *The Guns at Last Light: The War in Western Europe, 1944–1945* (New York: Henry Holt and Company, 2013): 301.
4. Max Hastings, *Armageddon: The Battle for Germany, 1944–1945* (New York: Alfred A. Knopf, 2004): 186.
5. Hastings, *Armageddon*, 187.
6. Paul Fussell, *Wartime: Understanding and Behavior in the Second World War* (New York: Oxford University Press, 1989): 279.
7. Peter Schrijvers, *The Crash of Ruin: American Combat Soldiers in Europe During World War II* (Washington Square, New York: New York University Press, 1998): 20.
8. Ibid., 20.
9. Geoffrey C. Ward, *The War: An Intimate History 1941–1945* (New York: Alfred A. Knopf, 2007): 329.
10. Schrijvers, *The Crash of Ruin*, 22.
11. Carlo D'Este, *Eisenhower: A Soldier's Life* (New York: Henry Holt and Company, 2002): 626.
12. Quoted in Richard M. Stannard, *Infantry: An Oral History of a World War II American Infantry Battalion* (New York: Twayne Publishers, 1993): 99. Stannard's book provides a good history of the 410th Infantry, 103 Division during the war and has interviews with soldiers Fussell served with as well as a detailed interview with Fussell.
13. Quoted in Fussell, *Doing Battle: The Making of a Skeptic* (New York: Little, Brown and Company, 1996), 171.
14. Stannard, *Infantry*, 108.
15. Fussell, *Doing Battle*, 172.
16. Stannard, *Infantry*, 103.
17. Fussell, *Doing Battle*, 123, 122.
18. Ibid., 125. Fussell does not answer the question why the Germans continued to fight in spite of the fact they know they were defeated. The historian Charles B. MacDonald in his volume *The Last Offense: U.S. Army in World War II, The European Theater of Operations,* in the U.S. Army's "United States Army in World War II" series, has surmised that "many Germans continued to believe if not in victory, then in a kind of nihilistic syllogism which said: Quit now, and all is lost; hold on, and maybe something will happen to help—a process of inductive reasoning that Allied insistence on unconditional surrender may not have promoted but did nothing to dissuade. Already the Germans had demonstrated amply the ability to absorb punishment, to improvise, block, mend, feint, delay" (Atlanta: Whitman Publishing, 2012: 9–10).
19. Stannard, *Infantry*, xviii, 87.
20. Ibid., 102.
21. Fussell, *Doing Battle*, 144.
22. Operation Undertone, the massive offense Fussell was taking part in the day he was wounded was a success. MacDonald writes that "the Seventh Army and its attached French units captured 22,000 Germans ... [it] probably incurred about 12,000 casualties, including almost a thousand killed" (2012, 264).

23. *The Century: America's Time 1941–1945: Homefront*, Part 7, 1999: https://video.search.yahoo.com/search/video;_ylt=AwrXnY.lAJpb2jsAGiNXNyoA;_ylu=X3oDMTE0OG5ubWFiBGNvbG8DZ3ExBHBvcwMxBHZ0aWQDQjQwMzdfMQRzZWMDGl2cw—?p=the+century%3A+america%27s+time&fr2=piv-web&fr=yset_chr_syc_hp-s#id=15&vid=042add4d572b8493fe548d4d1253604a&action=view. Accessed August 13, 2018.
24. Fussell, *Doing Battle*, 171.
25. Stannard, *Infantry*, 108.

Chapter 2

1. Fussell, *Doing Battle*, 171.
2. Ibid., 176.
3. Betty Fussell, *My Kitchen Wars* (New York: North Point Press, 1999): 62, 63.
4. Fussell, 1996, 177.
5. Ibid.,176.
6. Fussell, *My Kitchen Wars*, 61–63.
7. Paul Fussell, "More on Pseudo-Medical Educational Jargon," *American Speech* (29.3), October 1954, 235.
8. Fussell, *Doing Battle*, 208.
9. Ibid., 1996, 211.
10. Paul Fussell, "Thornton Wilder and the German Psyche," *The Nation*, May 3, 1958, 394.
11. Ibid., 394.
12. Paul Fussell, "Scholarship and Autobiography," *The Journal of the Rutgers University Libraries* (36:2), December 1977, 70.
13. Ibid., 70.
14. Quoted in *World Authors 1975–1980*, Edited by Vineta Colby (New York: The H.W. Wilson Company, 1985): 260.
15. Paul Fussell, *The Rhetorical World of Augustan Humanism: Ethics and Imagery From Swift to Burke* (Oxford: Oxford University Press, 1965): 5.
16. Ibid., 6.
17. Ibid., 6.
18. Ibid., 7.
19. Ibid., 7.
20. Ibid., 7.
21. Ibid., 8.
22. Ibid., 9.
23. Geoffrey Tillotson, Paul Fussell, Jr., Marshall Waingrow, & Brewster Rogerson, *Eighteenth Century English Literature* (New York: Harcourt, Brace & World, Inc., 1969): 18.
24. Sheldon Hackney, "The Initial Shock: A Conversation with Paul Fussell," *Humanities* (17.5), November/December, 1996, 4.
25. https://www.c-span.org/video/?155913-1/great-war-modern-memory. Accessed November 20, 2017.
26. Paul Fussell, *Samuel Johnson and the Life of Writing* (New York: Harcourt Brace Jovanovich, Inc., 1971): 278. See also, Fussell, *Doing Battle*, 262.
27. Steven Pinker, *Enlightenment Now: The Case For Reason, Science, Humanism, and Progress* (New York: Viking, 2018): 11.
28. Pinker, *Enlightenment Now*, 166. Pinker's position is not unusual. The noted British military historian Michael Howard has argued in the 2000 book *The Invention of Peace: Reflections on War and International Order* (London: Profile) that since the enlightenment the liberal projection based upon the notion of progress towards peace has greatly spread and become increasingly common. Kenneth Payne has written that this project has "sought to escape war through the extension of reason and empathy. Liberals pointed to the importance of commerce and representative, transparent government in building the mutual bonds between national societies—reducing the predatory motive for war, and the capacity of elites to wage it to their advantage over those of their constituents." (*The Psychology of Modern Conflict: Evolutionary Theory, Human Nature and a Liberal Approach to War*, New York: Palgrave Macmillan, 2015, p. 103). Francis Fukuyama in *The End of History and the Last Man* (London: Penguin, 1992) and John Mueller in *The Remnants of War* (Ithaca: Cornell University Press, 2007) have espoused similar views.
29. Paul Fussell, *A Bloody Game: An Anthology of Modern War* (London: Scribner's, 1991): 17.
30. Pinker, *Enlightenment Now*, 408.
31. Ibid., 5.
32. Paul Fussell, *The Boy Scout Handbook and Other Observations (*New York: Oxford University Press, 1982): vii.
33. *Poetry and Criticism of Matthew Arnold*, Edited by A. Dwight Culler (Boston: Houghton, Mifflin, Company, 1961): 427.
34. Ibid., 475.
35. Paul Fussell, "George Orwell," *The Sewanee Review*, 93.2, Spring 1985, 232.
36. Ibid., 237.
37. Ibid., 237.

38. Ibid., 237.
39. Peter Wilkin, *The Strange Case of Tory Anarchism* (Faringdon, Oxfordshire: Libri Publishing, 2010). See in particular chapters one, two, and five.

Chapter 3

1. Paul Fussell, *The Great War and Modern Memory*, Twenty-Fifth Anniversary Edition (New York: Oxford University Press, 2000): 336.
2. Fussell, *Doing Battle*, 265–266.
3. Fussell, *The Great War and Modern Memory*, 336.
4. Fussell, *Doing Battle*, 336.
5. Roger J. Spiller, "The Real War: An Interview with Paul Fussell," in *In the School of War* (Lincoln: University of Nebraska Press, 2010): 367.
6. Fussell, *Doing Battle*, 266.
7. Interview, Book TV, C-SPAN 2, March 8, 2000.
8. Fussell, *The Great War and Modern Memory*, ix.
9. James Campbell, "Interpreting the War," *The Cambridge Companion to the Literature of the First World War*, Edited by Vincent Sherry (New York: Cambridge University Press, 2005): 267.
10. E-mail to the author, April 7, 2017.
11. Martin Gilbert, *The First World War: A Complete History* (New York: Henry Holt and Company, 1994): 540.
12. One way of gauging the effects of the war is to consider the counterfactual of what the world would have been like if the Great War had not occurred. For an interesting attempt to answer this question, see Richard Lebow's *Archduke Franz Ferdinand Lives!* (New York: Palgrave Macmillan, 2014).
13. Christopher Moore-Bick, *Playing the Game: The British Junior Infantry Officer on the Western Front* (Solihull, West Midlands, England, Helion & Company, 2011): 206–207.
14. Liaquat Ahamed, *Lords of Finance: 1929, The Great Depression, and the Bankers Who Broke the World* (London: Windmill Books, 2009): 76. Ahamed claims the 1929 Great Depression was largely the result of the massive war debts of the major powers and Germany's reparations. He writes that "dealing with these massive claims consumed the energies of financial statesmen for much of the decade and poisoned international relations. More importantly, the debts left massive fault lines in the world financial system, which cracked at the first pressure" (p. 501).
15. John Keegan, *The First World War* (New York: Vintage Books, 1998): 8, 3.
16. For example, see the book, *Killing Time: Archaeology and the First World War* by Nicholas J. Saunders (Gloucestershire, England: Sutton Publishing, 2007).
17. Peter Doyle, *The First World War in 100 Objects* (Gloucestershire, England: The History Press, 2014): 9–10.
18. Fussell, *The Great War and Modern Memory*, 335.
19. Ibid., 35, 189.
20. Ibid., 7–8.
21. Ibid., 90.
22. Ibid., 115.
23. Ibid., 146, 147, 152. The allusions in Jones's work appear, at times, so fast and furious that he felt it necessary to attach 35 pages of endnotes to the poem.
24. Ibid., 147.
25. Jonathan Miles has maintained that Fussell completely misreads Jones's intention in *In Parenthesis*, stating that Jones is not using heroic allusions to celebrate war, but that "more often than not they function as ironic critiques ... Fussell misunderstands Jones's attempt to comprehend an experience which both shared similarities with what had gone before and yet was quite unlike anything that had gone before because of the more insidious nature of the technical role and the resultant magnitude of the suffering." *Backgrounds to David Jones: A Study in Sources and Drafts* (Cardiff: University of Wales Press, 1980), 83, 82. Miles also strangely asserts that "what badly biases Fussell's judgements ... is a personal taste for the bland and what may be called his particularly "American" sensibility" (p. 81). It is difficult, at times, when reading certain sniffy British critics of Fussell (especially military historians) that some of their remarks are rooted in the fact that a person who is not English is writing and gaining fame on such an important and thoroughly English subject as the British experience in World War One. For another critical take on Fussell's interpretation of Jones, see Elizabeth Ward's *David Jones: Mythmaker* (Manchester: Manchester University Press, 1983): 102–107.
26. Fussell, *The Great War and Modern Memory*, 156.

27. George Walter, *The Penguin Book of First World War Poetry* (London: Penguin Books, 2006): xi.
28. Fussell, *The Great War and Modern Memory*, 165.
29. Ibid., 189.
30. A perusal of British soldier slang in a reference book like John Brophy and Erick Partridge's classic *The Long Trail: What the British Soldier Sang and Said in The Great War of* 1914–18 (New York: London House and Maxwell, 1965), reveals numerous others words that continued to be used even today.
31. Fussell, *The Great War and Modern Memory*, 157, 160. The noted military historian John Keegan has written that the reason why the American Civil War did not produce a Robert Graves, Wilfred Owen, or Siegfried Sassoon, was because "Nineteenth century America had no such literary tradition of its own [when compared to the English] and no such literary class ... Americans were therefore not drawn to write of their experience of the war in poetic or psychological explorative terms, and there was no school of literary realism to guide American Civil War Writers into the right emotional and psychological path if they were to produce an explicitly imaginative narrative of the war." *The American Civil War: A Military History* (New York: Alfred A. Knopf, 2009): 359.
32. Fussell, *The Great War and Modern Memory*, 192.
33. Fussell oddly neglects to mention the frequent theatrical performances provided by civilians in camps and hospitals for British soldiers and even war zones in Europe, the Balkans, and the Middle East. L. J. Collins has noted that these entertainments filled a variety of important functions. "For personnel stationed in Britain, and under training, the theatre provided relief from the tedium of military existence. It was also, although without much success, employed as a mode of social control ...To the troops in the fighting areas, on the other hand, entertainment was much more than a release from the ennui of trench life. To both the servicemen in training at home, and personnel abroad, the theater helped to maintain morale, but to the fighting soldier ... the theater assumed a position of added importance. The sight of a pretty girl in a civilian concert party dressed in a colorful frock reminded of another world, another time. So desirous of this other peaceful, happier and brighter place were the soldiers, that they tried to recreate a theatrical version of home and "normality' by attempting in their own way to imitate the familiar—even to the point of dressing men up as women ...The theatrical productions also gave all ranks, particular the lower ranks, a legitimate opportunity to voice corporate feelings of dissent." *Theatre at War: 1914–1918* (New York: St. Martin's Press, 1998): 213. The existence of these performances reinforce Fussell's point about the British theatrical tendencies regarding the war.
34. Fussell, *The Great War and Modern Memory*, 210.
35. Ibid. It is odd that Fussell does not mention in this chapter the famous trench magazine *The Wiper Times* which was published from February 1916—December 1918 by British soldiers fighting in the Ypres region in France. This publication was noted for its satirical poems, essays, and lampoons mocking the military, and funny ironic writing style. Moreover, the magazine abounded in references to the theater and was well known for its advertisements for mock British music hall extravaganzas which featured humorous war related songs such as 'The Duck-Board Dangle," "Machine Gun Slither," and "Whizz-Bang Hop." (See *The Wipers Times*. Introduction and Glossary by Patrick Beaver (London: Peter Davies, 1974).
36. Graves, who loved to muddy the waters concerning the theme of *Goodbye to All That*, wrote in 1941 that it "was neither a war-book nor literary, but a reckless autobiography in which the war figured, written with small consideration for anyone's feelings." *The Long Weekend: A Social History of Great Britain 1918–1939* by Robert Graves and Alan Hodge (New York: The Macmillan Company, 1941): 208.
37. For example, J. M. Cohen in *Robert Graves* (New York: Barnes & Noble, Inc., 1967), inaccurately states that Grave's memoir is a "direct and factual autobiography" (69), and does not discuss the book's satirical elements. James S. Mehoke's *Robert Graves: Peace Weaver* (Paris: Mounton, 1975), devotes just a couple of pages to the book, and completes ignores Grave's ironic and theater-related techniques. This disregard has continued even after the publication of *The Great War and Modern Memory*. Katherine Snipe's *Robert Graves* (New York: Frederick

Ungar Publishing, 1979), offers a very short, and matter-of-fact analysis of the memoir, but says nothing about the points Fussell raises. While Robert H. Canary's *Robert Graves* (Boston: Twayne Publishers, 1980), spends a little over eight pages on the work, but he fails to discuss the stylistic elements Fussell notes, instead arguing that Graves's prose in the battle passages "is straightforward and matter-of-fact, with a casualness that does not have even the artistic pretensions of Hemingway...What counts is not the effect of any one incident but the cumulative effect of the whole" (pp. 35–36). Diane De-Bell in "Strategies of Survival: Robert Graves, *Goodbye to All That*, and David Jones, *In Parenthesis*," in *The First World War in Fiction*, Edited by Holger Klein (New York: Macmillan, 1976), argues that Graves utilizes a method that "relies upon a dramatic presentation of material accompanied by very little added comment, with rapid transitions occurring from one event to another. It is a method by which horror can be accommodated if not fully penetrated" (p. 163). While she is half right using the term dramatic, she also fails to take into account the satirical, ironic, and theatrical techniques Graves frequently employs when describing incidents. Adrian Caesar in *Taking it like a Man: Suffering, Sexuality, and the War Poets Brooke, Sassoon, Owen, Graves* (Manchester: University of Manchester Press, 1993), largely agrees with Fussell's analysis but also believes that Graves's memoir is not as anti-war as Fussell implies, but ambivalent (p. 215). Finally, even Richard Perceval Graves, in *Robert Graves: The Years with Laura Riding, 1926–1940* (New York: Penguin Books, 1990, the second volume of his impressive three volume biography of Robert Graves, when discussing the writing of *Goodbye to All That*, fails to mention the heavily satirical thrust and dark humor of *Goodbye to All That*, instead writing that "since Graves's account was undistinguished by heroic preconditions or sentimental preoccupations, it seemed to his readers to have captured very precisely the reality of wartime service" (p.105).

38. Robert Graves, *Good-Bye to All That: An Autobiography*, Edited, with a Biographical Essay and Annotations by Richard Perceval Graves (Providence: Berghahn Books, 1995): 5.

39. *The Poetical Works of Rupert Brooke*, Edited by Geoffrey Keynes (London: Faber and Faber, 1946): 112. Thanks to Terence Allred for bringing this poem to my attention.

40. Fussell, *The Great War and Modern Memory*, 206.

41. Paul Fussell, introduction, *Goodbye to All That* (New York: Vintage International, 1998): vii.

42. Fussell, *The Great War and Modern Memory*, 268.

43. Fussell, Ibid., 272.

44. Fussell, Ibid., 291. The quote from Bergonzi is from *Heroes Twilight: A Study of the Literature of the Great War* by Bernard Bergonzi (New York: Coward-McCann, 1966), 128.

45. Studies like Santanu Das's 2008 *Touch and Intimacy in First World War Literature* (Cambridge: Cambridge University Press), are possible in part because of *The Great War and Modern Memory*.

46. Bruce Cherry, *They Didn't Want to Die Virgins: Sex and Morale in the British Army on the Western Front 1914–1918* (Solihull, England: Helion and Company, 2016): 18.

47. Fussell, *The Great War and Modern Memory*, 335.

48. Fussell, afterword to 2000 edition of *The Great War and Modern Memory*, 341.

49. In fact, the emotional impact of this book has been so strong with many readers that they can clearly remember years later precisely when and where they had first read it. The British writer Martin Stephen, who is now quite critical of the work, recalls, "I cannot remember where I was Kennedy was assassinated, but I can remember when I first read *The Great War and Modern Memory* for over an hour in the long-suffering Heffner's Bookshop in Cambridge." *The Price of Pity: Poetry, History and Myth in the Great War* (London: Leo Cooper, 1996): 230. Stephen's experience was (and is) not unusual.

50. Gary Sheffield, *Forgotten Victory: The First World War- Myths and Realities* (London: Headline Book Publishing, 2001): 15.

51. James Campbell, "Interpreting the War," 267.

52. See chapter one of Janet Brennan Croft's *War and the Works of J.R.R. Tolkien* (London: Prager, 2004): 13–32 for a Fussellian analysis of Tolkien's *Lord of the Rings* trilogy.

53. Geoff Dyer, *The Missing of the Somme* (London: Hamish Hamilton, 1994): 84.

Chapter Notes—3

54. This is also occasionally true of works of fiction concerning the war. Recently, I picked up the 2014 novel *Wake* by Anna Hope which is about the two-year anniversary of Armistice Day in Britain. In the acknowledgment page, Hope mentions several books that helped her in her research, one of which was *The Great War and Modern Memory*.

55. The large influence of *The Great War and Modern Memory* and the wide and often strongly worded commentary it generated can be clearly seen in the fact that in 1991, a collection of essays was published by noted British military historians. It was according to its editor, "inspired by the need for a historical counterpart to Paul Fussell's celebrated literary study *The Great War and Modern Memory*. Many of Fussell's ideas are useful to historians but his approach is emphatically not historical nor is he is entirely reliable as a guide." *The First World War and British Military History*, edited by Brian Bond (Oxford: Clarendon Press, 1991): 1.

56. Robin Prior and Trevor Wilson, "Paul Fussell At War," *War in History*, 1.1 (1994): 68.

57. Prior and Wilson, "Debate: Paul Fussell At War," 63. Dan Todman has elaborated on this argument, writing, "*The Great War and Modern Memory* highlights the problem of using literature as the basis for historical understanding. Potentially, literature is an extremely useful source. It can demonstrate the ways in which individuals understood what was happening to them. A work that carries the force of lived experience can help the scholar empathize with the human beings involved in historical events ... In using works of literature we have, however, to be constantly aware that these are representations of an individual's reaction to events. As a result, they may tell us as much or more about the individual as they do about the event. We cannot assume that because a work has aesthetic merit it is necessarily representations of wider experiences or reactions ... In addition, we have to be careful not to allow our own subjective reading of a poem, novel, or memoir, which is shaped by the context in which we are reading it, to overwhelm our effort to use it as a piece of evidence." *The Great War: Myth and Memory* (London: Bloomsbury, 2005): 159–160.

58. Prior and Wilson, "Debate: Paul Fussell At War,", 68.

59. Ibid., 67.

60. While the term *learning curve* is frequently used by military historians, Dan Todman (*The Great War*) has offered a better and more nuanced metaphor. "Although the metaphor is less neat, it is better to picture the development of the army as being composed of a series of individual learning processes that included patterns plateaux, backward steps, and peaks at an insufficient level, as well as great leaps foreword. Overall, however, the fighting power of the army improved significantly" (p. 83).

61. These changes are considered so important that they are referred to by historians as a Revolution in Military Affairs (RMA). For details, see Gary Sheffield, *A Short History of the First World War* (London: Oneworld Publications, 2014): 81. For a collection of wide ranging essays by revisionist historians, see *A Part of History: Aspects of the British Experience in the First World War* (London: Continuum, 2008). For an informative visual representation of the complexities of coordinating an artillery barrages with the advancement of the infantry, which took the British army years to become proficient at, see *The Western Front Companion: The Complete Guide to How the Armies Fought for Four Devastating Years, 1914–1918* by Mark Adkin (London: Aurum Press Ltd., 2013): 254–261.

62. There are some historians who reject this revisionist interpretation of the war. See, for example, Niall Ferguson's *The Pity of War: Explaining World War One* (New York: Basic Books, 1999) and John Keegan's *The First World War* (New York: Vintage Books, 1998). Keegan, a renowned military historian, was a great defender of Fussell. Moreover, the distinguished Oxford University historian and scholar on the war, Hew Strachan, told me in a short conversation in 2015 at an academic conference at Ohio University, that he felt military historians had been "unfair to Fussell."

63. Moreover, as Robert Wohl notes, "Reading the literature on the [World War One's] lost generation, one seldom has reason to remember that of the 700,00 British Combatants who died during the war, only 37,452 were officers—and yet it these 37,000 and not the troops they commanded who are enshrined in the myth." *The Generation of 1914* (Cambridge: Harvard University Press, 1979): 121.

64. Tony Ashworth, *Trench Warfare 1914–1918* (London: Macmillan, 1980): 19.

Chapter Notes—3

65. Brian Bond, *The Unquiet Western Front: Britain's Role in Literature and History* (New York: Cambridge University Press, 2002): 99–100.

66. Dan Todman, *The Great War: Memory and Myth* (London: Bloomsbury, 2005): 187, 207.

67. Barbara W. Tuchman, *The Proud Tower: A Portrait of the World Before the War, 1890–1914* (New York: The Macmillan Company 1962): xiii.

68. Historians Jay Winter and Antonie Prost point out that it was not until the 1980s and 1990s that military history entered the revisionist phase. *The Great War in History: Debates and Controversies, 1914 to the Present* (New York: Oxford University Press, 2005): 73. See Bond, Todman, and Sheffield for histories or changing impressions of the Great War.

69. Todman, *The Great War*, 139. Fussell also relied upon Liddell Hart's *A History of the First World War* (London: Cassell, 1970). He also uses the popular histories, *In Flanders Fields: The 1917 Campaign* by Leon Wolfe (New York: Ballantine Books, 1958), and *The First Day of the Somme 1 July 1916* by Martin Middlebrook (New York: Norton, 1971). Moreover, Fussell quoted widely from the anthologies *Promises of Greatness: The War of 1914–1918*, Edited by George A. Panichas (New York: The John Day Company, 1968), *Vain Glory: A Miscellany of the Great War 1914–1918 Written by Those Who Fought it on Each Side and on All Fronts*. Edited by Guy Chapman (New York: Cassell, 1937), and *War Letters of Fallen Englishmen*, Edited by Laurence Housman (New York: E.P. Dutton, 1930), and the work *Passchendaele and the Somme: A Diary of 1918 by Hugh Quigley* (London: Methuen, 1928). Curiously, while he wrote that he spent several months researching *The Great War and Modern Memory* at the Imperial War Museum in London reading the diaries and letters of soldiers, he quoted from few of them. To be fair, it appears that Fussell felt no need to do much further reading on the subject of the Great War nor does it appear he ever read any revisionist accounts. His bibliography of suggested further readings for his afterword to the 25th anniversary edition of *The Great War and Modern Memory* does not contain any works written by historians of the revisionist school, and many of the books he listed are quite old.

70. When compared to such well-received works like John Ellis's *Eye-Deep in Hell: Trench Warfare in World War 1* (New York: Pantheon Books, 1976), and Denis Winter's *Death's Men: Soldiers of the Great War* (New York: Penguin Books, 1979).

71. Keegan, *The First World War*, 293–294.

72. Fussell, *The Great War and Modern Memory*, ix. Santanu Das has noted that "the trench accounts, it is true, cannot be used as the only narrative of the war or turned into a metaphor for 20th century consciousness. But, instead of simply challenging them, it is time that we might try to understand and analyze why those images persist." *Touch and Intimacy in First World War Literature* (New York: Cambridge University Press, 2008): 10.

73. To his credit, the historian Gary Sheffield has noted some of the differences between Fussell's approach and that of historians. As he notes, Fussell's approach or the cultural view is "based on empathy and emotion, [which] collides head on with the archive-based 'scientific' approach to the writing of history...The result is that there are now two distinct perceptions of the First World War. The majority of people view it as a unique cultural event, essentially 'outside' history. In contrast, a small group of historians see the war in the context of political and military history." *Forgotten Victory: The First World War: Myths and Realities* (London: Headline Book Publishing, 2001): xiv.

74. Fussell, *Doing Battle*, 267.

75. Fussell, *The Great War and Modern Memory*, 342, 338. Fussell's use of emotion does have a drawback. The English poet Philip Larkin in a letter that is very critical of *The Great War and Modern Memory*, stated that "Fussell does not seem to have made up his mind whether he approves of disapproves of the Great War." *Selected Letters of Philip Larkin, 1940–1985*. Edited by Anthony Thwaite (Boston: Faber and Faber, 1992): 531. Larkin's acid comment does touch on a pertinent point (but probably not in the way Larkin meant it). There are times when a reader of *The Great War and Modern Memory* might wonder if Fussell is not a bit too much, in John Keats's famous words, "half in love with easeful death."

76. Todman, *The Great War*, 159.

77. Prior and Wilson, "Debate: Paul Fussell At War," 69.
78. Ibid., 65.
79. Ibid., 1994, 69.
80. Ibid., 1994, 69.
81. Ibid., 1994, 69.
82. Ibid., 1994, 68.
83. Frederic Manning, *The Middle Parts of Fortune: Somme and Ancre, 1916*. Introduction by Paul Fussell (New York: Penguin Books, 1990): ix, xvi.
84. This can be clearly seen in the historian Brian Bond's injunction that "it is obvious literature cannot provide a substitute for the *history* of the war which embraces policy, strategy, and tactics as well as the dramatic personal experiences of the home and military fronts." Bond, *The First World War and British Military History*, 2.
85. Peter Hart, *The Battle of the Somme: The Darkest Hour on the Western Front* (New York: Pegasus Books, 2008): 528. Hart goes on to claim that "the Somme was so awful not because of the venality or stupidity of individuals, but because of the leaders of the great Western nations had set themselves to resolve long-standing problems through war, with the active or passive encouragement of much of their civilian populations ... The fighting was not futile unless the war was futile. The responsibility for all the manifold sacrifices lies not so much with the generals as with the enthusiasm with which the war was embraced in 1914" (p. 529). Needless to say, Fussell would find this absolving of the generals of responsibility highly dubious.
86. Fussell, *The Great War and Modern Memory*, 338.
87. Ibid., 169.
88. Ibid., 311.
89. Ibid., 312.
90. Ibid., 207.
91. Ibid., ix.
92. Ian Kershaw, *To Hell and Back: Europe 1914–1949* (New York: Penguin Books, 2015): 10, 11.
93. Samuel Hynes, *The Soldier's Tale: Bearing Witness to Modern War* (New York: The Penguin Press, 1997): 106–107.
94. E-mail to the author, April 7, 2017.
95. Catherine W. Reilly, *English Poetry of the First World War: A Bibliography* (New York: George Prior Publishers, 1978).
96. Elizabeth Vandiver, *Stand in the Trench: Classical Receptions in British Poetry of the Great War* (Oxford: Oxford University Press, 2010).
97. Jay Winter, *Sites of Memory, Sites of Morning: The Great War in European Cultural History* (Cambridge: Cambridge University Press, 1995).
98. James Campbell, "Interpreting the War," 265. Moreover, as George Walter has noted, literacy in England during this time was equated with literature, literature "which is this case meant poetry of a particular kind: what Elizabeth A. Marshland calls "the nation's treasury of patriotic and heroic poems."" Walter, *The Penguin Book of First World War Poetry*, xi
99. *The Bloody Game: An Anthology of Modern War*, Edited by Paul Fussell (New York: Scribner's, 1991): 34.
100. Told to the author, April 11, 2018.
101. Fussell, *The Bloody Game: An Anthology of Modern War*, ix.
102. Robert Darby, "Oscillations on the Hotspur-Falstaff Spectrum: Paul Fussell and the Ironies of War," *War in History*, 9.3 (2002): 312.
103. Fussell, *The Great War and Modern Memory*, 131.
104. Jay Winter, "Paul Fussell: Memories of a Friend and Scholar," *The Chronicle of Higher Education*, May 12, 2012.
105. Jay Winter, *Sites of Memory, Sites of Morning*, 3.
106. Drew Gilpin Faust, "War's Laureate," *The New Republic*, June 8, 2012.
107. Samuel Hynes, *The Soldier's Tale*, 106.
108. Paul Fussell, National Book Award in Arts and Letters Acceptance Speech, April 21, 1976. http://www.nationalbook.org/nbaacceptspeech_pfussell.html#.WiC8h0qnHIU. Accessed November 30, 2018.
109. Fussell, National Book Award in Arts and Letters Acceptance Speech.
110. Ibid.
111. Betty Fussell, *My Kitchen Wars* (New York: North Point Press, 1999), 198. Ironically, she claims in this memoir that the fame associated with Fussell's book greatly contributed to their later divorce, writing, "Paul reaped the merit badges for his prize-winning book, and I faded like an old Polaroid. I grew resentful, but not, as Paul assumed, because I was jealous of his fame. I had wanted something simpler and subtler, some sign of recognition from him that his achievement, which

was real and admirable, was the result of labor shared. The writing, research, the sensibility, the work itself, were all his, of course. But I had given him a gift he had used and discarded without thought. I had given him time. From the beginning, I had freed him from all the secretarial and familial and social chores that unravel concentrated work, The Work" (pp. 199–200). Betty Fussell would go on to write 12 books on food, and a biography of the 1920s silent film actress Mabel Normand.

112. Fussell, *Doing Battle*, 267.

Chapter 4

1. Evelyn Waugh, *When the Going Was Good* (Boston: Little, Brown and Company, 1934): 187.
2. Paul Fussell, *Abroad: British Literary Travel Between the Wars* (New York: Oxford University Press, 1980): vii.
3. Paul Fussell, "Patrick Brydone: The Eighteenth-Century Traveler as Representative Man." In *Literature as a Mode of Travel: Five Essays and a Postscript*, With an introduction by Warner G. Rice (New York: The New York Public Library, 1963): 67.
4. Fussell, *Abroad*, 4.
5. Ibid., 16.
6. Ibid., 1980, 108.
7. Ibid.. 1980, 41.
8. Ibid., 1980, 39.
9. Ibid., 1980, 41.
10. Another byproduct of the advent of modern low cost flights that Fussell does not mention is the flocks of mainly young tourists on a shoestring budget to areas like Europe and Southeast Asia who are primarily motivated to travel in order to drink and party. They commonly stay at resorts that cater to foreigners and have no interest in the countries they are visiting.
11. Fussell, *Abroad*, 219–220.
12. W. H. Auden and Christopher Isherwood, *Journey to a War* (New York: Random House, 1939): 152.
13. Alan Wilde, *Christopher Isherwood* (New York: Twayne Publishers, Inc., 1971):
14. Auden and Isherwood, *Journey to a War*, 231.
15. Michael Kernan, "Bygone Travelers," *The Washington Post*, October 7, 1980.
16. Peter Stansky, *The Washington Post Book World*, September 21, 1980.
17. Edward J. Curtin, "*Abroad*: British Literary Travelling Between the Wars," *America*, December 27, 1980: 433, 434.
18. Jonathan Rabin, "Live and Letters Between the War: Travel With the English," *The New York Times*, August 31, 1980: A1.
19. Ibid., A1.
20. Abe Weiss, "More on Fussell," *Los Angeles Times*, July 7, 1991, L22.
21. Fussell, *Abroad*, 71.
22. Ibid., 73.
23. Ibid., 203.
24. For example, these changes can easily be observed in the massive differences between the first edition of the Lonely Planet's guide to Korea and its latest.
25. Andrew Keen, *The Cult of the Amateur: How the Internet is Killing Our Culture* (New York: Crown Business, 2007).
26. Paul Fussell (Editor), *The Norton Book of Travel* (New York: W.W. Norton & Company, 1987): 14.
27. Ibid., 1987, 16.
28. Paul Fussell, "Bourgeois Travel: Techniques and Artifacts," in *Bon Voyage: Designs for Travel* (New York: Cooper-Hewitt Museum, The Smithsonian Institution's National Museum of Design, 1987): 77.
29. Ibid., 1987, 93.
30. Paul Fussell, "Travel, Tourism, and International Understanding," in *Thank God for the Atom Bomb and Other Essays* (New York: Ballantine Books, 1988): 129, 131.
31. Fussell, Ibid., 139.

Chapter 5

1. Paul Fussell, *The Great War and Modern Memory*, 338.
2. Paul Fussell, *Abroad*, 204.
3. Paul Fussell, *The Boy Scout Handbook and Other Observations*, vii.
4. Ibid., 1982, vii.
5. Paul Fussell, *Thank God for the Atom Bomb and Other Essays* (New York: Ballantine Books, 1988): i.
6. Fussell, *The Boy Scout Handbook and Other Observations*, 3.
7. Ibid., 6.
8. Ibid., 231.
9. Ibid., 225.
10. Edmund Wilson, *A Literary Chronicle: 1920–1950* (New York: Doubleday Anchor Books, 1956): 189.
11. Fussell, *The Boy Scout Handbook and Other Observations*, 68.

12. Ibid., 118, 120.
13. Ibid., 136.
14. Fussell, *Thank God for the Atom Bomb and Other Essays*, i.
15. Ibid., 247.
16. Ibid., 120.
17. Ibid., 41, 42.
18. James Cahill, "Nancy Wilson Ross, Stanley Young, a Book and a Song," http://jamescahill.info/the-writings-of-james-cahill/responses-a-reminiscences/201-79-nancy-wilson-ross-stanley-young-a-book-and-a-song. Accessed August 4, 2018.
19. For a concise overview of this controversy, see Chris McMachen's "My Sister and I: An Elaborate Literary Hoax," *Warfare History Network*, November 21, 2016. https://warfarehistorynetwork.com/daily/wwii/my-sister-and-i-an-elaborate-literary-hoax/
20. Fussell, *Thank God for the Atom Bomb and Other Essays*, 81.
21. Michiko Kakutani, "Books of the Times," *The New York Times*, October 8, 1982: C28.
22. Judith Chettle, "If the Scouts Ruled America," *The Christian Science Monitor*, September 10, 1982.
23. Noel Perrin, "Of Literature, War, and Travel," *The New York Times Book Review*, August 29, 1982.
24. Michael Gorra, "Dark, Ironical, Flip," *The Nation*, November 27, 1982: 567.
25. Mark Muro, "Rich Essays from an Experienced Moralist, the *Boston Globe*, June 9, 1988: 86.
26. Robert W. Smith, "Quite Contrary: More of Paul Fussell's Brash Attacks on Modern Icons," The *Washington Post*, July 4, 1988: D3.
27. Arne Weinstein, *The New York Times*, August 7, 1988: BR21.
28. James Yuenger, "Honestly Amusing Jabs at the Self-Righteous," *Chicago Tribune*, July 24, 1988: 9.

Chapter 6

1. William Manchester, *Goodbye Darkness: A Memoir of the Pacific War* (Boston: Little, Brown, and Company, 1979): 210.
2. "Thank God for the Atom Bomb," in *Hiroshima's Shadow*, Edited by Kai Bird and Lawrence Lifschultz (Stony Creek, Connecticut: The Pamphleteer's Press, 1998): 211.
3. Ibid., 211.

4. Ibid., 214.
5. Fussell continued to be highly irritated about Gray's remarks for many years. His 1996 autobiography contains several pages criticizing Gray's ideas about the bombings.
6. *Hiroshima's Shadow*, 213–214.
7. Ibid., 220.
8. Ibid., 216.
9. Fussell received complaints from some veterans regarding his description of the actions of American soldiers fighting in the Pacific. In 1987, he published a short article defending his accusation that some soldiers collected Japanese skulls as wartime trophies. It also appears in his *Thank God For the Atomic Bomb and Other Essays* (New York: Ballantine Books, 1988). MIT historian John W. Dower's influential study of the role of race in the war, *War Without Mercy: Race and Power in the Pacific War* (New York; Pantheon Books, 1986), supports Fussell's assertions regarding this matter.
10. *Hiroshima's Shadow*, 221.
11. Ibid., 222.
12. Robert Jay Lifton and Greg Mitchell, *Hiroshima in America: Fifty Years of Denial* (New York: G.P. Putnam's and Sons, 1995): 243.
13. *Hiroshima in America*, 243.
14. Ibid., 215.
15. Quoted in Lifton and Mitchell, *Hiroshima in America*, 242.
16. Ibid., 242.
17. "An Exchange of Views," in *Thank God for the Atom Bomb and Other Essays*, 1988, 27.
18. Ibid., 26
19. Richard B. Frank, *Downfall: The End of the Imperial Japanese Empire* (New York: Penguin Books, 1999): 334–335. These numbers, along with the Allied bombing of Dresden, lead the famous foreign and defense policy expert McGeorge Bundy to write, "I do not find myself find Hiroshima more *immortal* than Tokyo or Dresden, but I find the *political* question more difficult. The nuclear world as we now know it is grimly dangerous; might it be less dangerous if Hiroshima or Nagasaki had never happened? If so, a stretch out of the anguish of war might have been a small price to pay." *Danger and Survival: Choices about the Bomb in the First Fifty Years* (New York: Vantage Books, 1988): 96. Fussell would have strongly disagreed with Bundy's last sentence, which he would have

considered cavalier and yet another example of *ex post facto* reasoning.

20. Dower, *War Without Mercy*.

21. Henry L. Stimson, and McGeorge Bundy. *On Active Service in Peace and War* (New York: Harper and Brothers, 1947): 632.

22. Michael Kort, *The Columbia Guide to Hiroshima and the Bomb* (New York: Columbia University Press, 2007): 11.

23. Ibid., 11. Kort provides a concise overview of the development of the historiography regarding the atomic bombs on pages 3–13. His book is a valuable reference work which covers all the major issues of the bombings and also contains important primary documents.

24. Winston Churchill, *Triumph and Tragedy* (New York: Bantam Books, 1953): 552.

25. For details on Japan's defense strategy, see Frank, 178–213.

26. Robert James Maddox, "The Biggest Decision: Why We Had to Drop the Atomic Bom," *American Heritage*, May/June 1995: 73.

27. For details, see Kort, 110–111. It is has been argued that the U.S. wanted the Soviet Union to enter the war in large part in case the bomb failed to go off. See *The Accidental President: Harry S. Truman and the Four Months that Changed the World* by A.J. Baime (New York: Houghton Mifflin Harcourt, 2017: 315.

28. Frank, *Downfall: The End of the Imperial Japanese Empire*, 350.

29. Ibid., 359.

30. According to postwar interviews with the surviving members of the Supreme Council for the Direction of the War, as well as the Lord Keeper of the Privacy Seal, and the Emperor, the main reason why Japan's surrendered was the dropping of the atomic bombs.

31. Kort, *The Columbia Guide to Hiroshima and the Bomb*, 95. It is interesting to note that during this time, Japan had been doing their own atomic bomb research. While it was badly organized and ultimately a failure, there is little doubt that Japan would have used it if it had been successful. For a discussion of the program, see John Dower's essay "'NI' and 'F': Japan's Wartime Atomic Bomb Research," in his *Japan in War and Peace* (New York: HarperCollins, 1996): 55–100. Japan has continued to see itself as a victim because of the bombings. Gavan McCormack observes that "the perception in Japan … is complex. It is probably true to say that most people see it as a crime of such magnitude as to warrant analogy with Auschwitz." *The Emptiness of Japanese Affluence*. Revised Edition (New York: M.E. Sharpe, 2001): 241–242. See also chapter four of Ian Buruma's insightful *Wages of Guilt: Memories of War in Germany and Japan* (New York: Vintage, 1995).

32. Sean L. Malloy, *Atomic Tragedy: Henry L. Stimson and the Decision to Use the Bomb Against Japan* (Ithaca and New York: Cornell University Press, 2008): 107.

33. Ibid., 114.

34. Ibid., 114.

35. Waldo Heinrichs and Marc Gallicchio, *Implacable Enemies: The War in the Pacific, 1944–1945* (New York: Oxford University Press, 2017): 506–507.

36. Ibid., 2017, 595.

37. Stimson and Bundy, *On Active Service in Peace and War*, 633.

38. Paul Fussell, *Doing Battle*, 291.

Chapter 7

1. J. Anthony Lukas, *Big Trouble: A Murder in a Small Western Town Sets Off a Struggle for the Soul of America* (New York: Simon & Schuster, 1997): 13.

2. Paul Fussell, *Class: A Guide Through the American Status System* (New York: Summit Books, 1983): 50.

3. Ibid., 27.

4. Ibid., 56.

5. Ibid., 75–76. For an interesting history of Anglophilia in American life, see Christopher Hitchens's *Blood, Class, and Nostalgia: Anglo-American Ironies* (London: Chatto & Windus, 1990). Hitchens quotes in the book with approval an example Fussell gives in *Class* of America's widespread Anglophilia (see pages 49–50).

6. Fussell, *Class*, 90.

7. Ibid., 92.

8. Ibid., 117.

9. Ibid., 141.

10. Ibid., 152.

11. Ibid., 163.

12. Ibid., 169.

13. Ibid., 172.

14. Ibid., 179.

15. Ibid., 180.

16. Ibid., 185, 186.

17. For example, Dennis Gilbert and Joseph A. Kahl in their widely used textbook,

Chapter Notes—8

The American Class Structure: A New Synthesis, 4th Edition (Belmont, California: Wadsworth Publish Company, 1992), list *Class* in their recommended readings for their chapter "Socialization, Association, Lifestyles, and Values."

18. For example, W. Lloyd Warner and Paul S. Lunt have proposed a theory of six distinct classes in America that is similar to Fussell's taxonomy (See *Inequality: A Contemporary Approach to Race, Class, and Gender* by Lisa A. Keister and Darby E. Southgate (Cambridge: Cambridge University Press, 2012): 99. Gilbert and Kahl offer a theory that posits six classes which also has characteristics that are similar to Fussell's (p. 18).

19. Alison Lurie, "From the Bottom-Out-Sights on Up," *New York Times*, November 18, 1983, BR7.

20. Margaret Manning, "Telling an Upper From a High Prole," *Boston Globe*, November 27, 1983, 93.

21. Christopher Lehmann-Haupt, "Books of the Times," *New York Times*, November 18, 1983.

22. Ibid.

23. Jonathan Yardley, "Casting Proles Before Swine," *Washington Post*, November 6, 1983.

24. T. R. Hummer, "An Introduction to Class Consciousness and the American Writer," *New England Review*, 15.2 (1993): 5.

25. James Fallows, "Why Paul Fussell Thinks He's Better Than You," *The Washington Monthly*, December, 1983, 36.

26. Mimi Kramer, "Whoring after Self-Respect," *The New Criterion*, September, 1984.

27. Ibid..

28. Carlin Romano, *America: The Philosophical* (New York: Alfred A. Knopf, 2012): 267.

29. Quoted in Romano, *America: The Philosophical*, 270.

30. Quoted in "A Class Critic Takes Aim at America: The Slings and Arrows of Paul Fussell" by Curt Suplee, *Washington Post*, September 28, 1982: B1.

31. Quoted in "Class Raises Status to an Exact Science" by Elizabeth Mehren, *Los Angeles Times*, December 26, 1983, D33.

32. Evan Osnos, *Age of Ambition: Chasing Fortune, Truth, and Faith in the New China* (New York: Farrar, Straus, and Giroux, 2014): 63.

33. Dwight Garner, "On the Touchy Subject of Class in America," *New York Times*, July, 27, 2017, C13.

34. "Amy Chua: By the Book." *New York Times Book Review*, February 4, 2018, BR8.

35. Dan Balz, "A Fresh Look Back at 2016 Finds America With an Identity Crisis," *Washington Post*, September 15, 2018.

36. In several ways, *Class* is an useful complement to Charles Murray's popular 2012 book *Coming Apart: The State of White America, 1960–2010* (New York: Crown Forum), which discusses the formation of new American classes in terms of behavior and values and the socially harmful effects of this change, and Nancy Isenberg's *White Trash: The 400-Year Untold Story of Class in America (*New York: Viking, 2016).

37. For example, see Lisa Zeidner's "Can You Lead a Moral and Creative Life and Still Enjoy a Bit of Luxury?" *Washington Post*, June 20, 2017.

38. Suplee, "A Class Critic" B1.

39. Ibid.

40. Ibid., B1.

41. D. Keith Mano, "Paul Fussell: From His Bunker in Princeton N.J., a Wounded Literary Guerrilla Shoots at the 20th Century," *People*, 19.3, February 7, 1983.

42. Annie Paul, "The Last Curmudgeon," *Psychology Today*, 31.4, July/August 1998, 26.

43. Quoted in *The Portable Curmudgeon*, Compiled and Edited by Jon Winokur (New York: New American Library, 1987): 161.

Chapter 8

1. Paul Fussell, *Wartime*, ix.
2. Ibid., 268.
3. Ibid., 3.
4. Ibid., 8.
5. Ibid., 80.
6. Ibid., 80.
7. Gerald F. Linderman, *The World Within the War: America's Combat Experience in World War II* (New York: The Free Press, 1997): 185.
8. Fussell, *Wartime*, 136, 139.
9. Ibid., 146.
10. Ibid., 159.
11. Ibid., 251.
12. Ibid., 251.
13. For a history of the Armed Services Editions and a list of the books that were published, see Molly Guptill Manning's *When*

Books Went to War: The Stories that Helped U.S. Win World War II (Boston: Mariner Books, 2014).

14. Michael Shelden, *Friends of Promise: Cyril Connolly and the World of Horizon* (New York: Harper and Row, Publishers, 1979): 5.

15. *The Selected Essays of Cyril Connolly*, Edited and with an introduction by Peter Quennell (New York: Persea Books, Inc., 1984): 136.

16. Fussell, *Wartime*, 223.

17. Philip Ziegler, *Osbert Sitwell* (London: Chatto & Windus, 1998): 308.

18. Fussell, *Wartime*, 270.

19. Ibid., 282.

20. Ibid., 281, 282, 284

21. Ibid., 283.

22. Ibid., 55.

23. Evelyn Waugh, *Men at Arms* (Boston: Little, Brown and Company, 1952); 151.

24. Fussell, *Wartime*, ix.

25. Samuel Hynes, "Blood, Sweat, and Vulgarity," *New Republic*, November 13, 1989, 36.

26. Ibid., 36.

27. Jack Fuller, "Gone to Soldiers: Paul Fussell Puts the 'Good War' in Unsentimental Perspective," *Chicago Tribune*, August 13, 1989, L5.

28. Nina King, "A Savage, Insensate, Affair," *Washington Post*, August 13, 1989, M1.

29. Hillel Schwarz, "Chronicling the Four-Letter War," *Los Angeles Times*, December 25, 1989, E12.

30. Robert Wilson, "How an Ugly Conflict Became 'the Good War,'" *USA Today*, September 1, 1989, 4D.

31. Robin Prior and Trevor Wilson, "Paul Fussell at War," 76.

32. Ibid., 79.

33. Jonathan Marwil, "Paul Fussell's War," *Michigan Quarterly Review*, 29.3 (1990): 436.

34. Ibid., 441.

35. Richard Bernstein, "War as Abomination, and a Debate on Evil," *New York Times*, October 11, 1989.

36. Roger J. Spiller, "The Real War: An Interview with Paul Fussell," *In the School of War* (Lincoln: University of Nebraska Press, 2010): 363.

Chapter 9

1. Paul Fussell, *The Making of a Skeptic* (Boston: Little, Brown and Company, 1996): 229.

2. Paul Fussell, *BAD: Or, the Dumbing of America* (New York: Touchstone, 1991): 13.

3. Fussell, *BAD: Or, the Dumbing of America*, 17.

4. Martha Sherrill, "The Man From BAD; Professor Paul Fussell, Telling America Just Where It's Gone Wrong," *The Washington Post*, Dec. 17, 1991, B1.

5. Michael Kammen, *American Culture American Tastes: Social Change and the 20th Century* (New York: Alfred A. Knopf, 1999): 190.

6. Fussell, *BAD: Or, the Dumbing of America*, 17.

7. Fussell, *The Making of a Skeptic*, 73.

8. Fussell, *BAD: Or, the Dumbing of America*, 95.

9. It is revealing that Fussell during his career won the H. L. Mencken Award of the Free Press Association for his writings.

10. *A Mencken Chrestomathy: His Own Selection of His Choicest Writings*, Edited and Annotated by H. L. Mencken (New York: Vintage Books, 1982): 178. Fussell quotes most of this remark by Mencken in his autobiography, and it is worth bringing up because it reflects his thinking in *BAD*.

11. Fussell, *BAD: Or, the Dumbing of America*, 52.

12. Ibid., 64.

13. Ibid., 68

14. Ibid., 74.

15. Mark S. Ferrara, *Palace of Ashes: China and the Decline of American Higher Education* (Baltimore: Johns Hopkins University Press, 2015: 179. The quote within the quote is from *Take Back Higher Education: Race, Youth, and the Crisis of Democracy in the Post-Civil Rights Era* by Henry A. Giroux and Susan Searls Giroux (New York: Palgrave Macmillan, 2004): 10.

16. Fussell, *BAD: Or, the Dumbing of America*, 76.

17. Ibid., 79.

18. Ibid., 186.

19. Ibid., 200.

20. Ibid., 190, 198, 200–201.

21. Ibid., 201.

22. Alexis de Tocqueville, *Democracy in America*, Translated by George Lawrence, Edited by J.P. Mayer (New York: Harper and Row, Publishers, 1969): 537, 538.

23. Tom Wolfe, *From Bauhaus to Our House (*New York: Farrar Straus Giroux, 1981): 3.

24. Philip Jenkins, *Decade of Nightmares: The End of the Sixties and the Making of Eighties America* (New York: Oxford University Press, 2006).
25. Gertrude Himmelfarb, "The Bad-Mouthing of America," *The New Republic*, October 28, 1991, 27.
26. Ibid., 31.
27. Erich Eichman, "Basher," *The American Scholar*, 61.2, 1992, 303.
28. Joseph Coates, "Paul Fussell Attacks America's Idiocies," *Chicago Tribune*, October 6, 1991, 9.
29. Andrew Ferguson, "When Bad is BAD," *Wall Street Journal*, September 24, 1991, A16.
30. Ibid., A16.
31. Christopher Buckley, "Creeping Nincompoopism," *The New York Times*, October 13, 1991.
32. Jonathan Yardley, "Now For The 'BAD' News; Fussell's Incomplete Indictment of America," *The Washington Post*, October 30, 1991, C02.
33. Interestingly, some of the themes that Fussell discusses in *BAD* can be seen in recent books like Susan Jacoby's 2009 *The Age of American Unreason*, Mark Bauerlein's 2008 *The Dumbest Generation: How the Digital Age Stupefies Young Americans and Jeopardizes Our Future*, and Neal Gabler's 1999 *Life the Movie: How Entertainment Conquered Reality*.

Chapter 10

1. Paul Fussell, Introduction, *Articles of War: A Collection of Poetry About World War II*, Edited by Leon Stokesbury (Fayetteville: The University of Arkansas Press, 1990): xxv.
2. Paul Fussell, *The Anti-Egoist: Kingsley Amis, Man of Letters* (New York: Oxford University Press, 1994): 135, 149.
3. Ibid., 135.
4. Siegfried Sassoon, *The War Poems of Siegfried Sassoon* (London: William Heinemann, 1919): 91.
5. Fussell, *The Bloody Game: An Anthology of Modern War*, 25.
6. Paul Fussell, "The Culture of War," in *The Costs of War: America's Pyrrhic Victories*, Second Expanded Edition, Edited by John V. Denson (London: Transaction Publishers, 1999): 417.
7. Ibid., 418.
8. Ibid., 419.
9. Ibid., 419–420.
10. Paul Fussell, "My War: How I Got Irony in the Infantry," *Harper's Magazine*, January 1982: 40.
11. Vera Brittain, *Testament of Youth: An Autobiographical Study of the Years 1900–1925* (New York: Penguin Books, 2015): 251.
12. Ibid., 2015, 251–252.
13. Fussell, Introduction, *Articles of War*, xxix.
14. Dave Grossman, *On Killing: The Psychological Cost of Learning to Kill in War and Society* (Boston: Little, Brown and Company, 1999): xxix. Studies have also shown that due to this impulse, a large proportion of American soldiers in the Second World War never fired their weapons during combat (firing rates were estimated to be only 15–20 percent (See Grossman, 15–16).
15. Fussell, "The Culture of War," 419–420.
16. In *Wartime*, Fussell notes the stages soldiers commonly go through regarding being killed. The first is that "It *can't* happen to me," [then], "It *can* happen to me and I better be careful," [and finally], "It is *going to* happen to me, and only not being there is going to prevent it" (p. 282).
17. Grossman, *On Killing*, 75.
18. *Wilfred Owen: The Complete Poems and Fragments*, Edited by Jon Stallworthy (London: Chatto & Windus, The Hogarth Press, and Oxford University Press, 1983): 140.
19. Recently, Yale University psychologist Paul Bloom has written about the numerous pitfalls associated with empathy in *Against Empathy: The Case for Rational Compassion* (New York: Ecco, 2016).
20. Edmund Blunden, *Undertones of War* (Harmondsworth Middlesex, England: Penguin Books Limited, 1938): 7.
21. Katie Blair, "The Other Side of War," *Atlantic Monthly*, February, 1997.
22. Fussell, "My War," 48.
23. Paul Fussell, "The Great War and Cultural Modernism," in *A Weekend with the Great War: Proceedings of the Fourth Annual Great War Interconference Seminar Lisle, Illinois 16–18 September 1994*, Edited by Steven Weingartner (Cantigny First Division Foundation and White Mare Publishing Company Inc., 1994): 248–249.
24. Modris Eksteins, *Rites of Spring: The*

Great War and the Birth of the Modern Age (New York: Doubleday, 1989): xiv.
25. Ibid., 1989, xv.
26. Fussell, "The Great War and Cultural Modernism," 252.
27. Ibid., 252–253.
28. Ibid., 1994, 260.

Chapter 11

1. Paul Fussell, *The Anti-Egotist: Kingsley Amis, Man of Letters* (New York, Oxford University Press, 1994): i.
2. Paul Fussell, "Kingsley, As I Know Him," in *Kingsley Amis in Life and Letters*, Edited by Dale Salwak (New York: St. Martin's Press, 1990): 19.
3. *The Letters of Kingsley Amis*, Edited by Zachary Leader (New York: Hyperion, 2000): 981.
4. Terry Teachout, "The Old Devil Himself," *New York Times*, September 11, 1994, BR12. It is unclear which character Teachout is referring to, but he might have meant the sexually confused solicitor Tim Valentine, who is undergoing a misguided and brief homosexual phase which is similar to what Fussell underwent in the 1980s.
5. Fussell, *The Anti-Egotist*, i.
6. Ibid., 3.
7. Ibid., 6.
8. Ibid., 7.
9. Ibid., 7.
10. Kingsley Amis, *Memoirs* (London: Hutchinson, 1991): 197, 293.
11. According to the journalist James Wolcott, Fussell told him that one of Amis's best traits is that "compared to Americans, he doesn't have an ounce of sincerity about him—everything he says is figurative." "Kingley's Ransom: Why Have the British Been Bashing the Original Amis?" in *Critical Essays on Kingsley Amis*, Edited by Robert H. Bell (New York: G. K. Hall & Co., 1998): 260. The problem is discerning when Amis is serious and when he is just being figurative.
12. Fussell, *The Anti-Egotist*, 8.
13. Zachary Leader, *The Life of Kingsley Amis* (London: Jonathan Cape, 2006): 775.
14. Amis, in his defense, later claimed that he intended to be funny and honest in the book and wanted to settle some long-standing scores (Leader, 2006, 781).
15. Fussell, *The Anti-Egotist*, 10, 12.
16. Leader,, *The Life of Kingsley Amis*, 775.
17. *The Letters of Kingsley Amis*, Edited by Zachary Leader (New York: Hyperion, 2000): 1127. In a letter written in November of 1991 to a friend, Amis complains that "Paul Fussell is over here for a year, but he's gotten so odd that I can barely talk to him anymore." (Leader, 2002, 1106). Moreover, according to Betty Fussell in her memoir *My Kitchen Wars*, in the 1950s, Amis, who was a notorious womanizer, while on a trip to the U.S., made a pass at her during a party.
18. Amis, *Memoirs*, 78, 79.
19. Fussell, *The Anti-Egotist*, 66.
20. Ibid., 135.
21. Fussell must have been greatly pleased with Amis's posthumously published 1999 book *The King's English: A Guide to English Usage*.
22. Teachout, "The Old Devil Himself," BR12.
23. William H. Pritchard, "Appreciating Kingsley Amis," *The Hudson Review*, 48, Spring 1994, 139.
24. Brian Murray, "The Compleat Literary Man," *First Things: A Monthly Journal of Religion and Public Life*, November, 1995, 59.
25. William Laskowski, *Kingsley Amis* (New York: Twayne Publishers, 1998): 156.
26. Pritchard, "Appreciating Kingsley Amis," 138.

Chapter 12

1. Paul Fussell, *Doing Battle*, i.
2. William Manchester, *Goodbye Darkness: A Memoir of the Pacific War* (New York: Little, Brown and Company, 1979): 10.
3. Ibid., 10.
4. Ibid., 11.
5. Ibid., 395.
6. E. B. Sledge, *With the Old Breed: At Peleliu and Okinawa* (New York: Oxford University Press, 1990), 315.
7. George MacDonald Fraser, *Quartered Safe Out Here: A Recollection of the War in Burma* (London: Harvill, 1992): 222.
8. Quoted in Fraser, *Quartered Safe Out Here*, 223.
9. Fraser, *Quartered Safe Out Here*, xvii.
10. Ibid., xviii.
11. John Bodnar, *The "Good War" in American Memory* (Baltimore: Johns Hopkins University Press, 2011): 56.
12. Fussell, *Doing Battle*, 174.

13. Neil McCallum, *Journey with a Pistol: A Diary of War* (London: Victor Gollancz LTD, 1959): 107, 117–118.
14. Ibid., 1959, 142.
15. Ibid., 1959, 88.
16. Ibid., 1959, 95.
17. Ibid., 1959, 77.
18. Ibid., 1959, 77.
19. John C. Brereton, "Four Careers in English," *College English*, 61.1 (1998): 79.
20. Fussell, *Doing Battle*, 284.
21. Ibid., 284.
22. John Keegan, "Natural Warriors, *The Wall Street Journal*, March 27, 1997: A20.
23. Fussell, *Doing Battle*, 299.
24. Anthony Hecht, "At War with His Memories," *The Washington Post*, September 29, 1996.
25. Richard Bernstein, "Fighting Euphemism and Optimism," *The New York Times*, October 9, 1996.
26. Russell F. Weigley, "In Search of a Sense of Tragedy," *The Los Angeles Times*, October 20, 1996.
27. Brereton, "Four Careers in English," 78.
28. Ibid., 78.
29. Paul Fussell, *The Boy Scout Handbook and Other Observations*, vii.

Chapter 13

1. Paul Fussell, *Uniforms: Why We Are What We Wear* (Boston: Houghton Mifflin Company, 2002): 5.
2. Ibid., 6.
3. Ibid., 6.
4. Ibid., 2002, 6.
5. Erving Goffman, *The Presentation of Self in Everyday Life* (New York: Doubleday Anchor Books, 1959): 30, 75.
6. Fussell, *Uniforms*, 3–4.
7. Ibid., 51.
8. Ibid., 138.
9. Ibid., 181.
10. Ibid., 182.
11. Ibid., 198.
12. Ibid., 2002, 204.
13. Michiko Kakutani, "Clothes Make the Mandate: Love the Epaulets, General." *The New York Times*, December 13, 2002.
14. P .J. O'Rourke, "What About Casual Fridays?" *The New York Times Book Review*, December 22, 2002, 8.
15. Ibid., 8.
16. Anne Hollander, "Men in Tights: Why Guys in Uniform Get Girls." *The New Republic*, February 10, 2003.
17. Paul Fussell, "Patton," in *Past Imperfect: History According to the Movies*, Edited by Ted Mico, John Miller-Monzon, and David Rubel (New York: Henry Holt and Company, 1995): 242–245.
18. Fussell, *Uniforms*, 44–47.

Chapter 14

1. For a history of the GW/GG perspective on the war, see Michael C. Adams's *The Best War Ever: America and World War II*. Second Edition (Baltimore: Johns Hopkins University Press, 2015): 130–147.
2. Victor Davis Hanson, *The Soul of Battle: From Ancient Times to the Present Times, How Three Great Liberators Vanquished Tyranny* (New York: The Free Press, 1999): 412.
3. Ibid., 409.
4. Ibid., 1999, 5.
5. Paul Fussell, *The Boy's Crusade: The American Infantry in Northwestern Europe, 1944–1945* (New York: The Modern Library, 2003): xiii.
6. Susanna Rustin, "Hello to All of That," *The Guardian*, July 31, 2004.
7. Paul Fussell, "The Guts, Not the Glory, of Fighting the 'Good War,'" *The Washington Post*, July 26, 1998: C01.
8. Ibid., 1998, C01.
9. Ibid. One recent movie that Fussell might have liked is 2014's *Fury* which depicts the experiences of an American tank crew fighting in Germany in April 1945. The film is extremely realistic (except for its stock Hollywood ending), well researched and acted. The crew's experiences generally seem to reflect what Fussell has written about the war.
10. Fussell, *The Boy's Crusade*, 7.
11. Ibid., 8–10.
12. Charles Glass in *The Deserters: A Hidden History of World War II* (New York: The Penguin Press, 2013) has stated that nearly 50,000 American and 100,000 British soldiers deserted during the war (p. xi). Only one American, Eddie Slovak, was executed for desertion.
13. Fussell, *The Boy's Crusade*, 97.
14. Stephen Ambrose, *Citizen Soldiers: The U.S. Army From the Normandy Beaches to the Bulge to the Surrender of Germany June 7, 1944-May 7, 1945* (New York: Simon & Schuster, 1997): 340.

15. See also Phillip Knightley's classic study, *The First Casualty: The War Correspondent as Hero and Myth Maker From the Crimea to Kosovo* (Baltimore: Johns Hopkins University Press, 2002), especially chapters 12 and 13.
16. Fussell, *The Boy's Crusade*, 130.
17. Ambrose, *Citizen Soldiers*, 473.
18. Ibid.. 473, 14, 473.
19. William L. O'Neill, *A Democracy at War: America's Fight at Home and Abroad in World War II* (New York: The Free Press, 1993): 325.
20. Ibid., 325–326.
21. Fussell, *The Boy's Crusade*, 111.
22. Tom Brokaw, *The Greatest Generation* (New York: Random House, 1998): 388.
23. Ibid., 389.
24. Fussell, *The Boy's Crusade*, 161.
25. Ibid., 174. Ambrose does refer to this part of the military, but uses much different language than Fussell, calling them "Jerks, Sad Sacks, Profiters" (*Citizen Soldiers*, 331).
26. Fussell, *The Boy's Crusade*, 16–19, 40–41. Ambrose, who admitted that he was in awe of these soldiers, has argued that "war brings out the best in most men" (*Citizen Soldiers*, 331). Fussell would have retorted that at best, it has the *potential* to.
27. Brokaw, *The Greatest Generation*, 389.
28. Max Hastings, *Inferno: The World at War, 1939–1945* (New York: Vintage Books, 2011): 651.
29. Alan Riding, "Band of Children," *The New York Times*, October 12, 2003: C16.
30. Clancy Sigal, "A Soldier Remembers," *The Los Angeles Times*, December 21, 2003.
31. Mick Jackson, "Nowhere to Run," *The Guardian*, October 23, 2004.
32. Phillip Parotti, *The Sewanee Review*, 115: 4 (2007): ixxxix.
33. Benjamin Schwartz, "New & Newsworthy, What To Read this Month" *The Atlantic Monthly*, November, 2003.
34. Paul Marantz Cohen, "Remembering Christopher Hitchens, Nora Ephron, Paul Fussell, and Others," March 12, 2013, https://www.huffingtonpost.com/paula-marantz-cohen/remembering-christopher_b_3071386.html, Accessed October 22, 2018.
35. Samuel Wilson Fussell, *Muscle: Confessions of an Unlikely Body Builder* (New York: Poseidon Press, 1991): 59.
36. Ibid., 145.
37. If you type into the Google search box 'Paul Fussell Obituary', over 34,000 results will appear.
38. Matt Schudel, "Paul Fussell, Curmudgeonly Essayist and Scholar, Dies at 88," *Washington Post*, May 24, 2012.
39. Bruce Weber, "Paul Fussell, Literary Scholar and Critic is Dead at 88," *The New York Times*, May 23, 2012.
40. Drew Gilpin Faust, "War's Laureate: The Morbid Greatness of Paul Fussell," *The New Republic*, June 28, 2012: 10.
41. Nicholas Mills, "Paul Fussell, the Critic Who Fought the Cant of Military Sacrifice," *The Guardian*, May 24, 2012.
42. "Paul Fussell, Warrior Against War, Died on May 23rd, Aged 88," *The Economist*, June 9, 2012
43. "Literary Scholar Paul Fussell Dead at 88," *Associated Press*, May 24, 2012.
44. Eric Randall, "America Will Miss Its Public Curmudgeon, Paul Fussell," *The Atlantic Monthly*, May 24, 2012.
45. Jay Winter, "Paul Fussell: Memories of a Friend and Scholar," *The Chronicle of Higher Education*, May 29, 2012.
46. Ibid., 2012.

Chapter 15

1. The term political correctness is loosely and imprecisely used. One of the best definitions of this mind-set has been offered by professor Michel S. Cummings who has argued that "the essence of political correctness is not the specific beliefs and ideologies disliked by conservatives. It is, rather, the way in which (conservatives allege) liberals and radicals hold and act upon their beliefs: namely, narrowly, dogmatically, unfairly, intolerantly, self-righteously, and oppressively…[There are four dimensions to] PC: (1) its black and white oversimplification of the world in terms of right and wrong; (2) its discouragement of self-insight and perspective; (3) its substitution of ideological fervor for philosophical clarity; and (4) its flight from uncomfortable truths." *Beyond Political Correctness: Social Transformation in the United States* (Boulder: Lynne Rienner Publishers, 2001): 10, 12. This is the type of PCism that Fussell would have scorned.
2. Fussell, *BAD: or, The Dumbing of America*, 194.
3. Fussell, *The Anti-Egoist*, 105.

4. Roderick M. Chisholm, *Theory of Knowledge*, Second Edition (Englewood Cliffs, New Jersey: Prentice-Hall, Inc., 1977): 15, 14. Chisholm did attach the caveat that these intellectual requirements are "only a *prima facie* duty; it may be, and usually is, overridden by others, nonintellectual requirements, and it may be fulfilled more or less adequately" (p. 14).

5. Fussell, "The Culture of War," 421.

6. Andrew Bacevich, "Cheap Grace and American Patriotism," TomDispatch.com, July 28, 2011.

Bibliography

Adams, Michael C. *The Best War Ever: America and World War II*. Second edition (Baltimore: Johns Hopkins University Press, 2015).
Ambrose, Stephen. *Citizen Soldiers: The U.S. Army from the Normandy Beaches to the Bulge to the Surrender of Germany, June 7, 1944–May 7, 1945* (New York: Simon & Schuster, 1997).
Amis, Kingsley. *The Amis Collection: Selected Non-Fiction, 1954–1990* (New York: Penguin, 1991).
Amis, Kingsley. *Memoirs* (London: Hutchinson, 1991).
Atkinson, Rick. *The Guns at Last Light: The War in Western Europe, 1944–1945* (New York: Henry Holt, 2013).
Auden, W.H., and Christopher Isherwood. *Journey to a War* (New York: Random House, 1939).
Auerbach, Erich. *Mimesis: The Representation of Reality in Western Literature.* Fiftieth anniversary edition. Translated by William Trask (Princeton: Princeton University Press, 2003).
Beaver, Patrick. *The Wiper Times.* Introduction, notes, and glossary by Patrick Beaver (London: Peter Davies, 1974).
Bergonzi, Bernard. *Heroes' Twilight: A Study of the Literature of the Great War* (London: Constable, 1965).
Bird, Kai, and Lawrence Lifschultz. *Hiroshima's Shadow* (Stony Creek, CT: Pamphleteer's Press, 1998).
Blunden, Edmund. *Undertones of War* (Harmondsworth, Middlesex, England: Penguin, 1938).
Bodnar, John. *The "Good War" in American Memory* (Baltimore: Johns Hopkins University Press, 2011).
Bond, Brian. *The Unquiet Western Front: Britain's Role in Literature and History* (New York: Cambridge University Press, 2002).
Brittain, Vera. *Testament of Youth: An Autobiographical Study of the Years 1900–1925* (New York: Penguin, 2015).
Brokaw, Tom. *The Greatest Generation* (New York: Random House, 1998).
Brophy, John, and Eric Partridge. *The Long Trail: What the British Soldier Sang and Said in The Great War of 1914–18* (New York: London House and Maxwell, 1965).
Bundy, McGeorge. *Danger and Survival: Choices about the Bomb in the First Fifty Years* (New York: Vantage Books, 1988).
Bunyan, John. *The Pilgrim's Progress.* Introduction by Louis L. Martz (New York: Holt, Rinehart, and Winston, 1964).
Burns, John Horne. *The Gallery.* Introduction by Paul Fussell (New York: New York Review of Books Classics, 2004).

Bibliography

Buruma, Ian. *Wages of Guilt: Memories of War in Germany and Japan* (New York: Vintage, 1995).
Byron, Robert. *The Road to Oxiana.* Introduction by Paul Fussell (New York: Oxford University Press, 2007).
Campbell, James. "Interpreting the War." *The Cambridge Companion to the Literature of the First World War.* Edited by Vincent Sherry (New York: Cambridge University Press, 2005).
Chapman, Guy. *A Passionate Prodigality* (New York: Fawcett World Library, 1966).
Chapman, Guy, editor. *Vain Glory: A Miscellany of the Great War, 1914–1918* (London: Cassell, 1937).
Chisholm, Roderick M. *Theory of Knowledge.* Second edition (Englewood Cliffs, NJ: Prentice-Hall, 1977).
Colby, Vineta, editor. *World Authors 1975–1980* (New York: The H.W. Wilson Company, 1985).
Collins, L. J. *Theatre at War: 1914–1918* (New York: St. Martin's Press, 1998).
Cooper, Jilly. *Class: A View from Middle England* (London: Corgi, 1979).
Culler, A. Dwight, editor. *Poetry and Criticism of Matthew Arnold* (Boston: Houghton Mifflin, 1961).
Cummings, Michael S. *Beyond Political Correctness: Social Transformation in the United States* (Boulder: Lynne Rienner, 2001).
Das, Santanu. *Touch and Intimacy in First World War Literature* (New York: Cambridge University Press, 2008).
D'Este, Carlo. *Eisenhower: A Soldier's Life* (New York: Henry Holt, 2002).
Dower, John W. *War Without Mercy: Race and Power in the Pacific War* (New York: Pantheon Books, 1986).
Doyle, Peter. *The First World War in 100 Objects* (Gloucestershire, England: The History Press, 2014).
Dyer, Geoff. *The Missing of the Somme* (London: Hamish Hamilton, 1994).
Ehrhart, W. D. "Paul Fussell: A Remembrance." *War, Literature, and the Arts*, 24.1–2 (2012).
Eksteins, Modris. *Rites of Spring: The Great War and the Birth of the Modern Age* (New York: Doubleday, 1989).
Eliot, T. S. *Notes Toward a Definition of Culture* (New York: Harcourt Brace, 1954).
Ellis, John. *The Sharp End of War: Fighting Man in World War II* (London: Corgi, 1982).
Frank, Richard B. *Downfall: The End of the Imperial Japanese Empire* (New York: Penguin, 1999).
Fraser, George MacDonald. *Quartered Safe Out There: A Recollection of the War in Burma* (London: Harvill, 1992).
Frye, Northrop. *Anatomy of Criticism: Four Essays* (Princeton: Princeton University Press, 1957).
Fussell, Betty. *My Kitchen Wars* (New York: North Point Press, 1999).
Fussell, Paul. *Abroad: British Literary Travel Between the Wars* (New York: Oxford University Press, 1980).
Fussell, Paul. *The Anti-Egoist: Kingsley Amis, Man of Letters* (New York: Oxford University Press, 1994).
Fussell, Paul. *Bad: Or, the Dumbing of America* (New York: Simon & Schuster, 1991).
Fussell, Paul. *A Bloody Game: An Anthology of Modern War* (London: Scribner's, 1991).
Fussell, Paul. "Bourgeois Travel: Techniques and Artifacts," in *Bon Voyage: Designs for Travel* (New York: Cooper-Hewitt Museum, The Smithsonian Institution's National Museum of Design, 1987).
Fussell, Paul. *The Boy Scout Handbook and Other Observations* (New York: Oxford University Press, 1982).

Bibliography

Fussell, Paul. *The Boy's Crusade: The American Infantry in Northwestern Europe, 1944–1945* (New York: The Modern Library, 2003).

Fussell, Paul. *Class: A Guide Through the American Status System* (New York: Summit Books, 1983).

Fussell, Paul. "The Culture of War," in *The Costs of War: America's Pyrrhic Victories.* Second expanded edition. Edited by John V. Denson (London: Transaction, 1999).

Fussell, Paul. *Doing Battle: The Making of a Skeptic* (New York: Little, Brown, 1996).

Fussell, Paul. "George Orwell." *The Sewanee Review*, 93.2 (Spring 1985).

Fussell, Paul. "The Great War and Cultural Modernism," in *A Weekend with the Great War: Proceedings of the Fourth Annual Great War Interconference Seminar Lisle, Illinois 16–18 September 1994.* Edited by Steven Weingartner (Cantigny First Division Foundation and White Mare Publishing, 1994).

Fussell, Paul. *The Great War and Modern Memory.* 25th anniversary edition (New York: Oxford University Press, 2000).

Fussell, Paul. "Kingsley, As I Know Him," in *Kingsley Amis in Life and Letters.* Edited by Dale Salwak (New York: St. Martin's Press, 1990).

Fussell, Paul. "More on Pseudo-Medical Educational Jargon" *American Speech*, 29.3 (October 1954).

Fussell, Paul. "My War: How I Got Irony in the Infantry." *Harper's*, January 1982.

Fussell, Paul. National Book Award in Arts and Letters Acceptance Speech, April 21, 1976. http://www.nationalbook.org/nbaacceptspeech_pfussell.html#.WiC8h0qnHIU.

Fussell, Paul. "Patrick Brydone: The Eighteenth-Century Traveler as Representative Man," in *Literature as a Mode of Travel: Five Essays and a Postscript.* Introduction by Warner G. Rice (New York: The New York Public Library, 1963).

Fussell, Paul. "Patton," in *Past Imperfect: History According to the Movies.* Edited by Ted Mico, John Miller-Monzon, and David Rubel (New York: Henry Holt, 1995).

Fussell, Paul. *Poetic Meter and Poetic Form* (New York: Random House, 1965).

Fussell, Paul. *The Rhetorical World of Augustan Humanism: Ethics and Imagery from Swift to Burke* (Oxford: Oxford University Press, 1965).

Fussell, Paul. *Samuel Johnson and the Life of Writing* (New York: Harcourt Brace Jovanovich, 1971).

Fussell, Paul. "Scholarship and Autobiography." *The Journal of the Rutgers University Libraries*, 36.2 (December 1977).

Fussell, Paul. *Thank God for the Atom Bomb and Other Essays* (New York: Ballantine Books, 1988).

Fussell, Paul. *Theory of Prosody in Eighteenth Century England* (Hamden, CT: Archon Books, 1966).

Fussell, Paul. "Thornton Wilder and the German Psyche." *The Nation*, May 3, 1958.

Fussell, Paul. *Uniforms: Why We Are What We Wear* (Boston: Houghton Mifflin, 2002).

Fussell, Paul. *Wartime: Understanding and Behavior in the Second World War* (New York: Oxford University Press, 1989).

Fussell, Paul, editor. *English Augustan Poetry* (New York: Anchor, 1972).

Fussell, Paul, editor. *The Norton Book of Travel* (New York: W.W. Norton, 1987).

Fussell, Samuel Wilson. *Muscle: Confessions of an Unlikely Body Builder* (New York: Poseidon Press, 1991).

Gilbert, Martin. *The First World War: A Complete History* (New York: Henry Holt, 1994).

Gilbert, Martin. *The Second World War: A Complete History* (New York: Henry Holt, 1989).

Gittings, Robert. *War Poets: The Lives and Writings of Rupert Brooke, Siegfried Sassoon, Wilfred Owen, Robert Graves and the Other Great Poets of the 1914–1918 War* (New York: Orion Books, 1988).

Bibliography

Glass, Charles. *The Deserters: A Hidden History of World War II* (New York: Penguin, 2013).
Goffman, Erving. *The Presentation of Self in Everyday Life* (New York: Doubleday Anchor Books, 1959).
Graves, Robert. *Good-Bye to All That: An Autobiography.* Edited and with a biographical essay and annotations by Richard Perceval Graves (Providence: Berghahn Books, 1995).
Graves, Robert. *Good-Bye to All That: An Autobiography.* Introduction by Paul Fussell (New York: Vintage Books, 1998).
Grossman, Dave. *On Killing: The Psychological Cost of Learning to Kill in War and Society* (Boston: Little, Brown,, 1999).
Hackney, Sheldon. "The Initial Shock: A Conversation with Paul Fussell." *Humanities,* 17.5 (November/December 1996).
Hale, Alfred M. *The Ordeal of Alfred M. Hale: The Memoirs of a Soldier Servant.* Edited and with an introduction by Paul Fussell (London: Cooper, 1975).
Hanson, Victor Davis. *The Soul of Battle: From Ancient Times to the Present Times, How Three Great Liberators Vanquished Tyranny* (New York: The Free Press, 1999).
Hastings, Max. *Armageddon: The Battle for Germany, 1944–1945* (New York: Alfred A. Knopf, 2004).
Hastings, Max. *Inferno: The World at War, 1939–1945* (New York: Vintage Books, 2011).
Heinrichs, Waldo, and Marc Gallicchio, *Implacable Enemies: The War in the Pacific, 1944–1945* (New York: Oxford University Press, 2017).
Heller, Joseph. *Catch 22* (New York: Simon & Schuster, 1961).
Hynes, Samuel. *The Soldier's Tale: Bearing Witness to Modern War* (New York: Penguin, 1997).
Jones, David. *In Parenthesis* (London: Faber & Faber, 2010).
Keegan, John. *The First World War* (New York: Vintage Books, 1998).
Keen, Andrew. *The Cult of the Amateur: How the Internet Is Killing Our Culture* (New York: Crown Business, 2007).
Knightley, Phillip. *The First Casualty: The War Correspondent as Hero and Myth Maker from the Crimea to Kosovo* (Baltimore: Johns Hopkins University Press, 2002).
Kort, Michael. *The Columbia Guide to Hiroshima and the Bomb* (New York: Columbia University Press, 2007).
Kotlowitz, Robert. *Before Their Time: A Memoir* (New York: Knopf, 1997).
Leader, Zachary, editor. *The Letters of Kingsley Amis* (New York: Hyperion, 2000).
Linderman, Gerald F. *The World Within the War: America's Combat Experience in World War II* (New York: The Free Press, 1997).
Lloyd, George, D. *War Memoirs of David Lloyd George, Volumes 1 and 2* (London: Odhams Press, 1933–1936).
Lloyd, Nick. *Passchendaele: The Lost Victory of World War I* (New York: Basic Books, 2017).
Lurie, Alison. *The Language of Clothes* (New York: Henry Holt, 1981).
MacDonald, Charles B. *The Last Offense: U.S. Army in World War II, The European Theater of Operations* (Atlanta: Whitman, 2012).
Manchester, William. *Goodbye Darkness: A Memoir of the Pacific War* (Boston: Little, Brown,, 1979).
Manning, Fredrick. *The Middle Parts of Fortune: Somme and Ancre, 1916.* Introduction by Paul Fussell (New York: Penguin, 1990).
Manning, Molly Guptill. *When Books Went to War: The Stories That Helped Win World War II* (Boston: Mariner Books, 2014).
McCallum, Neil. *Journey with a Pistol: A Diary of War* (London: Victor Gollancz, 1959).
Mencken, H. L. *A Mencken Chrestomathy: His Own Selection of His Choicest Writings.* Edited and annotated by H. L. Mencken (New York: Vintage Books, 1982).

Bibliography

Middlebrook, Martin. *The First Day on the Somme* (London: Allen Lane/ Penguin, 1971).
Morris, William. *The Well at the World's End* (London: Longmans, Green, 1913).
O'Neill, William L. *A Democracy at War: America's Fight at Home and Abroad in World War II* (New York: The Free Press, 1993).
Orwell, George. *A Collection of Essays* (New York: Houghton Mifflin Harcourt, 1981).
Owen, Wilfred. *Wilfred Owen: The Complete Poems and Fragments*. Edited by Jon Stallworthy (London: Chatto and Windus, The Hogarth Press, and Oxford University Press, 1983).
Panichas, George A., editor. *Promise of Greatness: The War of 1914–1918* (London: Cassell, 1968).
Paul, Annie. "The Last Curmudgeon." *Psychology Today*, 31.4 (July/August 1998).
Pinker, Steven. *Enlightenment Now: The Case for Reason, Science, Humanism, and Progress* (New York: Viking, 2018).
Prior, Robin, and Trevor Wilson. "Paul Fussell at War." *War in History*, 1 (1994).
Pynchon, Thomas. *Gravity's Rainbow* (New York: Vintage, 1973).
Quiller-Couch, A. T., editor. *The Oxford Book of English Verse 1250–1900* (Oxford: Oxford University Press, 1900).
Romano, Carlin. *America: The Philosophical* (New York: Alfred A. Knopf, 2012).
Rose, Kenneth D. *Myth and the Greatest Generation: A Social History of Americans in World War II* (New York: Routledge, 2008).
Ruskin, John. *Modern Painters*. Volume one (London: J.M. Dent, 1906).
Sassoon, Siegfried. *Memoirs of a Fox-Hunting Man*. Introduction by Paul Fussell (New York: Penguin, 2013).
Sassoon, Siegfried. *Memoirs of an Infantry Officer*. Introduction by Paul Fussell (New York: Penguin, 2013).
Sassoon, Siegfried. *Sherston's Progress*. Introduction by Paul Fussell (New York: Penguin, 2013).
Sassoon, Siegfried. *Siegfried Sassoon's Long Journey: Selections from the Sherston Memoirs*. Edited by Paul Fussell (New York: Oxford University Press, 1983).
Sassoon, Siegfried. *The War Poems of Siegfried Sassoon* (London: William Heinemann, 1919).
Schrijvers, Peter. *The Crash of Ruin: American Combat Soldiers in Europe During World War II* (New York: New York University Press, 1998).
Sheffield, Gary. *Forgotten Victory: The First World War—Myths and Realities* (London: Headline Book Publishing, 2001).
Sherriff, R. C. *Journey's End*. Introduction by E.R. Wood (Oxford: Heinemann Educational Books, 1958).
Sledge, E.B. *With the Old Breed: At Peleliu and Okinawa*. Introduction by Paul Fussell (New York: Oxford University Press, 1990).
Smith, Gene. *Still Quiet on the Western Front Fifty Years Later* (New York: Morrow, 1965).
Spiller, Roger J. "The Real War: An Interview with Paul Fussell," in *In the School of War* (Lincoln: University of Nebraska Press, 2010).
Stannard, Richard M. *Infantry: An Oral History of a World War II American Infantry Battalion* (New York: Twayne, 1993).
Stimson, Henry L., and McGeorge Bundy. *On Active Service in Peace and War* (New York: Harper and Brothers, 1947).
Stokesbury, Leon, editor. *Articles of War: A Collection of American Poetry About World War II*. Introduction by Paul Fussell (Fayetteville: University of Arkansas Press, 1990).
Suplee, Curt. "A Class Critic Takes Aim at America: The Slings and Arrows of Paul Fussell." *The Washington Post*, September 28, 1982.
Terkel, Studs. *"The Good War": An Oral History of World War II* (New York: Patheon Books, 1984).

Bibliography

Tillotson, Geoffrey, Paul Fussell, Jr., Marshall Waingrow, and Brewster Rogerson. *Eighteenth Century English Literature* (New York: Harcourt, Brace & World, 1969).

Tocqueville, Alexis de. *Democracy in America.* Translated by George Lawrence, edited by J. P. Mayer (New York: Harper and Row, 1969).

Todman, Dan. *The Great War: Myth and Memory* (London: Bloomsbury, 2005).

Trilling, Diana. *Reviewing the Forties.* Introduction by Paul Fussell (New York: Harcourt Brace Jovanovich, 1978).

Vandiver, Elizabeth. *Stand in the Trenches: Classical Receptions in British Poetry of the Great War* (Oxford: Oxford University Press, 2010).

Veblen, Thorstein. *The Theory of the Leisure Class* (New York: The Modern Library, 1934).

Vonnegut, Kurt. *Slaughterhouse-Five: A Novel* (New York: Dell, 1984).

Walter, George. *The Penguin Book of First World War Poetry* (New York: Penguin Classics, 2007).

Ward, Geoffrey C. *The War: An Intimate History 1941–1945* (New York: Alfred A. Knopf, 2007).

Waugh, Evelyn. *Sword of Honor* (New York: Little, Brown, 1961).

Wilkin, Peter. *The Strange Case of Tory Anarchism* (Faringdon, Oxfordshire: Libri, 2010).

Winokur, Jon, editor. *The Portable Curmudgeon* (New York: New American Library, 1987).

Winter, Jay. "Paul Fussell: Memories of a Friend and Scholar." *The Chronicle of Higher Education,* May 12, 2012.

Winter, Jay. *Sites of Memory, Sites of Mourning: The Great War in European Cultural History* (Cambridge: Cambridge University Press, 1995).

Wolff, Leon. *In Flanders Field* (London: Longmans, 1960).

Index

Adams, Henry 141
Allred, Terry 209n35
Ambrose, Stephen 16, 178, 186, 191, 196
American Civil War 43, 208n31
Amis, Kingsley 3, 31, 123, 158–164
Arnold, Mathew 28–29, 45
Ashworth, Tony 53
Atomic Bombings of Japan 93–105
Auden, W.H. 72–74

Bacevitch, Andrew 202
Behringer, Harriette (second wife) 119, 197
Bell, Daniel 141
Benton, Walter 126
Bernstein, Richard 176
Blackmur, R.P. 2, 66
Bloom, Allan 142
Blunden, Edmund 45, 153
Bodnar, John 170
Bonhoeffer, Dietrich 202
"Boo-Hoo Brigade" 59, 191
Boorstin, Daniel J. 141
Brereton, John C. 174, 177
Brittain, Vera 146, 149–150
Brokaw, Tom 16, 186, 193–194
Brooke, Rupert 45
Buckley, Christopher 144
Bundy, McGeorge 214n19
Bunyan, John 40
Burns, John Horne 82
Burns, Ken 1, 9, 197
Byron, Robert 68, 70–71, 72

Cahill, James 88–89
Campbell, James 49
"Cheap Grace" 202
Chickenshit 122–123
Chisholm, Roderick 201, 222n4
Chua, Amy 118
Churchill, Winston 100, 173

Cohen, Paula Marantaz 197
commensurability, incommensurability 152
Connolly, Cyril 126
Conrad, Joseph 156
Cowley, Malcolm 2
Cummings, Michael S. 221n1
Curtin, Edward J. 74

Darby, Robert 64
Douglas, Keith 128
Douglas, Norman 69, 76
Dower, John W. 98, 214n9, 215n31
Dyer, Geoff 49, 63, 77

Ehrhart, W.D. 4
Eisenhower, Dwight 7, 8, 10, 182
Eliot, T.S. 19, 40, 147
Erkstein, Modris 155–156

Fallows, James 116
Faust, Drew Gilpin 65, 198
The First World War in 100 Objects 38
Forster, E.M. 40
Frank, Richard 102
Fraser, George McDonald 167–170
Frye, Northrop 28, 47–48
Fuller, Jack 130–131
Fury 220n9
Fussell, Betty (first wife) 17–18, 20, 66, 212n27, 219n17
Fussell, Paul: *Abroad, British Literary Travelling Between the Wars* 68–80; *The Anti-Egoist: Kingsley Amis, Man of Letters* 159–164; *Bad: Or, The Dumbing of America* 135–144, 179, 201; beliefs 3, 4, 15–16, 18, 22–29, 30, 34, 105–106, 120, 130, 143, 152–155, 157, 175, 177, 201 (*see also* "Boo-Hoo Brigade"; Chickenshit; Prole Drift and the Atomic Bombings of Japan; Tory Anarchism; X people); *"Bourgeois*

and Travel: Techniques and Artifacts" 79; *The Boy Scout's Handbook and Other Observations* 82–86, 90–91; *The Boy's Crusade: The American Infantry in Northwest Europe, 1944–1945* 106, 186–199, 203; childhood 6, 166; *Class* 107–120, 138, 159, 179, 203; criticisms 57–58, 117, 132–133, 149, 169–170, 177, 204, 207n25, 208n33, 208n35, 211n65, 214n9; "The Culture of War" 147–148, 151; death 197–198; *Doing Battle: The Making of a Skeptic* 3, 106, 165–177, 203; education 17–19; "The Great War and Cultural Modernism" 155–157; *The Great War and Modern Memory* 15, 32–67, 69, 106, 122, 129–130, 148, 184, 203; intellectual influences 18, 20–25, 30–31, 89–90; marriages 20, 119, 212n27 (see also Behringer, Harriette; Fussell, Betty); *The Norton Book of Modern War (The Bloody Game)* 145–147; *The Norton Book of Travel* 78; "Patrick Brydone: The Eighteenth Century Traveler as Representative Man" 68–69; *The Rhetorical World of Augustan Humanism: Ethics and Imagery From Swift to Burke* 22–23; *Samuel Johnson: The Life of Writing* 25; teaching 20, 89, 135, 174–17; *Thank God for the Atom Bomb and Other Essays* 82, 86–90, 93–105; *Theory of Prosody in Eighteenth Century England* 20–21; "Travel, Tourism, and International Understanding" 79–80; *Uniforms: Why We Are What We Wear* 179–185; view of the "Good War" and "Greatest Generation" interpretation of World War II 16, 176, 186–196; war experiences 5–16; *Wartime: Understanding and Behavior in the Second World War* 106, 121–134, 151, 203
Fussell, Samuel (son) 198

Galbraith, John Kenneth 94
Gallico, Paul 125
Gardner, Dwight 118
Gibbs, Spilman 11
Gilbert, Martin 58–59, 178, 191
Goffman, Irving 180, 182
Gosse, Edmund 156
Graves, Robert 43–46, 59, 153, 166–168, 170
Gray, J. Glenn 94–95
Greene, Graham 69, 85, 86
Grossman, Dave 151
Guest, John 128
Gulliver's Travels 34

Haig, Field Marshall Douglas 52
Hale, Alfred 82
Hanson, Victor Davis 16, 187, 195–196
Hart, B.H. Liddell 54
Hart, Peter 58, 212 n85

Hastings, Max 195
Hecht, Anthony 176
Heller, Joseph 130, 177–178
Hemingway, Ernest 18, 147
Himmelfarb, Gertrude 143
Hofstadter, Richard 141
Hollander, Anne 184–185
Hopkins, Gerald Manley 19
Horizon 126
Hudson, Edward 13, 56
Hummer, T.R. 116
Hynes, Samuel 35, 66, 130

Imperial War Museum 32
Implacable Enemies: War in the Pacific, 1944–1945 103–104
Indianapolis 500 87
The Insider's Guide to the Colleges by the Yale Daily News 112
Isherwood, Christopher 72–74

Jenkins, Philip 142
Johnson, Samuel 4, 24–25
Jones, David 41, 64
Jones, James 128
Joravsky, David 94

Kammen, Michael 136
Kazin, Alfred 2
Keegan, John 3, 55, 175, 208n31
Kershaw, Ian 61
King, Nina 131
Kort, Michael 102, 215n23
Kramer, Mimi 116
Kutani, Michiko 90–91, 183

Larkin, Philip 61, 211n75
Lasch, Christopher 141
Laskowski, William 163
Lawrence, D.H. 69
Leader, Zachery 161–162
Lehmann-Haupt, Christopher 115–116
LeMay, Curtis 98
Levi-Strauss, Claude 80
Linderman, Gerald F. 123
Lonely Planet Travel Guides 76–77, 213n24
Lurie, Allison 115

Maddox, Robert James 101
Mailer, Norman 128
Manchester, William 93, 166–168, 170
Manning, Frederick 57–58
Manning, Olive 128
Marshall, George 102–104
Marwil, Jonathan 132–133
Maudlin, Bill 147
McCallum, Neil 128, 172–173
McGinniss, Joe 141
McMaster, H.R. 82
Mencken, H.L. 5, 17, 137, 217n10

Index

Montgomery, Field Marshall Bernard 7, 182, 185
Moore-Bick, Christopher 37
Morris, William 40
Murray, Brian 163
My Sister and I: The Diary of a Dutch Boy 88–89

Naipaul, V.S. 80
National Rifle Association 86, 87
New Criticism 28
A New Literary History of America 122
The New York Review of Books 84
Nixon, Richard 141, 183

The Official Preppy Handbook 109
Oh! What a Lovely War 41–42
O'Neil, William L. 192–193
Operation Downfall (Cornet and Olympic) 95
Operation Undertone 12, 205n22
O'Rourke P.J. 183–84
Orwell, George 2, 30, 31, 70, 82, 87, 89–90, 108, 177
Owen, Wilfred 18, 46–47, 152
The Oxford Book of American Verse 43
The Oxford Book of English Verse 42, 45

Paglia, Camille 198
Patton 84, 185
Patton, George 123, 185
Perrin, Noel 91
Pinker, Stephen 25–27
Poe, Edgar Allan 161
Pope, Alexander 143, 161, 204
The Portable Curmudgeon 120
Pound, Ezra 135
Powell, Anthony 128
Prior, Robin 51, 57–58, 61, 131, 133
Pritchard, William H. 163, 164
Prole Drift 113
Pynchon, Thomas 47

Rabin, Jonathan 74–75
Randall, Eric 199
Romano, Carlin 117

Sassoon, Siegfried 18, 39–40, 45–46, 82, 146
Saul, John Ralston 142
Saving Private Ryan 84, 188
Scanlan, John 199
Schwartz, Benjamin 197
Schwartz, Hillel 131
Second Amendment 87–88

Sheffield, Gary 211n73
Sherry, Michael 94
Sigal, Clancy 196
Sitwell, Osbert 126
Sledge, E.B. 82, 128, 167–168, 170–171
Spiller, Roger J. 33, 133–134
Stallworthy, Jon 90
Stanksy, Peter 48, 74
Stimson, Henry L. 99, 105
Strachan, Hew 61, 210n62

Tarkington, Booth 85
Taylor, A.J. 54
Teachout, Terry 159, 163, 219n4
Terkel, Studs 90
Theroux, Paul 80, 85
Time-Life Series on the Second World War 84
Tocqueville, Alexis de 119, 141, 144
Todman, Dan 53–54, 210n60
Tolkien, J.R.R. 49, 209n52
Tory Anarchism 31
Trilling, Lionel 2, 48, 66
Truman, Harry 97, 99, 104–105
Trump, Donald 202
Tuchman, Barbara 54
Twain, Mark 141

Unforgeable Fire: Pictures Drawn by Atomic War Survivors 96

Vandiver, Elizabeth 62
Veblen, Thorstein 110

Wakeman, Frederick 136
Walter, George 42
Walzer, Michael 97–98
Waugh, Evelyn 31, 68, 85, 126, 128, 129
Weigley, Russell 10, 176–177
Whitman, Walt 135
Wilder, Thornton 21
Wilkin, Peter 30–31
Wilson, Edmund 2, 66, 84
Wilson, Robert 131
Wilson, Trevor 51, 57–58, 61, 131, 133
Winter, Jay 62, 64–65, 199
The Wiper Times 208n35
Wolfe, Tom 142
Wouk, Herman 83–84, 113

X People 113–114

Yardley, Jonathan 116, 144
Young, Stanley Preston 88–89

www.ingramcontent.com/pod-product-compliance
Lightning Source LLC
Chambersburg PA
CBHW021353300426
44114CB00012B/1201